The Honourable Dr. JODY WILSON-RAYBOULD, P.C.,O.B.C., K.C., served as the Independent Member of Parliament for Vancouver Granville, Minister of Justice and Attorney General of Canada, Minister of Veterans Affairs and Associate Minister of National Defence until her resignation in 2019. Wilson-Raybould is a Principal of JWR Group, a lawyer, an advocate and leader among Canada's Indigenous Peoples with a strong reputation as a bridge builder between communities, and a champion of good governance and accountability. She has been a provincial crown prosecutor, a councillor for the We Wai Kai Nation, a chair of the First Nations Finance Authority and has served as the BC regional chief of the Assembly of First Nations. Wilson-Raybould has written two bestselling books, *"Indian" in the Cabinet: Speaking Truth to Power* (2021) and *From Where I Stand: Rebuilding Indigenous Nations for a Stronger Canada* (2019).

Jody Wilson-Raybould is a descendant of the Musgamagw Tsawataineuk and Laich-Kwil-Tach peoples which are part of the Kwakwaka'wakw, also kno peoples. She is a member of the tional name, Puglaas, means "wo

T0205015

True Reconciliation

*How to Be
a Force for Change*

Jody Wilson-Raybould

MᶜCLELLAND & STEWART

LIBRARY AND ARCHIVES CANADA CATALOGUING IN PUBLICATION

Title: True reconciliation : how to be a force for change / Jody Wilson-Raybould.
Names: Wilson-Raybould, Jody, 1971- author.
Identifiers: Canadiana (print) 20220281106 | Canadiana (ebook) 20220281181 |
ISBN 9780771004384 (hardcover) | ISBN 9780771004407 (softcover) |
ISBN 9780771004391 (EPUB)
Subjects: LCSH: Reconciliation—Canada. | LCSH: Decolonization—Canada. |
LCSH: Canada—Race relations. | LCSH: Canada—Ethnic relations. | LCSH:
Indigenous peoples—Canada—Social conditions.
Classification: LCC E78.C2 W55 2022 | DDC 305.897/071—dc23

Book design by Terri Nimmo
Cover art: Illustration by Dylan Browne, based on Sun Hawk mask by John Henderson
Typeset in Adobe Caslon Pro by Daniella Zanchetta, Toronto

Printed in Canada

McClelland & Stewart,
a division of Penguin Random House Canada Limited,
a Penguin Random House Company

www.penguinrandomhouse.ca

1   2   3   4   5   28   27   26   25   24

Penguin
Random House
McCLELLAND & STEWART

This book was a project in collaboration with Roshan Danesh, and would not have been written otherwise. Roshan coined the term "inbetweener," and in more than thirteen years of working together—including during my years as Regional Chief of British Columbia and as minister of justice and attorney general of Canada—we have instinctively and pragmatically sought to define it and live it in the work of true reconciliation.

Dr. Roshan Danesh, K.C., has advised First Nations, the federal government, the British Columbia government, local governments, and industry on reconciliation. He has also advised governments, international organizations, and civil society on issues of peace education and peace-building. Roshan completed his doctoral studies in constitutional law at Harvard Law School.

For my beloved parents . . .
My dad, Hereditary Chief Hemas Kla-Lee-Lee-Kla
(William Lane Wilson)
My mumma, Sandra Raylene Wilson
Who raised me to be proud of who I am and
to always remember where I came from . . .
and who taught me how to live in two worlds
and strive to help bring them together.
With all my love.

CONTENTS

INTRODUCTION

This Moment in Time

This Moment in Time

In 2021, I received a letter that said: "Myself, and others like me . . . need guidance on how to help with the ongoing reconciliation that is needed in not only my area, but the rest of Canada."

It was a letter like so many others I have received over the years, where individuals are asking, in their own words, *What can I do to help advance reconciliation?*

This question is asked when people feel responsibility for the past, and the need to be a part of effecting real change into the future:

It is hard for me to know what to do so that I can move repentance and reconciliation ahead. (That may be why . . . people have looked to the government to do something.)

[S]ince it will probably take the government awhile to respond, I want you to know that my family and I are hearing [the] stories and are so sad and sorry for what [Indigenous] people have experienced [and] please let your families and relatives know that we do care and we want to make it better and we grieve with you for all that you lost.

It is asked by new Canadians as they become aware of the past and present reality of Indigenous Peoples and want to be a part of breaking patterns of harm:

I am just a first-generation immigrant and don't consider myself qualified to make any kind of comments/assertions on any aspect of our First Nations' relationship with the "Crown". I also realize that in a grand scheme of things my opinion or thoughts don't matter at all. However, I can very proudly claim that I don't subscribe to any of the (ignorant) stereotypes associated with our First Nations. I wish there were a way for immigrants (new Canadians) and our First Nations to connect and share experiences of colonialism, the damage it caused to the social fabric of the colonised societies and the healing brought forth by decolonization. I am saying this because most of the immigrants come from countries which were formerly colonized. I strongly believe that any kind of understanding and partnership between New Canadians and our First Nations would be extremely beneficial for both—but am not sure how that would be possible.

It is asked when people know they have a role to play and are ready to act, but don't know what action to take.

> I would like to be part of that [work of reconciliation] however small. I will do whatever I can, I have emailed my MP on many occasions but have never gotten a reply . . .

I have been asked this question—in one form or another—more than any other. In the boardroom. On the street. At family meals. In Indigenous communities. Around the Cabinet table. More than once, I have even been stopped while going into a restroom by engaged individuals wanting to discuss the challenges of reconciliation, how it relates to the state of politics and governance in this country, and how to get involved.

And I am asked this question—in one version or another, and by Indigenous and non-Indigenous people—more and more these days. It inspires and motivates me that you are asking what you can do to help advance reconciliation, that you are seeking answers. It is the right question. And when we ask the right questions, we can find ways to move forward.

Let's be honest: throughout most of the history of Canada, Indigenous Peoples have experienced the opposite of being asked that question. The more common experience has been for Indigenous Peoples to be told things, treated like we needed to be saved from ourselves because we, and our ways of life, were inferior. Our lives were placed under the control of government, and we were placed in isolated and often hidden places—the reserve down the poorly paved or gravel road, the houses on the other side of the tracks, the residential "school" in the field.

My grandmother, whose English name was Ethel Pearson and whose Kwakwaka'wakw name was Pugladee, had to struggle for change in the shadows, out of sight and invisible, to ensure our culture and our ways survived. To keep our traditions of the Big House alive—our governance system—she and others had to hide their gatherings and the work they were doing from agents of the federal government, including the Royal Canadian Mounted Police (RCMP), who had direction to stop those gatherings and that work. Our people had a system of lookouts that would let them know when the officials were close, so they could switch from the work they were doing to singing church hymns.

My grandmother's experience was not unique. First Nations, Inuit, and Métis Peoples, and our communities across the country, have had far more experience with having to hide our cultures, traditions, and ways of life than in feeling safe to share them.

It was reflecting on the experiences of my grandmother— which are so similar to the experiences of countless Indigenous people across this country over many generations—that gave me pause when considering whether I should write this book. "Reconciliation" is controversial. When I say this, I am speaking from my own perspective as an Indigenous person. For some Indigenous people, the whole notion of reconciliation is a sham. Even a four-letter word. Does one reconcile with one's oppressor? Does one reconcile when there has never been a proper relationship? Yes, we need justice. Yes, we need our rights upheld. Yes, we need #landback. Yes, we need fairness and equity. But reconciliation? With who? And why? And how?

What would my grandmother think of the word *reconciliation*? She, like so many, was focused more on survival than reconciliation. This included trying to make sure, as much as she could, that her kids were not subject to the same harm and threats she was. She (and my grandfather) did this by making sure my father avoided the residential "school" system that she was forced to go to, and instead attended the local public school. My dad was the first and, for a period of time, the only Indigenous student. I am not sure I ever heard the word *reconciliation* come out of my grandmother's mouth.

Understanding Distinctions Between First Nations, Inuit, and Métis

Terminology regarding Indigenous Peoples can be difficult to navigate. Often, we are uncertain about what term to use. Terminology also changes. Some terms go out of favour—and come to be seen as offensive—while others emerge as most common.

First Nations is a term that refers to Indigenous Peoples in Canada (sometimes referred to as Aboriginal Peoples) who are not Métis or Inuit. Within First Nations there is great diversity: more than seventy language groups, and sixty to eighty separate peoples or nations.

Inuit are the Indigenous Peoples living primarily in Inuit Nunangat—the Inuit homeland encompassing 35 percent of Canada's landmass and 50 percent of its coastline. Inuit are Indigenous people of the Arctic. The word *Inuit* means "the people" in the Inuit language of Inuktitut.

Métis are Indigenous Peoples of a "collective of cultures and ethnic identities that resulted from unions between Aboriginal and European people in what is now Canada."[1] Métis, including for legal purposes under the Constitution, are often identified as descendants of a specific historic Métis community, such as the Red River Métis from the Métis Nation homeland—a vibrant Métis community that was established with its own identity, language, culture, institutions, and way of life centred in the Red River Valley.[2]

The use of the term *Indigenous* has become most common in recent years. This is a shift from *Aboriginal*, which had previously been the most commonly used and is the term in our Constitution. This shift has occurred for a few reasons. First, it is accurate. *Indigenous* means, in this context, the original people from a particular place. Second, it is the terminology used and accepted internationally, including in the United Nations Declaration on the Rights of Indigenous Peoples (UNDRIP). When we use the term *Indigenous* when referring to Canada, it applies to three distinct peoples—First Nations, Inuit, and Métis.

Of course, we still encounter the use of other terms, such as *Indian*, in part because of the Indian Act. The use of the term *Indian* has its roots in the belief of early European arrivals in the Americas that they had reached India (they were confused). For many, the term *Indian* is colonial and racist.

But when I think about my dad, I gain a bit more perspective on why reconciliation may have a meaning and a role that is important. My dad's experience was a little different from my grandmother's. He was a political leader, and a very public one. At the core of his struggle, and the struggle of other leaders of his time, was a very public push for change. Part of this work was getting people to listen—and act—to support work that would help address the injustices, wrongs, and harms that had occurred and were continuing to occur. This included recognizing rights; returning lands and resources; removing laws and policies that tried to control how we govern and care for our people; creating much-needed economic, social, and cultural well-being; and addressing systemic anti-Indigenous racism. Doing these things meant struggling, and working, with governments and peoples who were now here and not going anywhere.

One way or another, we must all learn how to live together into the future in ways that address the legacy of colonialism, uphold rights, and transform the status quo. From this perspective, I think we need to define, understand, and talk about reconciliation as part of this work.

My experience as an Indigenous leader has reinforced for me that we need to take hold of what reconciliation truly means and reflect that in tangible action. There was a time not so long ago that I—like my dad—also experienced the challenge of getting Canadians, sometimes including those sitting around the federal Cabinet table, to listen and be interested in doing this transformative work. But here is the point: as any

Indigenous leader knows, there was no way we could wait on, or rely on, governments to help lead the changes that were needed. We needed Canadians from all walks of life to support us and join us in demanding, and acting to build, a just future for Indigenous Peoples.

I remember times as BC Regional Chief of the Assembly of First Nations—a role I served from 2009 to 2015—when I would be sitting around with other First Nations leaders and we would talk about how to get the public and the media to pay attention to the importance of upholding Indigenous rights. We would talk of non-Indigenous people working alongside us for justice as one of the core examples and meanings of reconciliation.

Use of the Term *Reconciliation*

Reconciliation is a word that is often used in Canada in reference to Indigenous Peoples, but rarely with a clear definition. This lack of a consistent and common understanding of the word is one reason why I felt it might be helpful to write a book like *True Reconciliation*.

What are some of the typical ways reconciliation has been defined and talked about in Canada?

Reconciliation is sometimes used to refer to building proper relationships, including repairing and healing the wrongs that have happened. For example, the Royal Commission on Aboriginal Peoples talked about how getting on with the work of reconciliation requires "a great cleansing of the wounds of the past."[3] The Truth and Reconciliation Commission (TRC) defined reconciliation as "establishing and maintaining a mutually respectful relationship between Aboriginal and non-Aboriginal Peoples in this country. For that to happen, there has to be awareness of the past, acknowledgement of the harm that has been inflicted, atonement for the causes, and action to change behaviour."[4]

The term *reconciliation* has also been central to how the courts have interpreted the rights of Indigenous Peoples under our Constitution. In this context, *reconciliation* is often used to speak about the proper political and legal relationship between Indigenous Peoples and their governments, and the federal and provincial governments. For example, the Supreme Court of Canada speaks of the need to "reconcile pre-existing Aboriginal sovereignty with assumed Crown sovereignty."[5] In other words, reconciliation is about the competing claims of Indigenous Peoples and the Crown (the federal and provincial governments) regarding who owns and governs the lands that make up Canada. Much of the law of title and rights that you read and hear about in the media is about this understanding of reconciliation—of what the balance is between Indigenous title and rights, including in treaties, and the powers of the Crown to make decisions and use lands and resources.

In recent years, the term *reconciliation* has also become closely associated with the United Nations Declaration on the Rights of Indigenous Peoples. While the UN Declaration does not use the term, the Truth and Reconciliation Commission called for the declaration to be adopted as the "framework for reconciliation"[6] by governments, communities, and organizations.

Reconciliation is not a term that makes sense to everybody as a way to describe the state of Canada and what must be done in relation to Indigenous Peoples. Some Indigenous Peoples, leaders, and scholars have criticized or rejected the term because, for example, it speaks to repairing a relationship when the fundamental realities of colonization, including its power structures, remain, or because it does not reflect the full scope of the fundamental changes that are needed. Here are a few examples:

> "Our struggle is far from over. If anything, the need for vigilant consciousness as Indigenous people is stronger than ever. Reconciliation is recolonization because it is allowing the colonizer to hold on to his attitudes and mentality, and does not challenge his behaviour towards our people or the land."[7]

※

> "Many Canadians want to see reconciliation between the settlers and Indigenous peoples. But that cannot be forced. Reconciliation has to pass first through truth. And we still have not had enough of that from . . . government or from Canada as a whole. . . .
>
> "Reconciliation . . . is only possible if we abandon our rights, which have since been enshrined in the UN Declaration of the Rights of Indigenous Peoples, or if the government recognizes our land rights and our fundamental right to self-determination. Without that, all of the hugs and tears, and increases in program and service money are meaningless."[8]

Related to this, one sometimes hears that "reconciliation is dead." One context where you will hear these words is in response to government actions, such as use of police to enforce land and resource decisions. They are often used to express a belief that struggle and resistance, not reconciliation, must be paramount.

Of course, *reconciliation* is not just a Canadian term. It has been used all over the world to speak to processes and efforts to address injustices, such as in South Africa with apartheid.

Here is another thing I believe, but that will also be controversial for some—in particular, for some Indigenous people. A lot has changed since the experiences of my grandmother and my dad, and even since my earlier years as an Indigenous leader.

In 2010, shortly after I was first elected BC Regional Chief, I gave a speech about what has changed in the last half century. I said then that "we truly have come a long way in the last fifty years." And we had.

Indigenous rights had been recognized in section 35(1) of the Constitution and upheld time and again by the Supreme Court of Canada. Inuit and First Nations individuals gained the right to vote in federal and provincial elections (even though this did not occur until the 1950s and 1960s, depending on which jurisdiction we are talking about). Our governing institutions had come to understand the diversity and distinctions between First Nations, Inuit, and Métis, and were working to address ignorant and harmful stereotypes that have long operated within government and across society. There had been important inquiries and investigations that helped to reveal the reality of our colonial history and its enduring legacy. There had been important agreements achieved, such as the land claims agreements in Inuit Nunangat and across the North, the James Bay and Northern Quebec Agreement, and the Nisga'a Final Agreement. First Nations across the country were in different stages of rebuilding their nations and governments, addressing the destruction caused by the Indian Act for more than a century.

As I look back on that speech today, I realize I would go even further now. I believe that there has been more change in the twelve years that have passed since I spoke than in the previous fifty years that I was reflecting on. The pace at which Indigenous communities are rebuilding their economies, governments, and social systems is accelerating. Greater numbers of Indigenous young people are driving creativity, innovation, and change across society, including in arts, culture, technology, and politics. Indigenous women are reclaiming their roles in leadership and public life. Indigenous businesses are starting to thrive in certain sectors. And from coast to coast to coast— in various ways—people from all backgrounds are listening. And learning. And sharing. And understanding. And acting. You want to make sure you are playing your role. And as even more comes to light about the ongoing colonial reality—like the public awareness that began in 2021 regarding unmarked graves of Indigenous children across this country who were forced to attend residential "schools"—you want to do more.

In this change exists another reason that there is reso-
nance in speaking of reconciliation. Canadians are reconciling themselves with Canada's true history—and through that
reconciliation, many are motivated to be forces for change in
constructive and essential ways.

The pace of change has also accelerated when it comes to
justice for Indigenous Peoples. One could say history has sped
up. And there are many forces that have driven this acceleration: Generations of advocacy by Indigenous Peoples. Strategic
action on the ground and in the courts. Efforts to change how
children are educated. Inquiries, commissions, and studies that
highlight the truth and propose solutions. Broader changes in
society have also driven change, including forces of integration
that have resulted in people having more interaction with each
other and more access to information; this includes through
social media, and an increasing awareness of how Indigenous
Peoples are reported on and presented in the media and arts.

The fact that you are asking this fundamental question—
What can I do?—reflects how much has accelerated and
demonstrates that we are in a critical moment of transition
and transformation. I said this in that speech in 2010, and I
believed it then. But now I can actually *feel* it. I understand
this moment as one in which we have finally recognized that
confronting the legacy of colonialism in Canada, and building
the future, is our shared work. This is a moment with significant transformative potential, a moment where we recognize
that we all have a role to play, and that we need to increasingly,
and urgently, act.

Do we need another book on reconciliation? Many have been written.

Reading About Reconciliation

Books *about* Indigenous Peoples and reconciliation used to be dominated by academia, such as in the fields of history or anthropology, or were general surveys about aspects of Indigenous Peoples in Canada. This has changed. Today, there are all kinds of books, for all ages, about Indigenous Peoples, cultures, rights, stories, languages, art, history, and also about the work of reconciliation.

The bigger change, however, has been in the proliferation of books *by* Indigenous Peoples, about our realities and experiences. We have told our stories in various styles of books over generations. But these works were typically quite marginalized, and rarely found in the mainstream of retail bookstores or on commercial bestseller lists. This is no longer the case. There is so much being shared by Indigenous Peoples that illuminates the reality and work of reconciliation, and that can be readily found. This is part of that acceleration of change I described.

Here are a few works—some by Indigenous authors and some by non-Indigenous authors, some fiction and some non-fiction—that explore different aspects of understanding reconciliation:

- *21 Things You May Not Know About the Indian Act: Helping Canadians Make Reconciliation with*

Indigenous Peoples a Reality by Bob Joseph—provides a lot of basic background on the Indian Act and how reconciliation requires addressing the act.

- *Aboriginal Peoples and Politics: The Indian Land Question in British Columbia, 1849–1989* by Paul Tennant—examines the "land question" in British Columbia.
- *Braiding Sweetgrass: Indigenous Wisdom, Scientific Knowledge, and the Teachings of Plants* by Robin Wall Kimmerer—explores our connection with nature and reveals dimensions of Indigenous worldviews.
- *The Inconvenient Indian: A Curious Account of Native People in North America* by Thomas King—examines racist and stereotypical views on Indigenous Peoples from historical and contemporary perspectives.
- *Indian Horse* by Richard Wagamese—a novel about dealing with the trauma inflicted by the residential school system.
- *A Mind Spread Out on the Ground* by Alicia Elliott—a book on trauma, legacy, oppression, and racism in North America.
- *Moon of the Crusted Snow* by Waubgeshig Rice—a novel about a small northern Anishinaabe community cut off from the outside world.
- *Seven Fallen Feathers* by Tanya Talaga—an examination of systemic racism, policing, and the lives of Indigenous Peoples and youth in northern Ontario.
- *Son of a Trickster* by Eden Robinson—a novel that blends humour with heartbreak in a coming-of-age novel.

- *They Called Me Number One: Secrets and Survival at an Indian Residential School* by Bev Sellars—a memoir of one Survivor's story.
- *Up Ghost River* by Edmund Metatawabin—a memoir that shares experiences in residential school and the journey of healing.

Some of these books are great and have had a profound impact. Importantly, these books are from very different perspectives. Reconciliation does not look the same for everyone. While there is much shared between First Nations, Inuit, and Métis Peoples, there are also critical distinctions, including with respect to history, experience, and current realities. Honouring and respecting these distinctions is part of responding to the legacy of colonialism.

My decision to write this book was made largely because of that question I keep getting asked—*What can I do?* The more people ask it—whether Indigenous or non-Indigenous— the more it becomes clear that there is still a struggle to find answers. In particular, people are struggling to translate their increasing knowledge, awareness, understanding, and desire into tangible action.

Times of transition and transformation can be confusing. So I understand why this question is being asked, and why answers are sometimes elusive.

We hear about how bad the Indian Act is. The first Indian Act was passed and imposed on First Nations by the federal government of the new Dominion of Canada in 1876. It divided First Nations into small "bands," segregated First Nations Peoples on "reserves," imposed a system of government and control by the federal government, restricted basic human rights, and established the residential "school" system. The Indian Act, with its 122 sections, was drafted as a means for the federal government to administer and control the lives of "Indians." It is a racist, colonial, and oppressive law of institutionalized wardship that has done massive harm to generations of First Nations people and continues to do so today. But it still exists, and we hear about how hard it is to get rid of it. And that is confusing.

We continue to hear about Indigenous communities that do not even have access to clean drinking water, despite government guarantees that this will be addressed by fixed dates. Yet the deadlines are never met. And that is confusing.

We complete study after study, report after report, that reveal the depths of the issues and the pathways for change. The *Report of the Royal Commission on Aboriginal Peoples*, released in 1996, was a comprehensive study and plan—including 440 recommendations—for what needed to happen in terms of Indigenous rights implementation and relationship-building in Canada.[9] In 2015, the Truth and Reconciliation Commission of Canada's report, *Honouring the Truth, Reconciling for the Future*, provided ninety-four "calls to action" in response to the history and impacts of the residential "school" system.[10] In 2019, the final report of the National Inquiry into Missing and Murdered Indigenous Women and Girls (MMIWG), *Reclaiming Power and Place*— had 231 "calls for justice," and laid out how to address disproportionate violence towards Indigenous women and girls.[11] Yet, with all this knowledge and development of solutions, the challenges still feel intractable. And that is confusing.

We hear about court case after court case involving Indigenous rights—literally hundreds of them over decades. The vast majority have upheld the rights of Indigenous Peoples. Yet we continue to hear about new court cases all the time, and they seem to go on and on. And that is confusing.

We see blockades and resistance to various natural resource projects by Indigenous Peoples and their governments. We also see acceptance, and indeed a full embrace of resource development projects, by other Indigenous Peoples and governments. And that is confusing.

We see multiple Indigenous leaders and governments claim to speak for the same people on the same issues, including hereditary and elected leaders. And that is confusing.

We see one Indigenous group claiming the same land as another group. In some cases, they are even from the same tribe; in others, they are not. And that is confusing.

We see new human rights and legal instruments come to the forefront in efforts such as the United Nations Declaration on the Rights of Indigenous Peoples, even though we already have recognized and affirmed the rights of First Nations,

Inuit, and Métis Peoples in section 35(1) of the Constitution Act (1982). And that is confusing.

We hear about increased commitments to make systemic change in the conditions of Indigenous Peoples, yet continue to see more and more protests demanding change, from Idle No More to those about police brutality against Indigenous people, including some instances where Indigenous people have been killed at the hands of police. And that is confusing.

And, as I mentioned earlier, we even find the word *reconciliation* confusing. It raises basic questions: What exactly does it mean? Whose responsibility is it to reconcile? Does reconciliation have a beginning, middle, and end? We hear people say that reconciliation is "dead." We hear of other terms we should use—such as *resurgence* or *rebuilding*. And that is confusing.

Cutting through this confusion is hard for all of us, including for Indigenous Peoples. When visiting Indigenous Peoples and communities across the country, I have asked individuals whether they would prefer the recognition of their constitutional rights and the implementation of the United Nations Declaration on the Rights of Indigenous Peoples, or more openings in the fishing season, or hunting opportunities, or other on-the-ground economic opportunities that would support their livelihood. I understand this is a binary choice, and a false dichotomy, really. But I think it says something that people, more often than not, pick the latter. This is a reflection of many things, including the reality of how much Indigenous Peoples have had to be concerned about addressing day-to-day realities of poverty and limited opportunities. Because of the immediacy of the challenges many people face to make ends meet, it is hard to focus effort and attention on the vital connection between how rights are upheld and implemented and the on-the-ground conditions of social, cultural, and economic well-being; on how both of these outcomes are interrelated, and how one supports the other.

As a First Nations leader, I—like many Indigenous leaders—see it as one of my responsibilities to help develop, share, and build answers to the many questions being asked, and to try to sort through the confusion people have. In one form or other, this is a responsibility shared by all Canadians, including Indigenous Peoples: finding ways to work together to tackle injustice, systemic racism, and the legacy of colonialism in a way that reflects and advances the vision we have of our society into the future—constructive, resilient, cohesive, just, thriving, and peaceful.

And so, I decided to write this book to give my answer to the question I am so often asked. To share my learnings about what each of us can do at this critical moment in time, and also to help address some of the confusion that many feel about what is happening, why it is happening, and what can be done about it. To be clear, this is my answer—and my definition of "true reconciliation"—based on what I have been taught and what I have learned. There are other answers—important ones—and we all benefit from hearing them.

I believe there are three core practices of true reconciliation: *learn, understand,* and *act.* These practices are interrelated and interconnected. They build on each other, yet they also should be operable in our lives at the same time; they are not linear. To be clear, these practices also have specific expressions and meanings. It is not about any learning, any understanding, or any action. I mean something very particular about each of these, and how they are practised will be distinct for individuals, communities, organizations, and governments.

I am not going to define *learn, understand,* and *act* yet. But I invite you to imagine what you think they mean, and how they may relate to what you are doing already. What is your initial reaction to them? Do the definitions seem obvious to you?

I admit, these three practices may sound simple and obvious, or too straightforward. But here is one thing I have learned: While effecting real change in our own lives as individuals and in groups is always hard, as human beings there is also often a tendency to believe this is even harder than it is (perhaps even impossible, we tell ourselves). And through that belief, we can make change harder than it already is. Sometimes, those beliefs can even become an excuse to not change. I can tell you that this attitude has plagued our governments in the work of reconciliation. *It is too hard. Too complicated. Not possible to know what to do. Or who to do it with.* This attitude is also not entirely foreign to Indigenous communities. *Change can't happen. It won't happen. They will never change.*

I reject these attitudes. They are unhelpful, wrong, and even harmful. Nothing is ever static in life. We are always moving forward—sometimes fast, sometimes slow—or falling back and being overtaken by struggle. Remember: doing little or nothing in the face of injustice, harm, or wrongs does not mean things stay the same; it means things are getting worse, and your action (inaction) can be or is a part of that worsening.

There is also the reality that because colonialism has wrought tremendous harms, and continues to do so, healing is a vital and necessary part of change; it is intrinsic to true reconciliation. Individuals, through no fault of their own, have experienced much suffering. This suffering has affected their well-being and must be grappled with every day. At the same time, there are intergenerational traumas, as well as systemic inequalities and injustices that have created painful realities for individuals, families, and communities. These also must be acknowledged and worked through if change is to move forward.

And I think there is another truth worth considering when exploring how change happens. History—at least the way it is often told—tends to talk of change through big moments and huge events. Or through leaders and the decisions and actions they take. But I do not think this is how change really unfolds. Most of the real change, especially social change, operates like a thief in the night; it does its work quietly, almost imperceptibly, until we realize that something is noticeably different. I recall a friend telling me a story of how, when he was a student in university, a lecturer, an expert in South Africa, told a few hundred politically active undergraduate students that he believed apartheid was about to end in the country, that Nelson Mandela would be released from prison, and that he would end up taking over the country in the not-too-distant future. The lecturer was booed and confronted. No one took a word he said seriously—they thought he was out of his mind. Not that long after, Mandela was freed. Apparently, very few could see the forces of change that were playing out and rapidly progressing. Only once the change had occurred was it broadly recognized. For many of us, that change came like a thief in the night.

The work of effecting change often happens out of sight—unrecognized and unrealized—because it happens through people in their own lives and realities doing things differently, making different choices, and often sacrificing in new ways. Real change is not the sole domain of leaders and so-called heroes; rather, change is driven forward by the choices and actions of each and every one of us. The big moments, the ones recorded for all time in the history books, are often moments where we suddenly realize how much has changed (and feel the effects of that change), or they are catalysts that significantly shift the direction or accelerate the work of change to come. But the changes themselves? They are chosen, advanced, acted upon, and implemented on the ground, including through what each of us chooses to do in our own lives.

I think one reason I say this about change is that it reflects how in my culture we talk and share about who we are, and about our histories. I am sure you have noticed how Indigenous people often introduce themselves by speaking of where they have come from, and their family lines. Like I do.

Whenever I speak publicly, I say, "My name is Jody Wilson-Raybould. My traditional name is Puglaas. I come from the Musgamagw Tsawataineuk and Laich-Kwil-Tach people of northern Vancouver Island, just off the coast of British Columbia. We are part of the Kwakwaka'wakw, also known as the Kwak'wala-speaking peoples."

In doing this I am recognizing that at the heart of our identity, and our history, are our personal stories and realities. I am recognizing that at the heart of human connection and understanding is knowing from whom and where another comes, and recognizing and respecting that. And that through that recognition and respect, connection and understanding are made. And that in that connection and understanding are the foundations of relating in good ways with each other and continuing to build even better relationships. One relationship that must be recognized is how what we do today—each and every one of us—will shape change in the future, just as the choices and actions of those before us shaped how things are in the present day.

This idea that change occurs through the actions of each and every one of us, and that the impacts of our actions must be viewed in relation to the past, the present, and the future, is reflected in many traditions and principles in Indigenous cultures. One example of this is the Seventh Generation Principle, which has roots in the Great Law of the Haudenosaunee Confederacy. In its simple form, the principle is that decisions should be made by thinking forward seven generations, and by ensuring that the decisions being made will effect the right kind of change that far into the future. One Haudenosaunee leader describes this way of thinking in the following terms:

> If you ask me what is the most important thing that I have learned about being a Haudenosaunee, it's the idea that we are connected to a community, but a community that transcends time.
>
> We're connected to the first Indians who walked on this earth, the very first ones, however long ago that was. But we're also connected to those Indians who aren't even born yet, who are going to walk this earth. And our job in the middle is to bridge that gap. You take the inheritance from the past, you add to it, your ideas and your thinking, and you bundle it up and shoot it to the future. And there is a different kind of responsibility. That is not just about me, my pride and my ego, it's about all that other stuff. We inherit a duty, we inherit a responsibility. And that's pretty well drummed into our heads. Don't just come here expecting to benefit. You come here to work hard so that the future can enjoy that benefit.[12]

The Inuit also describe a similar idea of actions and their impact over generations:

> Some might think that Inuit never plan for the future. They sometimes think that we lived from day to day with no plan.

We are here today because our ancestors were the ones who made sure that we could survive. They did not live one day at a time. We were made to become human beings right from birth. They taught us how to live a good life and what to do in difficult situations.[13]

And also from the Inuit:

We fear the weather spirit of earth . . . We fear Sila . . . Therefore it is that our fathers have inherited from their fathers all the old rules of life which are based on the experience and wisdom of generations. We do not know how, we cannot say why, but we keep those rules in order that we may live untroubled.[14]

The lesson I take from these teachings is that we are all forces of change, we all have a responsibility to advance change, and in order to do this we must locate ourselves in relation to the past, the present, and the future.

Before you read further—and learn, understand, and act— let me say something about what this book is and is not, and how you might read and best use it.

This book is not a policy manual or a legal treatise on section 35(1) of the Constitution of Canada—which protects and affirms the Aboriginal and treaty rights of Indigenous Peoples—or on what the courts have said. Nor is it a work of anthropology about the cultures and ways of life of the Indigenous Peoples of Canada, or a history of Indigenous-Crown relations.

Of course, I will address these topics in various ways—including by exploring Indigenous cultures and values, our colonial history, the law, and the nature and meaning of Indigenous rights. As the book unfolds, I will share my explanation of what "true reconciliation" means. But more than anything, this is a book about how you can take action in your own life and contexts to advance true reconciliation. It is about the roles we can play and the responsibilities we hold to achieve justice and build stronger communities. It is also about making our choices and actions meaningful—making them count. As you read, consider what you are doing now, and what you could be doing in the future. Of course, how one undertakes the interrelated and interdependent practices of learning, understanding, and acting will be different for each of us—it is about us, in our contexts, in our lives. But in undertaking those practices you are working for change, as are countless others. And, in so doing, change is happening.

A last word: thank you. By reading and responding to this book you are demonstrating how you care—for each other, our communities, our society, for Canada, and for humanity.

PART 1

Learn

Learn

It is often recognized that to build the future in the ways we wish, we must understand the past; that "you can't really know where you are going until you know where you have been."[1] Stated another way, "Those who cannot learn from history are doomed to repeat it."[2]

So it is for achieving a future of true reconciliation. We cannot fully advance reconciliation without knowing what has transpired thus far, and why. This is one reason that, in our recent Canadian history, reconciliation has always been talked about in connection to the "truth." We had a Truth and Reconciliation Commission to look at the residential school system. We place increasing focus on changes to ways of teaching children and sharing knowledge about the experience of Indigenous Peoples in Canada so that a more truthful understanding of history can be achieved. We have debates about the names of sports teams and the legacy of historical figures, about place names, and about different understandings of our past.

We accept, and rightfully so, that if there is to be reconciliation, first there must be truth.

Learning is the first foundation of true reconciliation.

But here is the challenge: Building awareness and, even more so, a shared understanding of the truths that are relevant to true reconciliation is a messy, complicated undertaking. There are diverse and distinct voices, experiences, and realities that must be listened to, learned from, and considered. There are tensions and conflicts about what or who should be emphasized, or what something does or does not mean. Sometimes, we are even unsure of whose voices to listen to if we want to better understand the truth. And, of course, we must also recognize that our understanding of the truth is continually evolving and growing. We can always learn more, know more, and understand better.

In this section, I share some of the realities, ideas, and truths I think we need to learn in order to advance true reconciliation, along with some thoughts on how each of us can go about further deepening our learning in our own lives. I think of these like the foundation of a house: we need a proper foundation if we are going to be able to design, and build, the house we want to live in. As time goes on, and as we continue to *Understand* and *Act*, we need to keep inspecting the foundation—to deepen our learning—to ensure that the house remains stable and capable of meeting our needs.

TRUE RECONCILIATION REQUIRES
LEARNING NEW STORIES

When I think of truth, I think of storytelling. It is through stories that various truths are revealed in my culture, and in many Indigenous cultures. It has been said that when Indigenous Peoples are not allowed to tell their stories, there is a breakdown of language and cultural traditions.[3] One example of how we reveal our understanding of the truth can be found in our creation stories. For example, the importance of creation stories for my people, the Kwakwaka'wakw, has been explained in the following way:

> The teachings and creation stories show the next generation how to live, share and maya'xala (treat others and all things the way you want to be treated [respect]) all things. In Indigenous cultures, teaching every generation is illustrated in stories, songs and ceremonies. Each listener takes away the teachings and meanings from the stories and songs, and uses the principles to help them in their own lives.[4]

Creation stories articulate how and why humans were created, and how we ended up where we are. With that, they help explain a way of comprehending our reality and how we should act in the world. Many Indigenous creation stories describe, for example, how original people were created but then started fighting, and, as such, purification was needed— such as through a flood or other natural events. What was required to survive, and thrive, was for humans and animals to work together. Here is one telling of part of one of these stories, from the Anishinaabe:

Gladly, all the animals tried to serve the spirit woman. The beaver was the first to plunge into the depths. He soon surfaced out of breath and without the precious soil. The fisher tried, but he too failed. The marten went down, came up empty handed, reporting the water was too deep. The loon tried. Although he remained out of sight for a long time, he too emerged, gasping for air. He said that it was too dark. All tried to fulfill the spirit women's request. All failed. All were ashamed.

Finally, the least of the water creatures, the muskrat, volunteered to dive. At this announcement the other water creatures laughed in scorn, because they doubted this little creature's strength and endurance. Had not they, who were strong and able, been unable to grasp the soil from the bottom of the sea? How could he, the muskrat, the most humble among them, succeed when they could not?

Nevertheless, the little muskrat volunteered to dive. Undaunted, he disappeared into the waves. The onlookers smiled. They waited for the muskrat to emerge as empty handed as they had done. Time passed. Smiles turned to worried frowns. The small hope that each had nurtured for the success of the muskrat turned into despair. When the waiting creatures had given up, the muskrat floated to the surface more dead than alive, but he clutched in his paws a small morsel of soil. Where the great had failed, the small succeeded.[5]

This story holds contemporary meaning, including how we can learn from animals how to counsel together, listen to one another, and draw hope from the depths below us.

Creation stories are just one example of the oral traditions that are the foundation for how teachings, knowledge, and history are passed on in Indigenous cultures. To say it another way: in Indigenous cultures, we emphasize the role of the spoken word more than the written word. This is different than, for example, in European cultures. Consider these descriptions by Indigenous people of why storytelling and oral traditions are important and how they are used:

> "The most important qualities of our culture are our language and our stories. In oral traditions such as ours, telling stories is how we pass on the history and the teachings of our ancestors. Without these stories, we would have to rely on other people for guidance and information about our past. Teachings in the form of stories are an integral part of our identity as a people and as a nation. If we lose these stories, we will do a disservice to our ancestors—those who gave us the responsibility to keep our culture alive."[6]

✳

> "Patience and trust are essential for preparing to listen to stories. Listening involves more than just using the auditory sense. Listening encompasses visualizing the characters and their actions and letting the emotions surface. Some say we should listen with three ears: two on our head and one in our heart."[7]

—

When I think about the work of reconciliation, then, I naturally think about it in terms of stories. Of course, part of reconciliation is helping to build non-Indigenous people's understanding of Indigenous cultures, knowledge, and traditions. This is why, when it is appropriate (because sharing our stories is not always culturally appropriate or permitted), Indigenous Peoples will share stories as part of helping to convey who we are, how we view the world, and what values and teachings we hold. This is why I sometimes will share parts of my Kwakwaka'wakw stories.

But I also think of reconciliation as involving, using, and examining a different type of story; namely, those stories we each tell ourselves, individually and collectively, about who we are, where we come from, what we stand for, and where we are headed. We form and tell ourselves these stories because they help us make sense of our reality, the place we have ended up in life, why we have experienced what we have, what may come next, and who we are connected to and a part of.

Think about how you respond to someone when they ask you to "tell me about yourself" or "what is your background." We each answer these fundamental questions in our own way—a way that reflects the perceptions we have of ourselves based on our experiences, our ways of understanding our experiences, and what we have been told throughout our lives. When we do this we are expressing aspects of our personal "truth."

Let me give you an example of how I answer such questions, and how rooted those answers are in a story I was told about myself from as early as I can remember. It's a story I was told by my parents, family, and community, starting at a young age, about the expectations I should have for myself in terms of the roles and responsibilities I should aspire to meet. I truly believe it has shaped how I view myself and the choices I have made throughout my life.

In my culture, we start telling the story of what the life of an individual should come to represent from the earliest age. The story I was told about myself was that I was born to and expected to lead. It was not—is not—a choice. It is a responsibility I hold to my community, my people, and, indeed, to myself. Of course, as an individual I still have free will, and there are also many other forces that shape one's path in life. But for me, being told and told again this story of my future greatly influenced the choices I have made.

I'd like to share a bit of this story with you.

I come from a matrilineal society—where descent is traced, and property inherited, through the female line, and where women carry high rank, roles, and knowledge.

We have Hereditary Chiefs—always men—who are groomed from the time they are born for leadership, but they are groomed by women. My father is the Hereditary Chief of our clan, the Eagle Clan. His name is Hemas Kla-Lee-Lee-Kla, which means "Number one amongst the Eagles, the Chief that is always there to help."

He was given his name in a Potlatch, which is our traditional form of government—one that we still practise today. The Potlatch is where our names are passed down or given from generation to generation. It is where laws are made, disputes are settled, people are married, and wealth is redistributed.

In our Potlatch, the highest-ranking male leaders are called *Hamatsa*.

Rank is reflected in positions and names—which bring with them considerable responsibility and obligations. My grandmother's name, Pugladee, was the highest-ranking name—male or female—in our clan. It means "a good host." As I said earlier, my name, Puglaas, means "a woman born to noble people." My grandmother used to joke that, when it came to the respective roles of women and men in our society, women were simply too busy and too important to be Chiefs.

My grandmother ensured that my sister and I knew our culture, our values, the laws of our Big House, and how to conduct ourselves as leaders. I am grateful to have come from a very strong and loving family. I was raised to be proud of who I am, to know where I came from, to believe in myself, and to recognize my rights and responsibilities. From a very young age, I was raised to lead. I was raised with a sense of community, duty, and a need to give back and use my skills and abilities to improve quality of life.

In our Potlatch system, I am a *Hiligaxste*—a role always held by women. One of my jobs is to lead the Hamatsa, the Chief, into the Big House. "Hiligaxste" can be translated as one who "corrects the Chief's path." We show them the way—a metaphor for life—and, in our Potlatch ceremonies, the power of the Hamatsa is symbolically "tamed" as he readies to be Chief.

Given that I was told and taught that my story in life was about leadership roles and responsibilities, it is not so surprising to see the general direction in which my journey has evolved. I ended up in multiple leadership roles, from a councillor of my own First Nation, to BC Regional Chief, to a member of Parliament and minister of justice and attorney general of Canada.

Of course, I am not saying that my life was determined or fixed by this story. At times, I was unsure about the directions to follow, and what would or should come next. I struggled with certain decisions, including whether to try to transition from Indigenous to federal politics. But stories do have a power. They act like a compass that keeps pointing us in a certain direction, even when other forces may be pulling or pushing us in other directions.

And, of course, our stories are challenged by events throughout our lives; sometimes these events are tragic and awful, and other times they are wonderful and miraculous. Though it's often hard work, we are constantly revisiting, retelling, and deepening our own stories. In doing that, we are learning— about who we really are, our strengths, and how we can be even better in our own lives and for those in our family and communities. This was the reality for me at various points in my life, where in order to honour the expectations of the story

I had been told, and which I told myself, about who I was and what my responsibilities were as a human being, I had to make sacrifices, change directions, or give things up.

Of course, stories and their power are not just individual. They are also collective. In fact, most stories are collective. All peoples, and all societies, have shared stories that are told about who they are, where they come from, and why they are important. Countries have them as well. And these stories are used as a type of glue to try to keep us bound together.

This is true of Canada. A narrative has been constructed of Canada: how our country came to be, what the important passages and moments in history have been, and how those things combined to forge a particular identity of who we are. We reflect these stories in the monuments and testimonials we build—in our buildings and place names, on our money and postage, in our decisions regarding which leaders, events, or memories to honour.

Our collective national stories are powerful. They define us and they differentiate us from others. But here's the thing: In much of history, these collective stories have never been truly collective. They have tended to be constructed by the few, and then taught and passed on from generation to generation. As this happens, they gain a "taken for granted" quality, a sense that they simply are "the" story. When this occurs, the stories grow more powerful, and a story that started out being told by the few becomes the story of the many.

These stories told by the few that are accepted, over time, as the stories of the many are typically exclusive. They leave some peoples and their experiences out. This is particularly the case in societies with diverse populations. Sometimes—even often—the vast majority of people are excluded. So the stories are incomplete, and not necessarily reflective of the full range of experiences and understandings of the different peoples or a country as a whole. They are far from the truth. In some cases, the prevailing narrative seeks to rewrite the history and even deny the existence of the plurality of peoples.

Canada, like many other countries, has constructed a predominant story of our history that is exclusive and incomplete. Sure, aspects of this story have changed and shifted over time. No story is ever totally static or fixed. But core elements of this story that were originally told by a few have, over time, come to be taken for granted as foundational to "our" national story—critical to the story we collectively share as Canadians.

But the fact is that the predominant story is also, when it comes to Indigenous Peoples, a myth. And myths need to be dispelled.

In examining that story and talking about the ways in which it may be a myth, and building shared understandings of how the predominant story may need to change further, we are contributing to the work of building a new, more inclusive and accurate, vision of Canada.

Let me give you an example. We have certain ways of talking about the founding of Canada. About how the "Fathers" of Confederation moulded a country by bringing together English and French traditions. Much of how we identify and think about Canada today is informed by this founding story: the idea that we were founded on "two solitudes"—francophones and anglophones; our focus on recognizing and maintaining harmony between these traditions, including through policies of bilingualism, or guaranteed seats and language requirements on the Supreme Court of Canada, or the balance between federal and provincial powers, or the way culture is supported and shaped, including what we identify with and respond to as "Canadian."

But here is the thing: Indigenous Peoples were also present at the time of Canada's founding, at Confederation. But Indigenous Peoples were left out of the founding of Canada. We were not there. We were out of sight and out of mind. Those "Founding Fathers" focused on francophones and anglophones at that time. But what about those who spoke Inuktitut, or Michif, or Cree, or any number of other Indigenous languages? Canada was born as a federation, which divided power between a federal government and provincial governments. But Indigenous governments—and our laws, jurisdictions, and authorities—were ignored, creating a massive and enduring obstacle for Indigenous Peoples. Indeed, not only were we, and our governments, left out, but the experience of the founding of Canada was an intensification, and a deepening, of colonization and oppression. It is after the founding of Canada that harsh, racist national policies were imposed on Indigenous Peoples, including the Indian Act. It is after the founding of

Canada that a complex and diverse set of interactions between Europeans and Indigenous Peoples—some with arguably positive elements, and some awful and tragic—became even more insidious and deeply entrenched.

Consider for a moment what you know about Indigenous Peoples at the time of the founding of Canada.

Other than perhaps the great Métis leader Louis Riel, can you name any Indigenous person from the time of the founding of Canada?

Did you know that at the time of Confederation the number of Indigenous people far outnumbered those who were settlers from Europe?

Did you know that when Europeans came to what would become Canada, they found complex and organized Indigenous societies with their own systems of government, legal orders, and family and kinship systems?

Did you know that prior to Confederation, treaties had been entered into with many First Nations by the British Crown?

Did you know that in 1763, King George III recognized Indigenous land rights and declared that land could not be taken without agreement with Indigenous Peoples?

When I grew up on Vancouver Island in the Comox Valley, going to schools where I was one of only a few Indigenous kids, I think I had an experience typical of many Indigenous kids in this country. I was learning two siloed stories about Canada.

One was the history I was taught in school, which in many respects reflected a predominant narrative in which Indigenous Peoples were absent. Our appearances in the curriculum were few and far between. Yes, I did have some great teachers who would occasionally break away from curriculum and share more of the Indigenous experience—but they were the courageous few who had gained some knowledge and experience that allowed them to do that. The exception, not the rule.

At the same time, I learned the history of the country based on Indigenous experience. This teaching came from my grandmother, father, community, my First Nations friends, and some wonderful non-Indigenous teachers (including my mumma). This story was one of oppression and injustice, of a struggle that is still ongoing.

The reality of silos is something that affects all of us— Indigenous and non-Indigenous—and it is destructive.

Siloed stories reinforce silos in society. They separate and divide people because we fail to understand each other's experience: how we came to be where we are, what responsibilities we bear for doing better, and also the positive and constructive things we actually do share. The silos about the Indigenous experience in our history are the deepest and oldest, characterized by a particular form of colonialism. But Canada is an immensely diverse country, and there are vital and important experiences of other peoples and populations that must form part of our shared story. Many peoples have suffered harms and wrongs in our history and have also contributed in vital ways that have not been recognized. And the work of reconciliation today is not what it would have been in 1867. It is not just about francophones, anglophones, and Indigenous Peoples. It is a responsibility we all bear, and work that we all can and must contribute to. It is part of renewing and revitalizing our vision for Canada and its future.

We should not underestimate how siloed we are, and how much work we still need to do.

Let's think about what happened in the summer of 2021, when reports came out regarding unmarked graves on the grounds of the former Kamloops Indian Residential School at Tk'emlúps te Secwépemc. Even though public awareness about the history of the residential school system in Canada has grown exponentially in the past decade, the realization that thousands of children never returned from these schools because they died there was a horrific shock for the public. It was, for many Canadians, a direct challenge to and rupture in the story that they had been told, and had believed, about this country. This was borne out in letters I received following the revelations—reflections of how countless Canadians felt from coast to coast to coast:

> "I always prided myself on having been fortunate to grow up in Canada and was proud of our Canadian history and peaceful global efforts. Now I feel ashamed and remorseful. How could we not have been taught of it, I am even more upset that my upbringing didn't include any awareness of what was happening in my own backyard. I really do believe that when you know better, you do better."

✳

"First I must say that growing up in a small town in Saskatchewan we knew nothing of the residential schools and learning all of this now makes our hearts very sad for the native population of this country. This is eye-opening for most of us and puts a lot of troubles of the First Nations into perspective for us. We pray for the healing in this land!"

✳

"The recent revelations of mass grave sites of the thousands of children from residential schools have finally caught Canadians attention and made many aware of the generations of injustice and abuse suffered by Indigenous peoples for the past hundreds of years. Even though the TRC and other commissions have clearly outlined the terrible wrongs and injustices."

✳

"I'm a 100% settler/colonialist/British background and I 100% apologize for what my ancestors have done and continue to do to your ancestors and you."

Residential School Buildings Today

The residential school system was extensive, with more than 130 schools attended by approximately 150,000 First Nations, Inuit, and Métis children. While these schools criss-crossed the country and many people knew they existed—even just a few miles from their neighbourhoods—few Canadians had any idea of what was going on inside. Despite the comprehensive study of the residential school system by the Truth and Reconciliation Commission, that idea that these schools would have graveyards and, in most cases, numerous unmarked graves, came as a shock to many non-Indigenous people.

Indigenous communities across the country are now making decisions about whether and how to search the grounds of former residential schools for unmarked graves. This process is complex and heart-wrenching and will be addressed differently in different places. Fundamental to these processes is the involvement of Survivors, who will be from a wide range of First Nations, Métis, and Inuit communities, as children were sent to schools across the country.

The discovery of unmarked graves has also refocused dialogue and understanding about the status of buildings and sites formerly used as residential schools. Over a number of decades, Indigenous communities have had extensive discussions about what to do with residential school buildings after they ceased being used for that purpose. For many, it has been a critical part of healing to tear the schools down. Speaking of St. Michael's Indian Residential School in Alert Bay, British Columbia, Hereditary Chief Robert Joseph said: "It really has cast a dark shadow for so long. Symbolically, it's [tearing it down] a liberation from the haunting past. Symbolically, it's really important for the survivors because it allows us to have hope and optimism."[8]

The journey to demolishing schools has often been painful. For example, a residential school in Île-à-la-Crosse, Saskatchewan—attended by thousands of Métis children from the 1880s until the mid-1970s—became an alcohol rehabilitation centre. This was described as "ironic" and an obstacle to proper treatment, as many of the people seeking rehabilitation were those who had been forced to attend the residential school as children. Ultimately, the decision was made to demolish it.[9]

In some instances, residential schools have been transformed to suit another purpose—as part of an act of reclaiming what was taken from Survivors. This is the case at Tk'emlúps te Secwépemc, where the former Kamloops Indian Residential School is used for offices and administrative purposes, or the Kootenay Indian Residential School, which has become a resort. Former Chief Sophie Pierre, who attended residential school for nine years, describes it like this: "St. Eugene Golf Resort and Casino is on the site of the Kootenay Indian Residential School . . . That building stood for so much loss, hurt, grief. We made the decision to take that back, and give to ourselves what we'd lost there."[10]

Another example is the Muskowekwan Residential School in Saskatchewan, where a process involving Survivors resulted in the school building remaining: "We held a working conference, and 334 people attended, almost all residential school survivors. The question was put to them: Do you want us to tear it down? . . . The loud answer to that was: No."[11] Plans have been advancing to transform the school into a museum, archive, and youth training centre. This has similarities to other schools, such as the Shingwauk Residential School in Ontario, which has been turned into an educational and research centre that helps with healing and honouring the past.

A few residential schools and their grounds have been designated as National Historic Sites through the leadership and advocacy of Indigenous Peoples. One of these is on the land of the Long Plain First Nation near Portage la Prairie, Manitoba. The First Nation owns the school, which houses offices and a small residential school museum. A memorial garden and statue are planned. The second is in Shubenacadie, Nova Scotia. The school has been torn down, and other works now sit there, but the designation as a National Historic Site is viewed as part of the process of addressing what was lost through the wrongs that occurred at the residential school.[12]

But consider this. While the reports were indeed horrific for Indigenous Peoples, they were not shocking. Yes, they are triggering and extremely painful, on a personal level, for many. But in our communities, it has always been known that children never returned from residential schools, that they died there. In various ways, these missing children have always been spoken of, as part of our telling of our history in this country. Sometimes their names would be shared. Sometimes

Survivors would identify the places where they knew others were buried. Sometimes stories would be shared of those who never came home.

The existence of unmarked graves is but one illustration of how different the predominant story of Canada is for Indigenous Peoples. It reveals how much work we still must do and how much learning has to take place in order to form shared stories that are inclusive of Indigenous Peoples, and more grounded in truth.

Think about how many other times there have been some shifts in our siloed stories. For example, consider what you knew about the residential school system before the apology by Prime Minister Stephen Harper in 2008, or the release of the Truth and Reconciliation Commission report in 2015. In the apology, the prime minister acknowledged that the "burden" of harms created by residential schools had been on the shoulders of Indigenous people, and that this was wrong and that the "burden is properly ours as a government, and as a country."[13] This was an expression of how siloed stories—which had kept non-Indigenous Canadians largely ignorant of the residential schools—had created even more harm for those who suffered at the schools. By learning the truth, and breaking down silos, some of these burdens and the perpetuation of harms they create can be addressed.

Consider also how many other dimensions and aspects of our siloed stories still need to be addressed: what the early experience and orientation was of Indigenous Peoples to those who arrived from Europe; how treaties are understood and talked about; how events in Canadian history were experienced and understood; how advances in the health care system that were to the benefit of Canadians generally were part of and tied to further marginalization, disease, and even medical experimentation on Indigenous people; how the adoption of the Charter of Rights and Freedoms and the repatriation of the Constitution in 1982 was viewed with significant trepidation and resistance by some Indigenous people, and so on.

Our collective challenge—if we want to advance true reconciliation—is to break down these silos and to be able to tell a shared story of Canada that is based not on the experience of the few but of the many, including Indigenous Peoples. This is pursuing the truth—a more inclusive and accurate telling of the story of Canada and where it is going.

In order to break down those siloed stories and move towards a more complete, inclusive, and true story, we must listen, learn, and understand each other's experiences. While it is fine to have different stories that reflect our different experiences, it is not fine to be siloed in our understandings of the experiences of others, and how those experiences inform and may change the stories we tell ourselves. To build a shared future, we need to build shared ways of thinking about and understanding the history of our country.

Changing Curricula

One area where work is being done to break down silos is in education. While this effort has been going on for decades, a recent driver of change has been the response to the calls to action of the Truth and Reconciliation Commission.

Call to Action 62 states:

We call upon the federal, provincial, and territorial governments, in consultation and collaboration with Survivors, Aboriginal peoples, and educators, to:

i.   Make age-appropriate curriculum on residential schools, Treaties, and Aboriginal peoples' historical and contemporary contributions to Canada a mandatory education requirement for Kindergarten to Grade Twelve students.

ii. Provide the necessary funding to post-secondary institutions to educate teachers on how to integrate Indigenous knowledge and teaching methods into classrooms.

iii. Provide the necessary funding to Aboriginal schools to utilize Indigenous knowledge and teaching methods in classrooms.

iv. Establish senior-level positions in government at the assistant deputy minister level or higher dedicated to Aboriginal content in education.[14]

Partially in response to this work, efforts to change how children and youth are taught about Canada's history, and the reality and experience of Indigenous Peoples, have become more widespread across the country. The changes being worked on are multi-faceted—affecting what is taught, how it is taught, and who is teaching it. Even a generation ago, one could go through school learning almost nothing about Indigenous Peoples. This is certainly no longer the case. Not only is learning about Indigenous Peoples increasingly taking place throughout all grades and in many parts of the curriculum, but Indigenous people are more often in the classroom leading and helping with this process.

As well, mandatory requirements are increasingly being instituted. For example, in British Columbia, a redesigned K–12 curriculum was implemented in 2019, which explores Indigenous worldviews, perspectives, cultures, and histories across multiple grade levels. That province has also announced that in the 2023/24 academic year, a mandatory graduation requirement will be implemented regarding Indigenous-focused coursework. This work is being co-developed and implemented with First Nations.

While progress of this sort is vitally important, it should not distract us from recognizing the challenges that remain. For example, there are relatively frequent reports of overtly racist curricula material continuing to be taught—whether it be assignments about "positive experiences with residential schools"[15] or to create justifications for Europeans to be able to stay on Indigenous land.[16]

There are also significant challenges with systemic racism within schools and school systems, just like there are in other sectors. For this reason, jurisdictions are undertaking inquiries, reviews, and investigations into anti-Indigenous racism and how to address it. For example, British Columbia recently committed to "conduct an external review of Indigenous-specific racism and discrimination in the provincial public education system, and create a strategy, including resources and supports, to address findings."[17]

So let me share with you what I think is fundamental to that shared way of thinking and understanding our history— a way of telling the history of this country that incorporates and shares aspects of the Indigenous experience as well as our Canadian experience.

This telling of history is not in my words. It is an "oral" history, told through the words of Indigenous and non-Indigenous people. In telling this history through the voices of others, I am doing so in a manner that reflects how we do our work in the Big House, and is different from the way history is often told.

In the telling, we must acknowledge the countless voices that could not be included because of the reality that they have been ignored or not heard in our past, and what they said has not been recorded or remembered. As well, the way the story is told also reflects fundamental aspects of our history— about who holds power, about what beliefs were held, about what voices matter, about traditions and cultural practices, including of how knowledge was transmitted, and about the course of events. At times, Indigenous voices are predominant.

At other times, the voices of those of European descent are predominant. While the story reflects shifts and change, it also reveals things that stay the same.

This oral history weaves together voices from our past and present to try to tell our story.

And you, the reader, are being called to witness.

THIS STORY BEGINS with glimpses of the ways in which First Nations and the Inuit lived and organized their societies for thousands of years—long before there was ever any contact with Europeans. For Indigenous Peoples, the passing on of knowledge of our ways of life, teachings, cultures, and societies is commonplace. This is one of the roles of Elders and knowledge-keepers in our various traditions—and in all our communities we have mechanisms for ensuring that children are offered this knowledge from a young age.

This knowledge is also vital because it is a foundation of our work today of decolonization. When we speak of revitalizing our own systems of government and law, we are talking about translating these traditions into structures, mechanisms, and processes for today's world. The stories I have told in this book of my grandmother, and how she preserved the Potlatch, and how she and her peers passed on that knowledge to others from my generation and those younger than me, is part of that transmission of knowledge, and part of the work of revitalizing our governing traditions.

When you read the first part of this oral history, about Indigenous societies before the arrival of Europeans, I encourage you to imagine not only what these societies may have been like, but also how they may be similar or different from how your people may have lived and organized themselves in the past. Finally, I ask that you always reflect on your assumptions—the ones you may have had about Indigenous Peoples and their history and their way of life in the past, and the ones that come to mind as you read ahead.

*For the thousands of years before the arrival of Europeans,
Indigenous Peoples owned, occupied, and governed the lands now
known as North America. Those who lived here were the ancestors
of the peoples now referred to as First Nations and Inuit. In some
First Nations traditions, the story of creation is often told as the
story of the creation of "Turtle Island," a name commonly used by
some First Nations to refer to these lands. While there are diverse
and distinct versions of this story, one of the characteristics they
share is a deep respect for the natural world and the environment.
Ancient Inuit legends, such as the legend of Sedna, also speak to
the overwhelming power of nature.*

FROM THE IROQUOIS

Long before the world was created there was an island,
floating in the sky, upon which the Sky People lived. They
lived quietly and happily. No one ever died or was born
or experienced sadness. However one day one of the Sky
Women realized she was going to give birth to twins.
She told her husband, who flew into a rage. In the center
of the island there was a tree which gave light to the entire
island since the sun hadn't been created yet. He tore up
this tree, creating a huge hole in the middle of the island.
Curiously, the woman peered into the hole. Far below she
could see the waters that covered the earth . . . She fell
through the hole, tumbling towards the water below.

Water animals already existed on the earth, so far below the floating island two birds saw the Sky Woman fall. Just before she reached the waters they caught her on their backs and brought her to the other animals. Determined to help the woman they dove into the water to get mud from the bottom of the seas. One after another the animals tried and failed. Finally, Little Toad tried and when he reappeared his mouth was full of mud. The animals took it and spread it on the back of Big Turtle. The mud began to grow and grow and grow until it became the size of North America.

Then the woman stepped onto the land. She sprinkled dust into the air and created stars. Then she created the moon and sun.[18]

FROM THE INUIT

Sedna was a beautiful Inuit girl who was pressured into marriage by her father. Unknown to Sedna, her new husband was actually a raven who fed her fish and kept her in a nest on an island far away from her family. Her father, who missed Sedna terribly, went in his kayak to rescue her but the raven, with his special powers, called up a storm. The father panicked and pushed Sedna into the cold water.

As she clung to the kayak, her frozen fingers and hands were broken off and fell into the sea where they became seals, whales and other sea mammals. Sedna could no longer struggle and sank into the water where she became a goddess of the sea. Her frustration and anger continue to be expressed through the creation of storms and high seas. Inuit hunters have treated Sedna with respect for centuries to ensure she will allow Inuit to harvest her bounty. Today some hunters still sprinkle a few drops of fresh water into the mouths of sea mammals they harvest to thank Sedna for her generosity.[19]

As First Nations and Inuit had predominately oral traditions, we do not have written records by Indigenous Peoples about their way of life from prior to contact with Europeans. But First Nations and Inuit have continued to pass on orally, and in writing after Europeans arrived, their knowledge of life prior to contact. There was tremendous diversity among these peoples and societies. They had complex systems of governance, law, social organization, and family that were reflections of their distinct worldviews, spiritualities, and cultures. These included, for example, diplomatic protocols, structures, and processes governing relations between and among First Nations, such as the well-known Great Law of Peace.

TECUMSEH, A SHAWNEE CHIEF

Before the palefaces came among us, we enjoyed the happiness of unbounded freedom and were acquainted with neither riches, wants, nor oppression.[20]

CHIEFS OF THE SHUSWAP, OKANAGAN, AND COUTEAU
TRIBES OF BRITISH COLUMBIA, WRITING TO PRIME
MINISTER WILFRID LAURIER, DESCRIBING HOW
THEIR LIFE WAS BEFORE EUROPEANS ARRIVED, 1910

When they first came amongst us there were only Indians here. They found the people of each tribe supreme in their own territory, and having tribal boundaries known and recognized by all. The country of each tribe was just the same as a very large farm or ranch (belonging to all the people of the tribe) from which they gathered their food and clothing, and so on, fish which they got in plenty for food, grass and vegetation on which their horses grazed and the game lived. And much of which furnished materials for manufacture, stone which furnished pipes, utensils and tools and so on, trees which furnished firewood, materials for houses and utensils, plants, roots, seeds, nuts and berries which grew abundantly and were gathered in their season just same as the crops on a ranch; minerals, shells, and so on, which were used for ornament and for plants, and so on.

All the necessaries of life were obtained in abundance from the lands of each tribe, and all the people had equal rights of access to everything they required. You will see the ranch of each tribe was the same as its life, and without it the people could not have lived.[21]

HAUDENOSAUNEE (IROQUOIS), EXCERPTS FROM THE
GREAT LAW OF PEACE, DESCRIBING DEMOCRATIC
POLITICAL RELATIONS BETWEEN THE SENECA,
CAYUGA, ONEIDA, ONONDAGA, AND MOHAWK, 1451

2. Roots have spread out from the Tree of the Great Peace,
    one to the north, one to the east, one to the south and one
    to the west. The name of these roots is the Great White
    Roots and their nature is Peace and Strength.

    If any man or any nation outside the Five Nations
    shall obey the laws of the Great Peace and make their
    disposition to the Lords of the Confederacy, they may
    trace the Roots to the Tree and if their minds are clean
    and they are obedient and promise to obey the wishes of
    the Confederate Council, they shall be welcomed to take
    shelter beneath the Tree of the Long Leaves.

    . . .

24. The chiefs of the League of Five Nations shall be mentors
    of the people for all time. The thickness of their skins shall
    be seven spans, which is to say that they shall be proof
    against anger, offensive action and criticism. Their hearts
    shall be full of peace and good will and their minds filled
    with a yearning for the welfare of the people of the league.
    With endless patience, they shall carry out their duty.
    Their firmness shall be tempered with a tenderness for
    their people.

    . . .

92. If a nation, part of a nation, or more than one nation within the Five Nations should in any way endeavor to destroy the Great Peace by neglect or violating its laws and resolve to dissolve the Confederacy such a nation or such nations shall be deemed guilty of treason and called enemies of the Confederacy and the Great Peace.

93. Whenever a specially important matter or a great emergency is presented before the Confederate Council and the nature of the matter affects the entire body of Five Nations threatening their utter ruin, then the Lords of the Confederacy must submit the matter to the decision of their people and the decision of the people shall affect the decision of the Confederate Council. This decision shall be a confirmation of the voice of the people.[22]

Additionally, some Europeans set out to study the ways of life, cultures, and traditions of First Nations and Inuit, and, in the process of those studies, recorded what they heard from First Nations and Inuit about life prior to contact. The birth of the field of study known as anthropology has many of its foundations in Europeans studying Indigenous Peoples in different parts of the world, including what is now Canada. These descriptions by early anthropologists reflect attitudes and beliefs of Europeans, while also providing descriptions of Indigenous culture and society, including as described to them by the peoples they were studying. For example, Franz Boas, sometimes called the "father" of anthropology, spent time with the Inuit, Kwakwaka'wakw, and the Nuu-chah-nulth, among others.

"After all the many little adventures, and after a long and intimate intercourse with the Eskimos, it was with feelings of sorrow and regret that I parted from my Arctic friends. I had seen that they enjoyed life, and a hard life, as we do; that nature is also beautiful to them; that feelings of friendship also root in the Eskimo heart; that, although, the character of their life is so rude as compared to civilized life, the Eskimo is a man as we are; that his feelings, his virtues, and his shortcomings are based in human nature, like ours."[23]

＊

"The structure of the 'namima is best understood if we disregard the living individuals and rather consider the 'namima as consisting of a certain number of positions to each of which belongs to a name, a 'seat' or 'standing place,' that means rank, and privileges. Their number is limited, and they form a ranked nobility. I am told that among the thirteen tribes of the region extending from Fort Rupert to Nimpkish River and Knight Inlet, there are 658 seats. These names and seats are the skeleton of the 'namima, and individuals in the course of their lives, may occupy various positions and with these take the names belonging to them."[24]

＊

"It is good that you should have a box in which your laws and stories are kept. My friend, George Hunt, will show you a box in which some of your stories will be kept. It is a book I have written on what I saw and heard when I was with you two years ago. It is a good book, for in it are your laws and your stories. Now they will not be forgotten."[25]

Based on our knowledge of the lives of First Nations and Inuit that has been passed on from generation to generation, there are many summary descriptions of how their societies were structured and organized prior to the arrival of Europeans.

ROYAL COMMISSION ON ABORIGINAL PEOPLES, AND
PAUKTUUTIT INUIT WOMEN OF CANADA, DESCRIBING
LIFE PRIOR TO THE ARRIVAL OF EUROPEANS

In the southeastern region of North America, the Cherokee were organized into a confederacy of some 30 cities—the greatest of which was nearly as large as imperial London when English explorers first set eyes on it. Further south, in Central and South America, Indigenous peoples had carved grand empires out of the mountains and jungles long before Cortez arrived.

In northern North America, Aboriginal cultures were shaped by environment and the evolution of technology:

◊   The plentiful resources of sea and forest
    enabled west coast peoples to build societies
    of wealth and sophistication.

◊   On the prairies and northern tundra,
    Aboriginal peoples lived in close harmony with
    vast, migrating herds of buffalo and caribou.

◊   In the forests of central Canada, Aboriginal
    peoples harvested wild rice from the marshes
    and grew corn, squash and beans beside the
    river banks, supplementing their crops by
    fishing, hunting and gathering.

◊   On the east coast and in the far north, the
    bounty of the sea and land—and their own
    ingenuity—enabled Aboriginal peoples to
    survive in harsh conditions.[26]

✻

Prior to contact with Europeans, Inuit were entirely
self-sufficient. They lived in small, autonomous, nomadic
groups, dependent upon hunting, fishing and gathering for
survival and for all their physical needs. Customary law
was followed, characterized by its informal nature, flexibility,
and its reliance upon social pressures to ensure that people
acted appropriately. Inuit had developed a rich material culture, based primarily upon hunting and fishing technology.
Spirituality centered upon beliefs in animal and human-like
spirits, including the spirits of deceased relatives.[27]

WITH CONTACT BETWEEN Indigenous Peoples and
Europeans came massive changes. But change was not linear
or one-dimensional. This is not just a story of the racism,
violence, and colonization perpetuated by European powers,
though that is certainly a major part of the story. As you
can imagine, responses to contact between peoples who did
not know previously of each other's existence were complicated and dynamic. There were efforts to learn about each
other, to learn each other's languages, and to understand
differences in respective ways of life and social organization.
There was the development of visions and patterns of what
living together might look like. There were efforts to define a
common future. At times, there was mutual support to help
each other survive.

Over time, however, patterns of harm—fuelled by attitudes and ambitions that were destructive—became more
paramount, and opportunities for constructive relations
became more remote. A major factor in this was the ongoing
proliferation of imposed structures, laws, policies, and institutions—driven by competition between European powers
and an increase in their population—that had foundations in
racist ideas and economic self-interest. Colonization deepened, and with it, the systematization of patterns of harm.
Even where European laws and traditions required certain
forms of recognition and respect for Indigenous Peoples,
these came to be readily violated or ignored altogether.

As such, it is not surprising that as one moves forward
from initial contact towards Confederation, things grow

darker and more difficult for Indigenous Peoples. This is reflected in our oral history in a variety of ways; note, for example, how Indigenous voices recede as those of the Europeans begin to dominate.

Before you continue reading, pause for a moment and think about what I just wrote.

With a few slight nuances, I could have been describing our more recent history. Efforts at learning and building a common future still give way to patterns of harm that continue to exist and need to be addressed.

I do not mean to suggest that nothing has changed; you already know of my firm belief that much has changed, and that the pace of change is accelerating. Rather, I say it because I want to emphasize our connection to the past, and our responsibility and capacity to not repeat it. In this story, in the past, the response over time to differences and change was deepening patterns of harm and injustice. Today, in response to differences and change, we are focused on the work of true reconciliation, and breaking from those past responses.

Europeans came to the lands that are now known as North America as part of efforts to build economic wealth, spread Christianity, and address struggles for power between rulers. It was these dynamics that set off centuries of European conquest and colonization of different parts of the world. The "Doctrine of Discovery," which has its roots in directives from the papacy, provided a justification for this movement across the globe. At the core of their doctrine was the belief that any lands where there were no Christians living were considered uninhabited and therefore could be "discovered." Any non-Christians who happened to be on those lands were viewed as not inhabiting them as human beings. As such, the lands and resources could be taken as if they were empty—terra nullius—and any people on those lands were treated as slaves, and to be converted to Christianity.

POPE NICHOLAS V, 1452

. . . invade, search out, capture, vanquish, and subdue all Saracens, Pagans whatsoever. Reduce their persons to perpetual slavery. Convert them to his and their use in profit.[28]

ROMANUS PONTIFEX AUTHORIZING KING AFONSO V OF PORTUGAL TO TAKE POSSESSION OF TERRITORIES ALONG THE AFRICAN COAST AND BEYOND, AND TO ENGAGE IN THE SLAVE TRADE, 1455

. . . to invade, search out, capture, vanquish, and subdue all Saracens and pagans whatsoever, and other enemies of Christ wheresoever placed, and the kingdoms, dukedoms, principalities, dominions, possessions, and all movable and immovable goods whatsoever held and possessed by them and to reduce their persons to perpetual slavery, and to apply and appropriate to himself and his successors the kingdoms, dukedoms, counties, principalities, dominions, possessions, and goods, and to convert them to his and their use and profit.[29]

In 1496, King Henry VII of England gave direction to explorer John Cabot and his sons reflecting the Doctrine of Discovery. This resulted in the first English claim to "discover" lands that would eventually make up Canada. The first French claim to "discover" these lands was by explorer Jacques Cartier in the 1530s. These lands, which were occupied by Indigenous Peoples, were granted by European powers to their own people. A well-known example of this practice can be found in the Hudson's Bay Company, founded in 1670, which was a central force in the English settlement of what would become known as Canada. They were given a monopoly by King Charles II over "Rupert's Land," a region drained by all rivers and streams flowing into Hudson Bay. This effectively gave the Hudson's Bay Company control of the fur trade, allowing them to play a government-like role over a vast area for almost two centuries. The Hudson's Bay Company sold "Rupert's Land" to Canada in 1869, while continuing to operate elsewhere.

KING HENRY VII, DIRECTION TO THE EXPLORER JOHN CABOT AND HIS SONS FOR THE DISCOVERY OF NEW AND UNKNOWN LANDS, 1496

We have also granted to them and to any of them, and to the heirs and deputies of them and of any one of them, and have given licence to set up our aforesaid banners and ensigns in any town, city, castle, island or mainland whatsoever, newly found by them . . . And . . . may conquer, occupy and possess whatsoever such towns, castles, cities and islands by them thus discovered that they may be able to conquer, occupy and possess, as our vassals and governors lieutenants and deputies therein, acquiring for us the dominion, title and jurisdiction of the same towns, castles, cities, islands and mainlands so discovered . . .[30]

While the Doctrine of Discovery was a foundation for Europeans coming to what would become North America, some of the early contact and interaction between First Nations and Europeans was marked by peace, friendship, military alliances, and mutual support.

THE CHIEFS OF THE SHUSWAP, OKANAGAN, AND
COUTEAU TRIBES, WRITING PRIME MINISTER
WILFRID LAURIER, DESCRIBING SOME OF
THEIR RELATIONS WITH THE FRENCH, 1910

We speak to you more freely because you are a member of the white race with whom we first became acquainted, and which we call in our tongue "real whites" to the latter. . . .

The "real whites" we found were good people. We could depend on their word, and we trusted and respected them. They did not interfere with us nor attempt to break up our tribal organizations, laws, and customs. They did not try to force their ideas of things to us to our harm. Nor did they stop us from catching fish, hunting and so on. They never tried to steal or appropriate our country and treated our chiefs as men. They were the first to find us in this country. We never asked them to come here, nevertheless we treated them kindly and hospitably and helped them all we could.

They had made themselves (as it were) our guests. We treated them as such, and then waited to see what they would do.

As we found they did us no harm our friendship with them became lasting. Because of this we have a warm heart to the French at the present day. We expect good from Canada.[31]

Growing conflict between the French and the English, beginning in the latter part of the seventeenth century and continuing through the Seven Years' War (1756–63), was a factor in many of the changes in their relations with Indigenous Peoples, as European powers looked for allies to bolster their positions. The English also started formalizing roles and offices to conduct "Indian Affairs," and eventually, in the 1750s, established an "Indian Department" and appointed a "Superintendent for Indian Affairs." The mandate included "political relations with Indian people, protection of traders, boundary negotiations and the enlistment of Indian people during times of war."[32]

These shifts to more formal relations with Indigenous Peoples were one reason for the emergence of treaty-making. Some First Nations indicated their assent to treaty by presenting wampum to officials of the Crown. Although not a part of all First Nations cultures, Wampum—made of white and purple seashells from the Atlantic—is woven into belts. Particular patterns symbolize events, alliances, and peoples. Wampum was used to form relationships, propose marriage, atone for murder, or even ransom captives. The Two Row Wampum Belt of the Iroquois symbolizes an agreement of mutual respect and peace between the Iroquois and European newcomers. The principles embodied in the belt

are a set of rules governing the behaviour of the two groups.
The wampum belt tells us that neither group will force their
laws, traditions, customs, or language on each other, but will
coexist peacefully.

ONONDAGA NATION, DESCRIBING
TWO ROW WAMPUM, C. 1613

It is agreed that we will travel together, side by each, on the
river of life . . . linked by peace, friendship, forever. We will
not try to steer each other's vessels.[33]

ELLEN GABRIEL, MOHAWK ACTIVIST AND
ARTIST, DESCRIBING THE IMPORTANCE
OF THE TWO ROW WAMPUM TREATY

Ka'swènh:tha or the Two Row Wampum Treaty is a significant agreement in the history of the relationship between
European monarchs and Indigenous peoples. *Ka'swènh:tha*
is more than visionary. As a principled treaty it is grounded
in an Indigenous intellect providing an insight and a vigilant
awareness of the inevitability of the evolution of society.
Ka'swènh:tha is an instrument of reconciliation for contemporary times if openness, honesty, respect, and genuine
concern for present and future generations is a foundational priority.[34]

74

In the early era of constructive relations and treaty-making, Europeans grappled with the inevitable fact that First Nations owned and occupied the lands of North America. Some recognized that a framework was necessary for relations that would address First Nations sovereignty and rights. Various attempts were made at this. For example, the English colonizers—over time— were instructed that the Doctrine of Discovery did not and could not be applied. The Royal Proclamation of 1763 from King George III made clear that for Indigenous lands to be acquired, they must be ceded or purchased—they could not just be taken.

KING GEORGE III, EXCERPTS FROM THE ROYAL PROCLAMATION, 1763

[I]t is just and reasonable and essential to our Interest, and the Security of our Colonies, that the several Nations or Tribes of Indians with whom We are connected, and who live under our Protection, should not be molested or disturbed in the Possession of such parts of our Dominions and Territories as not having been ceded to or purchased by Us, are reserved to them, or any of them, as their Hunting Grounds . . . any Lands whatever, which, not having been ceded to or purchased by Us as aforesaid, are reserved to the said Indians, or any of them. . . .

[A]nd We do hereby strictly forbid, on Pain of our Displeasure, all our loving Subjects from making any Purchases or Settlements whatever, or taking Possession of any of the Lands above reserved, without our especial leave and Licence for that Purpose first obtained.

And We do further strictly enjoin and require all Persons whatever who have either wilfully or inadvertently seated themselves upon any Lands within the Countries above described or upon any other Lands which, not having been ceded to or purchased by Us, are still reserved to the said Indians as aforesaid, forthwith to remove themselves from such Settlements.[35]

Treaty-making continued after the Royal Proclamation, including the Treaty of Niagara (1764) between more than twenty First Nations in parts of what would become Ontario and Quebec. The Treaty of Niagara was affirmed through the gifting of wampum by the Crown official to the assembled Chiefs. It was to establish peace and alliance, which was of particular concern to the British, as conflict was increasing with the French.

MINAVAVANA, AN OJIBWA CHIEF FROM WEST OF MANITOULIN AT MICHILIMACKINAC, REGARDING TREATY-MAKING, 1761

Englishman, although you have conquered the French you have not yet conquered us! We are not your slaves. These lakes, these woods and mountains, were left to us by our ancestors. They are our inheritance; and we will part with them to none. Your nation supposes that we, like the white people, cannot live without bread, and pork and beef! But, you ought to know, that He, the Great Spirit and

Master of Life, has provided food for us, in these spacious lakes, and on these woody mountains.

Englishman, our Father, the king of France, employed our young men to make war upon your nation. In this warfare, many of them have been killed; and it is our custom to retaliate, until such time as the spirits of the slain are satisfied. But, the spirits of the slain are to be satisfied in either of two ways; the first is the spilling of the blood of the nation by which they fell; the other, by covering the bodies of the dead, and thus allaying the resentment of their relations. This is done by making presents.

Englishman, your king has never sent us any presents, nor entered into any treaty with us, wherefore he and we are still at war; and, until he does these things, we must consider that we have no other father or friend among the white man, than the king of France . . .

You have ventured your life among us, in the expectation that we should not molest you. You do not come armed, with an intention to make war, you come in peace, to trade with us, to supply us with necessities, of which we are in much want. We shall regard you therefore as a brother; and you may sleep tranquilly, without fear of the Chipeways. As a token of our friendship we present you with this pipe, to smoke.[36]

SIR WILLIAM JOHNSON, SUPERINTENDENT
OF INDIAN AFFAIRS, UPON THE GIVING
AND RECEIVING OF WAMPUM BELTS
TO ASSEMBLED CHIEFS, C. 1764

Brothers of the Western Nations, Sachems, Chiefs and
Warriors;

You have now been here for several days, during which
time we have frequently met to renew and Strengthen
our Engagements and you have made so many Promises
of your Friendship and Attachment to the English that
there now remains for us only to exchange the great Belt
of the Covenant Chain that we may not forget our mutual
Engagements.

I now therefore present you the great Belt by which
I bind all your Western Nations together with the English,
and I desire that you will take fast hold of the same, and
never let it slip, to which end I desire that after you have
shewn this Belt to all Nations you will fix one end of it with
the Chipeweighs at St. Marys [Michilimackinac] whilst the
other end remains at my house, and moreover I desire that
you will never listen to any news which comes to any other
Quarter. If you do it, it may shake the Belt.[37]

In specific places, relations between Europeans and Indigenous Peoples resulted in the emergence of a people with their own community, culture, and homeland. In the Red River Settlement, for example, the Métis Nation was born, with other Métis settlements stretching outward. The Métis would emerge as a vital political, cultural, and social force in the historic and contemporary reality of Canada, and as a distinct Indigenous People recognized in Canada's Constitution.

LOUIS RIEL, DESCRIBING THE RESISTANCE OF THE MÉTIS PEOPLE

We may be a small community and a Half-breed community at that—but we are men, free and spirited men, and we will not allow even the Dominion of Canada to trample on our rights.[38]

AUDREY POITRAS, DESCRIBING THE PRIDE, RESILIENCE, AND ROOTS OF THE MÉTIS

Our flag represents the faith that the Métis culture shall live on forever. We are Indigenous to this country because we were born of the land long before Canada was a country.[39]

Despite some early progress in the relations between Europeans and the Indigenous Peoples, destructive and oppressive forces also continued to grow. This included disease, violence, and the taking of lands and resources in other parts of what would become Canada. As the debate, dialogue, and effort to further settle and form the country emerged, Indigenous Peoples were increasingly marginalized. Smallpox was particularly destructive. For example, it is estimated the Haida went from an estimated population of twenty thousand prior to 1770 to less than six hundred by the end of the nineteenth century, primarily as a result of the disease. In some instances, the intentional spreading of smallpox was used against Indigenous Peoples as a weapon of war by Europeans.

NORTH COAST HAIDA CHIEF KOWE DESCRIBING THE DEVASTATION OF DISEASE, 1795

[T]he small Pox swept off two-thirds of the people.[40]

A HUDSON'S BAY COMPANY REPORT DOCUMENTING DISEASE, 1829

Immense numbers of them were swept off by a dreadful visitation of the smallpox, that from the appearance of some individuals that bear marks of the disease, may have happened fifty or sixty years ago [1769–79]. The same disease committed a second ravage, but less destruction than the first about ten years afterwards.[41]

LORD JEFFREY AMHERST, A BRITISH
MILITARY LEADER IN THE AMERICAS, 1763

You will Do well to try to Innoculate the Indians by means
of Blankets, as well as to try Every other method that can
serve to Extirpate this Execrable Race. I should be very
glad your Scheme for hunting them Down by Dogs could
take effect.[42]

*Out west, the newest of the colonies, the Colony of Vancouver
Island, was established in 1849. The original instructions to
James Douglas, the chief factor of the Hudson's Bay Company
and the first governor of the new colony, resulted in fourteen
treaties being completed. This early recognition of First Nations'
connection to their lands would soon change. Treaty-making
stopped, and land was increasingly taken up by settlers on
Vancouver Island and the mainland of what would eventually
become British Columbia.*

SECRETARY OF THE HUDSON'S BAY COMPANY
ARCHIBALD BARCLAY, INSTRUCTIONS TO
JAMES DOUGLAS TO COMPLETE TREATIES, 1849

With respect to the rights of the natives, you will have to
confer with the chiefs of the tribes on that subject, and in
your negotiations with them you are to consider the natives

as the rightful possessors of such lands only as they are occupied by cultivation, or had houses built on, at the time the island came under the undivided sovereignty of Great Britain in 1846. All other land is to be regarded as waste, applicable for the purposes of colonization. The right of fishing and hunting will be continued to the natives, and when their lands are registered, and they conform to the same conditions with which other settlers are required to comply, they will enjoy the same rights and privileges.[43]

JOSEPH TRUTCH, CHIEF COMMISSIONER OF LAND AND WORKS, DESCRIBING THE SHIFT AWAY FROM TREATY-MAKING TO DENIAL OF FIRST NATIONS' CONNECTION TO LANDS, 1870

[F]or the past 10 years at least during which I have resided in this Colony—the Government appears to me to have striven to the extent of its power to protect and befriend the Native race, and its declared policy has been that the Aborigines should, in all material respects, be on the same footing in the eye of the law as people of European descent, and that they should be encouraged to live amongst the white settlers in the country, and so, by their example, be induced to adopt habits of civilization. . . .

But the title of the Indians in the fee of the public lands, or any portion thereof, has never been acknowledged by Government—but, on the contrary, is distinctly denied.

In no case has any special arrangement been made with any of the tribes of the Mainland for the extinction of their claims of possession—but these claims have been held to have been fully satisfied by securing to each tribe, as the progress of the settlement of the country seemed to require, the use of sufficient tracts of land for their wants for agricultural and pastoral purposes. . . .

I will only remark further, on the general subject of the condition of the Indians in the Colony, that it is unhesitatingly acknowledged to be the peculiar responsibility of Government to use every endeavour to promote the civilization, education, and ultimate Christianization of the native races within our territory, and that any practical scheme for advancing this object which it would be within the scope of the pecuniary ability of the Colony to carry into effect would be adopted with alacrity. . .[44]

On the Prairies, what was called the Red River Resistance was forming in the late 1860s as a result of the arrival of new anglophone settlers, whose very existence increased tensions with the Métis and First Nations populations. The health and welfare of the Métis, especially, was becoming increasingly precarious, as their land was being appropriated and previous promises by the Europeans broken. Resistance emerged as a recurring aspect of Métis life and culture, as part of protecting their identity and reality as "une nouvelle nation"—a "new" nation of people both part of but distinct from Indigenous and European traditions.

A MÉTIS VOYAGEUR, DESCRIBING
THE MÉTIS IDENTITY, 1850s

Where do I live? I cannot say. I am a Voyageur—I am
a Chicot mister. I live everywhere. My grandfather was a
Voyageur; he died on the voyage. My father was a Voyageur;
he died on the Voyage. I will also die while on voyage and
another Chicot will take my place. Such is the course of
our life.[45]

LOUIS RIEL

We have allowed ourselves to fall into the hands of a
Government which only thinks of us to pillage us. Had he
only understood what God did for us before Confederation,
we should have been sorry to see it coming. And the half-
breeds of the North-West would have made conditions
of a nature to preserve for our children that liberty, that
possession of the soil, without which there is no happiness
for anyone; but fifteen years of suffering, impoverishment
and underhand, malignant persecution have opened our
eyes; and the sight of the abyss of demoralization into which
the Dominion is daily plunging us deeper and deeper every
day, has suddenly, by God's mercy, as it were, stricken us
with horror.[46]

As England continued to become more dominant over the French in North America through the second half of the eighteenth century, the focus further shifted from alliances with Indigenous Peoples for military purposes to a desire to control, subjugate, and "civilize" them.

DUNCAN CAMPBELL SCOTT, A CAREER CIVIL SERVANT WHO IMPLEMENTED "INDIAN" POLICY IN THE EARLY TWENTIETH CENTURY, DESCRIBING ASPECTS OF THAT POLICY FROM BEFORE CONFEDERATION

The civilization of the Indian became the ideal; the menace of the tomahawk and the firebrand having disappeared, the apparent duty was to raise him from the debased condition into which he had fallen owing to the loose and pampering policy of former days. Protection from vices which were not his own, and instruction in peaceful occupations, foreign to his natural bent, were to be substituted for necessary generosity.[47]

ARCHIBALD ACHESON, GOVERNOR GENERAL OF BRITISH NORTH AMERICA, DESCRIBING POLICY TOWARDS INDIGENOUS PEOPLES, 1837

[I]nducing the Indians to change their present ways for more civilized Habits of Life, namely their Settlement . . . compact Settlements should be formed . . . giving them Agricultural Implements, but no other Description of Presents.[48]

In Britain, the 1837 House of Commons Select Committee on Aborigines began considering new policies based on a worldwide view of Britain's imperial role. The committee was informed by field reports from North American missionaries stating that Indigenous Peoples were in urgent need of Christianity and the other trappings of civilization. Reflecting ideas of racial superiority and the need to civilize Indigenous Peoples, the attitudes and beliefs that would be the basis of the residential school system also were becoming deeply rooted and expressed in policy.

REPORT OF THE HOUSE OF COMMONS
SELECT COMMITTEE ON ABORIGINES, 1837

In the foregoing survey we have seen the desolating effects of unprincipled Europeans with Nations in a ruder state. There remains a more gratifying subject—the effect of fair dealing and of Christian instruction upon heathens. True civilization and Christianity are inseparable: the former has never been found, but as a fruit of the latter. As soon as they were converted, they perceived the evils attendant upon their former ignorant wandering state; they began to work, which they never did before; they perceived the advantage of cultivating the soil; they totally gave up drinking; they became industrious, sober and useful.[49]

SIR JAMES KEMPT, GOVERNOR GENERAL OF BRITISH
NORTH AMERICA, 1828-30, ON "INDIAN" POLICY

1st To collect the Indians in considerable numbers, and settle them in villages with a due portion of land for their cultivation and support.

2nd To make such provision for their religious improvement, education, and instruction in husbandry as circumstances may from time to time require.

3rd To afford them such assistance in building their houses; ration; and in procuring such seed and agricultural implements as may be necessary, commuting when practicable a portion of their presents for the later.[50]

REPORT OF THE COMMITTEE OF
THE EXECUTIVE COUNCIL RESPECTING
THE INDIAN DEPARTMENT, 1836

Before the Conquest of this Country the Indians were under the Especial care and Direction of the Jesuit missionaries . . . who became themselves their Instructors in so much of the Knowledge of Arts and Life as they thought it advisable to impart to them. Believing it however to be incumbent on the State to prepare the younger Generation of Indians for another and more useful Mode of Life, the Committee [Committee of the Executive Council,

Quebec City] would earnestly press upon His Majesty's
Government the necessity of establishing Schools among
them in which the Rudiments of Education shall be
taught . . . But though in natural Capacity, in Docility,
and the Faculty of Observation, the Indians do not yield
to any Race of Men . . . a considerable Time must probably
elapse before Ancient Habits and Prepossessions can be so
far broken through that they become sensible to the Benefits
of such Training for their Children. It may therefore be necessary to make it a condition of their continuing to receive
Presents either for themselves or to their families, that they
should send their Children to such Schools: and it may be
hoped that the Clergy will lend their Aid in recommending
and enforcing the Measure, as a necessary Part of any Plan
for assimilating the Indians as much and as soon as possible
to the rest of the Inhabitants of the Province? [51]

*At around the same time, harms and challenges also began to
increase for the Inuit. While there had been contact between the
Inuit and Europeans, it had been relatively light in nature and
seasonal, primarily related to the European whaling industry.
But in the 1850s, year-round shore stations were established.
Among the harmful impacts of contact with the Europeans
was a rising rate of disease that was soon decimating the
Inuit population.*

CHARLES FRANCIS HALL, AN ARCTIC EXPLORER
WHO TOOK MUCH INUIT TESTIMONY, C. 1861-62

The days of the Inuit are numbered. There are very few of
them left now. Fifty years may find them all passed away,
without leaving one to tell that such a people ever lived.[52]

A MISSIONARY STATIONED IN
CUMBERLAND SOUND, EARLY 1900S

I have more than once . . . pointed out to these wretched
people the whalers, the sure and certain goal to which they are
traveling. The extermination of the whole of the Eskimo population in Cumberland Sound and elsewhere is only a matter
of time, if some check is not put to these awful practices.[53]

WITH THE FOUNDING of Canada in 1867 came both conti-
nuity and rupture. Things we consider particularly destructive
towards Indigenous Peoples in the history of Canada—the
Indian Act, the residential school system, systemic racism
in public services, the taking up and exploitation of lands
and resources, the denial of basic human rights—were
already present or had their foundations established prior
to Confederation.

But the formation of the new country of Canada was
also a rupture from what had come before. In creating

Canada—as when forming any new country—there was a tremendous amount of bartering, negotiation, and, ultimately, compromises. Much of that involved issues of power, control, and jurisdiction of lands. With this rupture, Indigenous Peoples became even more marginalized. A major issue in the founding of Canada was debate over how power would be allocated between provinces and the federal government. With this focus, and in many ways even more so than before, Indigenous Peoples and any claims they may have had to authority, lands, and resources, had to be specifically and actively denied. In the complicated and challenging work of creating Canada, Indigenous Peoples and their continued existence were, more than anything, a problem. The easiest solution to this problem, in the eyes of Canada's founders, was to assimilate Indigenous Peoples and to effectively sever all enduring connections or claims they had to their land and resources. Assimilation and denial became the core, foundational framework of Canada, around which relations with Indigenous Peoples—First Nations, Métis, and Inuit—were built.

You already know we are still reckoning with the weapons that were used to effect assimilation and denial, such as the Indian Act. But that reckoning began long ago. After Confederation, as these policies deepened, Indigenous Peoples started to push back through new forms of advocacy and organization—including, at times, with non-Indigenous allies.

As you reflect on this period in the oral history, consider what has changed, and what has not. You will see that there are certain patterns that remain deeply entrenched and have not shifted much—including those involved in how government interacts with Indigenous Peoples—while other patterns have shifted, such as the degree to which Canadians from all walks of life are now engaged in issues and relations with Indigenous Peoples.

Indigenous Peoples were not present at Confederation, neither physically nor in spirit. There had been little debate or discussion about Indigenous Peoples—and none with Indigenous Peoples—in the process of making the decision to form the country of Canada. In fact, there was only one provision of the British North America Act regarding Indigenous Peoples, which was about the jurisdiction of the federal government over "Indians."

BRITISH NORTH AMERICA ACT, 1867

91 (24). Indians, and Lands reserved for the Indians.[54]

After Confederation, the formation of laws, policies, and practices of oppression deepened. A policy goal became to fully assimilate Indigenous Peoples, and to deny any official relationship of Indigenous Peoples to their lands. This included, for example, governments saying they would grant voting rights to Indigenous Peoples (at the time meaning men) as part of

a policy of creating a Canada where there were no "Indians,"
no Indigenous Peoples that were recognized in law or viewed as
having their own cultures, societies, and traditions, no treaties
or treaty rights, and no claims to land.

DUNCAN CAMPBELL SCOTT, DESCRIBING
A PROPOSED BILL ON CANADA'S POLICY
TOWARDS INDIGENOUS PEOPLES, 1920

Our objective is to continue until there is not a single Indian
in Canada that has not been absorbed into the body politic
and there is no Indian question, and no Indian Department,
that is the object of this Bill.[55]

JOSEPH TRUTCH, REGARDING THE CONNECTION
OF INDIGENOUS PEOPLES TO THEIR LANDS, 1867

The Indians really have no right to the lands they claim,
nor are they of any actual value or utility to them, and
I cannot see why they should either retain these lands to
the prejudice of the general interest of the Colony, or be
allowed to make a market of them either to the Government
or to Individuals.[56]

WILLIAM SPRAGUE, DEPUTY SUPERINTENDENT
GENERAL OF INDIAN AFFAIRS, DESCRIBING THE
PURPOSE OF CANADA'S EARLY LEGISLATION
REPLACING TRADITIONAL INDIGENOUS
POLITICAL INSTITUTIONS WITH ELECTED
BAND COUNCILS, LATE 1800S

The Acts [to provide for the organization of the Department of the Secretary of State of Canada and for the Administration of the Affairs of the Indians, and for the gradual enfranchisement of Indians] framed in the years 1868 and 1869, relating to Indian affairs, were designed to lead the Indian people by degrees to mingle with the white race in the ordinary avocations of life. It was intended to afford facilities for electing, for a limited period, members of bands to manage, as a Council, local matters; that intelligent and educated men, recognized as chiefs, should carry out the wishes of the male members of mature years in each band, who should be fairly represented in the conduct of their internal affairs.

Thus establishing a responsible, for an irresponsible system, this provision, by law, was designed to pave the way to the establishment of simple municipal institutions.[57]

CHIEF DAN GEORGE OF THE TSLEIL-WAUTUTH
NATION, REFLECTING ON CANADA'S POLICIES
TOWARDS INDIGENOUS PEOPLES, 1967

When I fought to protect my land and my home, I was
called a savage. When I neither understood nor welcomed
his way of life, I was called lazy. When I tried to rule my
people, I was stripped of my authority.[58]

*The Christian churches played a central role in implementing poli-
cies of assimilation and oppression, including operating most of the
residential school system. This role of the churches in "civilizing" and
assimilating Indigenous Peoples, which had been present in various
forms since the arrival of Europeans, continued as part of official
government policy after the formation of Canada.*

MEMORANDUM OF THE CONVENTION OF
CATHOLIC PRINCIPALS, DESCRIBING ATTITUDES
TOWARDS INDIGENOUS PEOPLES, 1924

All true civilization must be based on moral law, which
Christian religion alone can give. Pagan superstition could
not suffice . . . to make the Indians practice the virtues of
our civilization and avoid its attendant vices. Several people
have desired us to countenance the dances of the Indians
and to observe their festivals; but their habits, being the
result of free and easy mode of life, cannot conform to the
intense struggle for life which our social conditions require.[59]

REPORT OF THE ALBERTA METHODIST
COMMISSION, DESCRIBING ATTITUDES
TOWARDS INDIGENOUS PEOPLES, 1911

The Indian is the weak child in the family of our nation
and for this reason presents the most earnest appeal for
Christian sympathy and cooperation . . . [W]e are convinced that the only hope of successfully discharging this
obligation to our Indian brethren is through the medium
of the children, therefore education must be given the
foremost place.[60]

*Building on legislation that was passed prior to Confederation,
the Indian Act was the foundation for a deepening oppression of
Indigenous Peoples. The original Indian Act had 122 sections,
which formalized and entrenched the segregation of First Nations
people onto reserves, limited basic human rights including mobility
rights, imposed a system of administrative control from Ottawa,
and was the legislative foundation for removing children from
their parents and establishing the residential school system.*

ROYAL COMMISSION ON ABORIGINAL PEOPLES,
DESCRIBING THE INDIAN ACT, 1996

In the midst of the treaty-making process going on in
western Canada, the first *Indian Act* as such was passed in
1876 as a consolidation of previous Indian legislation. Indian
policy was now firmly fixed on a national foundation based
unashamedly on the notion that Indian cultures and societies
were clearly inferior to settler society. The annual report of
the department of the interior for the year 1876 expressed the
prevailing philosophy that Indians were children of the state.

> Our Indian legislation generally rests on the principle,
> that the aborigines are to be kept in a condition of tute-
> lage and treated as wards or children of the State. . . . the
> true interests of the aborigines and the State alike require
> that every effort should be made to aid the Red man
> in lifting himself out of his condition of tutelage and
> dependence, and that is clearly our wisdom and our duty,
> through education and every other means, to prepare him
> for a higher civilization by encouraging him to assume
> the privileges and responsibilities of full citizenship.

The transition from tribal nation in the tripartite
imperial system to legal incompetent in the bilateral federal/
provincial system was now complete. While protection
remained a policy goal, it was no longer collective Indian
tribal autonomy that was protected: it was the individual

Indian recast as a dependent ward—in effect, the child of the state. Moreover, protection no longer meant maintaining a more or less permanent line between Indian lands and the settler society; it meant the very opposite. By reducing the culture of distance through civilizing and assimilating measures that would culminate in enfranchisement of Indians and reduction of the reserve land base in 50-acre chunks, it was hoped Indian lands would in this piecemeal fashion soon lose their protected status and become part of the provincial land regime.

In keeping with the clear policy of assimilation, the *Indian Act* made no reference to the treaties already in existence or to those being negotiated at the time it was passed. The absence of any significant mention of the treaty relationship continues in the current version of the *Indian Act*. It is almost as if Canada deliberately allowed itself to forget the principal constitutional mechanism by which the nation status of Indian communities is recognized in domestic law.[61]

PRIME MINISTER SIR JOHN A. MACDONALD,
DESCRIBING THE PURPOSE OF THE INDIAN ACT, 1887

[N]othing in their way of life that was worth preserving . . . [and] . . . the great aim of our legislation [the Indian Act] has been to do away with the tribal system and assimilate the Indian people in all respects with the other inhabitants of the Dominions as speedily as they are fit to change.[62]

HECTOR-LOUIS LANGEVIN, ONE OF THE "FATHERS"
OF CONFEDERATION AND A LEADING POLITICIAN,
DESCRIBING THE NECESSITY TO ESTABLISH
RESIDENTIAL SCHOOLS

In order to educate the ('Indian') children properly we must separate them from their families. Some people may say that this is hard but if we want to civilize them we must do that.[63]

✳

The fact is that if you wish to educate the children you must separate them from their parents during the time they are being taught. If you leave them in the family they may know how to read and write, but they will remain savages, whereas by separating them in the way proposed, they acquire the habits and tastes . . . of civilized people.[64]

PRIME MINISTER SIR JOHN A. MACDONALD,
DESCRIBING THE POLICY TO ESTABLISH
RESIDENTIAL SCHOOLS, 1883

When the school is on the reserve the child lives with its parents, who are savages; he is surrounded by savages, and though he may learn to read and write his habits, and train-ing and mode of thought are Indian. He is simply a savage who can read and write. It has been strongly pressed on myself, as the head of the Department, that Indian children should be withdrawn as much as possible from the parental influence, and the only way to do that would be to put them in central training industrial schools where they will acquire the habits and modes of thought of white men.[65]

Indigenous Peoples continued to raise the alarm about the mounting harms, dispossession, and violence they were subjected to. As time passed, the concerns increased.

COAST SALISH CHIEFS TO GOVERNOR FREDERICK SEYMOUR, PETITIONS FOR CHANGE, 1860S AND '70S

We know the good heart of the Queen for the Indians. You bring that good heart with you, so we are happy to welcome you. We wish to become good Indians, and to be friends with the white people. . . . Please to protect our land, that it will not be small for us: many are well pleased with their reservations, and many wish that their reservations be marked out for them.

✳

[10 years later] For many years we have been complaining of the land left to us being too small. We have laid our complaints before the Government officials nearest to us: they sent us to some others; so we had no redress up to the present; and we have felt like men being trampled on, and are commencing to believe that the aim of the white men is to exterminate us as soon as they can, although we have always been quiet, obedient, kind, and friendly to the whites.

✳

The white men have taken our land and no compensation has been given us, though we have been told many times that the great Queen was so good she would help her distant children the Indians. White men have surrounded our Villages so much as in many instances especially on Fraser River but a few acres of Land have been left us.

✳

We are now obliged to clear heavy timbered land, all prairies having been taken from us by white men. We see our white neighbors cultivate wheat, peas, &c., and raise large stocks of cattle on our pasture lands, and we are giving them our money to buy the flour manufactured from the wheat they have grown on same prairies.

✳

What have we received for our good faith, friendliness and patience? . . . They have stolen our lands and everything on them and continue to use same for their own purposes . . . We demand that our land question be settled . . . We desire that every matter of importance to each tribe be a subject of treaty, so we may have a definite understanding with the government on all questions of moment between us and them.

✳

We have also learned lately the British Columbia government claims absolute ownership of our reservations which means that we are practically landless. We only have a loan of those reserves in life rent, or at the option of the B.C. government. Thus we find ourselves without any real home in this our own country.[66]

CHIEF DAVID MACKAY OF THE NISGA'A,
DESCRIBING HOW THE LAND WAS TAKEN, 1887

What we don't like about the Government is their saying this: "We will give you this much land." How can they give it when it is our own? We cannot understand it. They have never bought it from us or our forefathers. They have never fought and conquered our people and taken the land in that way, and yet they say now that they will give us so much land—our own land. These chiefs do not talk foolishly, they know the land is their own; our forefathers for generations and generations past had their land here all around us; chiefs have had their own hunting grounds, their salmon streams, and places where they got their berries; it has always been so. It is not only during the last four or five years that we have seen the land; we have always seen and owned it; it is no new thing, it has been ours for generations. If we had only seen it for twenty years and claimed it as our own, it would have been foolish, but it has been ours for thousands of years. If any strange person came here and saw the land for twenty years and claimed it, he would be foolish. We have always got our living from the land; we are not like white people who live in towns and have their stores and other business, getting their living in that way, but we have always depended on the land for our food and clothes; we get our salmon, berries, and furs from the land.[67]

The Métis Resistance of 1870 and the Northwest Resistance of 1885 arose as the Métis, who constituted a majority of the area's population, became increasingly marginalized. While some resistance objectives were achieved in 1870, including those that resulted in the formation of the Province of Manitoba, Métis nationality continued to be ignored, and the suffering and disenfranchisement of the Métis people continued. Louis Riel and other leaders remained exiles and continued to drive for recognition and change, including through the 1885 resistance.

LOUIS RIEL, DESCRIBING THE ROOTS
OF THE 1885 RESISTANCE

When I came into the Northwest in July, the 1st of July 1884,
I found the Indians suffering. I found the half-breeds eating
the rotten pork of the Hudson Bay Company and getting
sick and weak every day. Although a half-breed, and having
no pretension to help the whites, I also paid attention to
them. I saw they were deprived of responsible government,
I saw that they were deprived of their public liberties.
I remembered that half-breed meant white and Indian and
while I paid attention to the suffering Indians and the half-
breeds I remembered that the greatest part of my heart and
blood was white and I have directed my attention to help
the Indians, help the half-breeds and to help the whites
to the best of my ability. We have made petitions, I have
made petitions with others to the Canadian government
asking to relieve the condition of this country.[68]

*After Confederation, the federal government also focused on
expanding the reach of their authority over Indigenous Peoples.
This meant looking west and looking north. A priority was placed
on entering into treaties with First Nations as part of securing
land surrenders from them, and economic expansion for the government of Canada. Eleven numbered treaties were entered into
between 1871 and 1921. The treaties covered a vast geographic
area—between the Lake of the Woods and the Rocky Mountains*

to the Beaufort Sea.[69] *While the treaties have distinctions, the common elements included payments (annuities), land reserves, rights to hunt and fish, and statements regarding land status.*

THE FINAL REPORT OF THE TRUTH
AND RECONCILIATION COMMISSION,
DESCRIBING TREATY-MAKING

At the Treaty 1 talks, [A.G.] Archibald [then lieutenant governor of Manitoba and the North-West Territories] said that although the Queen thought it best for her "red children" to "adopt the habits of the whites," she had "no idea of compelling you to do so. This she leaves to your choice, and you need not live like the white man unless you can be persuaded to do so of your own free will."[70] This promise was at odds with the laws of the time, which limited First Nations participation in all aspects of Canadian society unless they went through the process of enfranchisement— which did require them to "live like the white man." In coming years, First Nations people would be compelled to send their children to residential schools, where those children would also be made to "live like the white man."

[Alexander] Morris [then lieutenant-governor of Manitoba and the North-West Territories] also stressed the permanent nature of the government commitments, saying, "What I offer you is to be while the water flows and the sun rises."[71] In 1876, Morris told the Cree, "What I trust and hope we will do is not for to-day and tomorrow only; what I will promise, and what I believe and hope you will take, is to last as long as the sun shines and yonder river flows."[72] This concept of an agreement that lasts as long as the sun shines and the water flows was symbolized in the Treaty medals that were distributed at the signing of Treaty 3 through to Treaty 8. They showed a chief and an imperial officer shaking hands; a hatchet was buried in the ground and, in the background, the sun shone.[73]

The First Nations negotiators demanded fair treatment. During the Treaty 3 talks, Chief Mawe-do-pe-nais reminded Morris, "The white man has robbed us of our riches, and we don't wish to give them up again without getting something in their place."[74]

First Nations have always viewed the treaties as recognizing their systems of government and law, and their relationship to their territories, and as part of a sacred and enduring relationship with the Crown. Concerns over violations of the numbered treaties by Canada began almost immediately after they were entered into. They remain to this very day and are the subject of ongoing litigation, negotiation, and conflict.

ELDER ALMA KYTWAYHAT, DESCRIBING
THE MEANING OF TREATIES

We were told that these treaties were to last forever.
The government and the government officials, the
Commissioner, told us that, as long as the grass grows,
and the sun rises from the east and sets in the west, and
the river flows, these treaties will last.[75]

ELDER JACOB BILL, DESCRIBING
THE MEANING OF TREATIES

We say it's our Father (wiyohtawinmaw); the White man
says "our Father" in his language, so from there we should
understand that he becomes our brother and we have to live
harmoniously with him. There should not be any conflict,
we must uphold the word "witaskewin," which means to
live in peace and harmony with one another.[76]

MAWE-DO-PE-NAIS TO LIEUTENANT GOVERNOR
ALEXANDER MORRIS AND HIS FELLOW COMMISSIONERS,
AS PART OF TREATY-MAKING, 1873

Now you see me stand before you all: what has been done
here to-day has been done openly before the Great Spirit
and before the nation, and I hope I may never hear any
one say that this treaty has been done secretly: and now

in closing this council, I take off my glove, and in giving you my hand I deliver over my birthright and lands: and in taking your hand I hold fast all the promises you have made, and I hope they will last as long as the sun rises and the water flows, as you have said.

Lieutenant governor, taking up his hand, then said in reply:
I accept your hand and with it the lands, and will keep all my promises, in the firm belief that the treaty now to be signed will bind the red man and the white together as friends for ever.[77]

LIEUTENANT GOVERNOR ALEXANDER MORRIS TO THE PLAINS CREE AT FORTS CARLETON AND PITT, AS PART OF NEGOTIATING AND CONCLUDING TREATY 6

What I have offered does not take away your living, you will have it then as you have now, and what I offer now is put on top of it.

＊

The instructions of the Queen are to treat the Indians as brothers, and so we ought to be. The Great Spirit made this earth we are on. He planted the trees and made the rivers flow for the good of all his people, white and red; the country is very wide and there is room for all.

❋

Now the whole burden of my message from the Queen is that we wish to help you in the days that are to come, we do not want to take away the means of living that you have now, we do not want to tie you down . . .[78]

CHIEF POUNDMAKER OF THE PLAINS CREE,
DESCRIBING THE CONNECTION TO THE LAND,
AND HOW TREATIES CANNOT DESTROY THAT

This is our land, not a piece of pemmican to be cut off and given in little pieces. It is ours and we will take what we want.[79]

In the years after Confederation, the RCMP began to play a larger role in the life of Indigenous Peoples across Canada. Often, the stated rationale for this overreach was that it was to "protect" Indigenous Peoples; rather, these actions were part of an extension of colonial social controls and law enforcement designed specifically with the goal of assimilation in mind.

This particular use of the RCMP originated in the North, where interactions between the Inuit and Europeans in Inuit Nunangat were dramatically increasing. It extended south as well, with the police enforcing bans on First Nations governing systems, such as the Potlatch in parts of British Columbia, and with the Indian Act allowing for the appointment of RCMP officers as "truant officers" to enforce attendance at residential schools. In one instance (of many), the RCMP arrested forty-five Indigenous participants in the Potlatch in Village Island (off Vancouver Island) on Christmas Day and charged them with a criminal offence. Twenty ended up serving time.

SPECIAL HOUSE OF COMMONS COMMITTEE, 1924

It is necessary to protect our rights against foreigners; to protect our fisheries, and to take care of our property generally. I think it is wise for us to exercise some oversight over the Canadian tribes, because . . . if you do not protect them, the traders who are not particularly anxious about the welfare of the native Eskimo, get in amongst them and debauch them, carry in liquor and exercise an evil influence among the tribes, and then the responsibility is ours. The Eskimo problem is beginning to be a rather serious one for us to handle, and we are establishing police posts at various points along the coast to protect the Eskimo and preserve their game.[80]

INDIAN AGENT WILLIAM MAY HALLIDAY,
DESCRIBING THE REASONS TO HAVE THE RCMP
ENFORCE A BAN OF THE POTLATCH, 1935

[The Potlatch is a] particularly wasteful and destructive custom, and created ill-feeling, jealousy and in most cases great poverty . . . [T]he good obtained from it was small, and the evils associated with it were so great.[81]

HARRY ASSU, FROM CAPE MUDGE, DESCRIBING THE
SHUTTING DOWN OF THE POTLATCH BY THE RCMP

The scow came around from the cannery and put in at the village to pick up the big pile of masks and headdresses and belts and coppers—everything we had for potlatching. I saw it pull out across Discovery Passage to the Campbell River side where more stuff was loaded on the Princess Beatrice for the trip to Alert Bay. Alert Bay was where the potlatch gear was gathered together. It came mainly from our villages around here and from Alert Bay and Village Island. It was sent to the museums in Ottawa from Alert Bay by the Indian agent. Our old people who watched the barge pull out from shore with all their masks on it said: "There is nothing left now. We might as well go home." When we say "go home" it means to die.[82]

First Nations, Métis, and Inuit advocacy continued to increase
in an effort to stop these mounting harms and to continue to
advance claims to their lands and resources—what would come
to be referred to as the "Indian Land Question," or what we often
refer to today as the issue of "Title." The Allied Tribes of British
Columbia, a political organization formed by Nisga'a and the
Interior Tribes in 1927, was a major force in this push to press
the Indian Land Question. This advocacy resulted in the Special
Joint Committee of the House of Commons and Senate on Indian
Affairs, which heard representations from Indigenous Peoples.

FEDERAL INDIAN AGENT OF THE NAAS AGENCY, DESCRIBING TENSIONS AROUND LAND, 1913

The management of nearly all the bands in this agency, as
is the case with many other bands in British Columbia, has
become much more difficult of recent years owing to the
great agitation that has been going on, a claim being made
that the Indians do not own merely the reserves they have
been assigned, but the whole province. Many of the bands
object to control of their affairs by the government, being
under the impression that to acknowledge the authority of
the government would be to surrender their alleged rights
to land.[83]

ALLIED TRIBES OF BRITISH COLUMBIA,
PETITION TO THE SPECIAL JOINT COMMITTEE
OF THE SENATE AND HOUSE OF COMMONS, 1926

2. When British Columbia entered Confederation Section
    109 of the British North America Act was made applicable
    to all public lands with certain specific exceptions. By virtue
    of the application of this Section it was enacted that the
    public lands belonging to the Colony of British Columbia
    should belong to the new Province. By virtue of the appli-
    cation of the same Section as explained by the Minister of
    Justice in January, 1875, all territorial land rights claimed
    by the Indian Tribes of the Province were preserved and it
    was enacted that such rights should be an "interest" in the
    public lands of the Province. The Indian Tribes of British
    Columbia claim actual beneficial ownership of their terri-
    tories, but do not claim absolute ownership in the sense of
    ownership excluding the title of the Crown. It is recognized
    by the Allied Tribes that there is in respect of all the public
    lands of the Province an underlying title of the Crown,
    which title at least for the present purposes it is not thought
    necessary to define.[84]

JOHN CHILIHITZA, AN INTERIOR CHIEF, TO THE SPECIAL JOINT COMMITTEE ON THE CROWN'S PROMISE TO RESPECT THE TITLE OF FIRST NATIONS, 1926

I am going to refer to the time when [Gilbert Malcolm] Sproat came as a messenger from the Queen. . . . The Indians were told by Sproat that the Queen would not touch their Indian rights and their rights would include the right to keep their native titles. Sproat told a lot of things to the Indians of what the Queen said, but I will not speak about that, as it will take too much time, but the Indians have kept in mind what Sproat told them concerning the white man.[85]

SPECIAL JOINT COMMITTEE, 1927

[T]he claims of the Indians were not well founded, and that no Aboriginal title, as alleged, had ever existed.[86]

As part of the response to these efforts, the Indian Act was amended in 1927 to make it illegal to obtain funds or legal counsel to advance Aboriginal Title cases. Increasingly, advocacy was forced to move underground.

INDIAN ACT, 1927, SECTION 141

Every person who, without the consent of the Superintendent General expressed in writing, receives, obtains, solicits
or requests from any Indian any payment or contribution
for the purpose of raising a fund or providing money for the
prosecution of any claims which the tribe or band of Indians
to which such Indian belongs, or of which he is a member,
has or is represented to have for the recovery of any claim
or money for the benefit of the said tribe or band, shall be
guilty of an offence and liable upon summary conviction for
each such offence to a penalty not exceeding two hundred
dollars and not less than fifty dollars or to imprisonment
for any term not exceeding two months.[87]

ONE OF THE THEMES of this oral history is how the lives of
Indigenous Peoples and the reality of colonialism have gradually
moved from the background of the Canadian consciousness to
the foreground. From being invisible to ever more visible. This
shift has not been quick; though as we have discussed, it has
greatly picked up pace in recent years.

For decades, the various shifts in attitude and awareness have
mostly been limited to political and legal processes. Many Canadians started hearing more about Indigenous Peoples as a result
of legal cases and/or constitutional reform. For this reason, the
perceptions of non-Indigenous Canadians was that the issues
affecting Indigenous Peoples were, naturally, of a largely political and legal nature, played out in legislatures and courtrooms.

In recent years, this foregrounding has further shifted into a broader realization that Indigenous issues are societal issues—about what Canada means and what it means to be Canadian.

The last part of the oral history reflects this shift. As such, you will notice the presence of various Indigenous voices, speaking to their experiences, realities, and the change that is needed. Of course, Indigenous voices have always been here, but now we are listened to, heard, or recorded. Note also the change in the rhetoric of the politicians and leaders, and the increasing distance from racist, assimilationist, and denial-based language.

As you read this part of the oral history, reflect on how much has tangibly changed, and how much the change may be in words only.

After the Second World War, because of growing public scrutiny, shifts began to occur in government policy and practice, including reviews of the living conditions of Indigenous Peoples. One example: During the war the American military had built a system of airfields in the North, which had the effect of accelerating changes to Inuit life. This included a separation from their land due to relocation to settlements. Around the same time, laws and policies were also being introduced that interfered more and more with the Inuit way of life, including enforced limitations being placed on the use and culling of dogs, which were critical for transportation, hunting, and the Inuit economy. This changing reality in the North brought the challenges faced by the Inuit more "forcefully to the attention of the Government and the country as a whole." [88]

In response, Prime Minister Louis St. Laurent announced in 1953
that the government would create a Department of Northern
Affairs and Natural Resources. Jean Lesage was the first minister
to head the new department.

ONE INUIT INFORMANT,
TO AN ANTHROPOLOGIST, 1958

The [government] didn't want Eskimos to have dogs any
more. Eskimos sometimes have dogs untied, they get
hungry and run around looking for food . . . The Eskimos
can't feed them regularly because the hunting around
Frobisher Bay is no longer good. Everyone is working so
no dog meat can be hunted for. But they need the dogs for
hunting in the winter.[89]

AKEESHOO JOAMIE, DESCRIBING
THE INCREASE IN NON-INUIT

In the '40s, there was a whole bunch of Qallunaat [people
who are not Inuit]; that is when we really came in contact
with Qallunaat. We would come into a community to seek
some work for the summer. Perhaps for about three months,
as part of the wage economy, during the re-supply season, we
would come to work during the summer time. In October,
we would go back to our wintering camps. We travelled by
boat; it was the only way to get back to our camps.[90]

SAMMY JOSEPHEE, DESCRIBING
THE INCREASE IN NON-INUIT

There was a bunch of Inuit moved to an island so that they could make room for the Americans. There were no more Inuit in Iqaluit. They wanted us out of the way to make room for the army.[91]

JEAN LESAGE, MINISTER OF NORTHERN AFFAIRS
AND NATURAL RESOURCES, DESCRIBING SOME
OF THE POLICY FOR THE NORTH

It is pointless to consider whether the Eskimo was happier before the white man came, for the white man has come and time cannot be reversed. . . . [it is government's responsibility to help the Inuit] climb the ladder of civilization.[92]

After commissioned studies and committees on the issue, which in various instances included Indigenous leaders making submissions, the occasional change in law and policy took place. The Indian Act was amended in various ways, including getting rid of the provision limiting the hiring of lawyers, lifting bans on ceremonies, reducing the discretionary power of the minister, and increasing some of the powers of Indian Act Band Councils. Changes to voting rights were also included—specifically that the Inuit were granted the right to vote in federal elections in 1950.

However, there was nowhere to vote in most Inuit communities until 1962, when ballot boxes were finally provided. In 1960, First Nations people subject to the Indian Act were granted the same right to vote. Given this history—with enfranchisement of Indigenous Peoples masking a policy linked to assimilation and the denial of status as an Indigenous person—there was suspicion of government motivations in extending these rights. At various times, all provinces except Nova Scotia and Newfoundland had legislation that in some way disqualified status Indians from voting. After the Second World War, this changed in all provinces, though in Quebec for example, this did not occur until as late as 1969.

PRIME MINISTER JOHN DIEFENBAKER,
DESCRIBING AMENDMENTS TO THE INDIAN ACT
REGARDING VOTING, 1960

The other measure, the provision to give Indians the vote, is one of those steps which will have an effect everywhere in the world—for the reason that wherever I went last year on the occasion of my trip to Commonwealth countries, it was brought to my attention that in Canada the original people within our country, excepting for a qualified class, were denied the right to vote. I say that so far as this long overdue measure is concerned, it will remove everywhere in the world any suggestion that color or race places any citizen in our country in a lower category than the other citizens of our country.

I say this to those of the Indian race that in bringing forward this legislation the Minister of Citizenship and Immigration (Mrs. Fairclough) will reassure, as she has assured to date, that existing rights and treaties, traditional or otherwise, possessed by the Indians shall not in any way be abrogated or diminished in consequence of having the right to vote. That is one of the things that throughout the years has caused suspicion in the minds of many Indians who have conceived the granting of the franchise as a step in the direction of denying them their ancient rights.[93]

ELLEN L. FAIRCLOUGH, SUPERINTENDENT GENERAL OF INDIAN AFFAIRS AND MINISTER OF CITIZENSHIP AND IMMIGRATION, DESCRIBING AMENDMENTS TO THE INDIAN ACT REGARDING VOTING, 1962

I should like to state for the record, so there will be no possibility of misunderstanding on the point, that the rights of Indians under treaty and the rights of Indians not under treaty are not in any way diminished or affected by the legislation passed in 1960 which conferred on persons of Indian status the right to vote in federal elections. The legislation in question takes nothing at all away from the Indians; instead, it confers an additional right or benefit, the right to vote in exactly the same way as any other citizen of Canada.

I would now like to give you my personal assurance that none of your rights will be affected by your voting and I urge you to exercise this privilege of citizenship.[94]

BILL ERASMUS, NATIONAL CHIEF OF THE DENE
NATION, DESCRIBING WHY GRANTING OF VOTING
RIGHTS WAS SOMETIMES SEEN AS PART OF
A PLAN FOR ASSIMILATION, 2010

That's what the whole exercise was about. It was to make us Canadians, and we never had a discussion about that.[95]

In the 1960s, with the limitations on the hiring of lawyers removed from the Indian Act, Indigenous Peoples began to access the courts for claims regarding their rights, including rights to land. One of the earliest cases involved hunting, wherein two men, Clifford White and David Bob, were charged under the provincial Game Act with hunting deer out of season. In response to the charges, White and Bob claimed that a pre-Confederation treaty had been entered into in 1854 with James Douglas, the first governor of the Colony of Vancouver Island and the Hudson Bay Company's chief factor. The judge at their trial balked at their assertion. Indeed, Canada, British Columbia, and the entire justice system apparently had no knowledge or memory that a treaty—one of fourteen signed up and down Vancouver Island prior to Confederation—had ever been entered into. The British Columbia Court of Appeal, however, accepted that the treaty existed and that it protected the right to hunt. The Supreme Court of Canada agreed and affirmed the treaty and its protection of rights.

CLIFFORD WHITE AND DAVID BOB, IN ANSWER TO THE CHARGE OF HUNTING OUT OF SEASON, 1963

The peace treaty signed years ago between the crown and the Indians, gives us the right to hunt and fish any time of the year.[96]

HIS WORSHIP MAGISTRATE L. BEEVOR-POTTS, EXPRESSING FRUSTRATION AT THE CLAIM THAT A TREATY EXISTED AND PROTECTED HUNTING RIGHTS

You have had ample opportunity, two and a half months, nearly three months to bring material cause forward in this matter. Nothing was done so Counsel retired from the case. We had no information whatsoever and I now hold, it is too late and I hold that the alleged Treaty as read by Mr. Elliot, does not apply to this case. You are both found guilty as charged. It is on the face, pure pigishness. You could have permits for a reasonable amount. You go out and get six deers.[97]

The Nisga'a brought their longstanding claims to the court under the leadership of Frank Calder, who would go on to become the first Indigenous person elected to a legislature in the Commonwealth, and the first to hold a Cabinet post. The 1973 Calder decision of the Supreme Court of Canada was the first time the court acknowledged the existence of Aboriginal title at the time of the Royal Proclamation of 1763. The court was split three to three in its judgment on the issue of whether the Nisga'a's claims to hold title were valid.

As part of the response to the decision, the federal government adopted the Comprehensive Claims Policy in the same year; this stated the government's intention to settle rights claims of Indigenous Peoples, including those related to land. The first modern land claim agreement was completed with the James Bay Cree in 1975. But the pace of settling claims would remain glacially slow. The Nisga'a finally completed a treaty with the federal government and the Province of British Columbia in 2000. It took 113 years for the Nisga'a to settle their land claim.

JOHN BORROWS, LEGAL SCHOLAR AND PROFESSOR,
DESCRIBING THE IMPORTANCE OF THE
CALDER DECISION

[The Calder case made it clear that] the Crown has legally binding obligations towards Aboriginal peoples in Canada.[98]

PRIME MINISTER PIERRE ELLIOTT TRUDEAU,
IN REACTION TO THE CALDER DECISION
AND INDIGENOUS CLAIMS

[Aboriginal peoples have] a lot more Rights than I thought you did, but it will take us a decade to define what they are.[99]

JEAN CHRÉTIEN, MINISTER OF INDIAN AFFAIRS
AND NORTHERN DEVELOPMENT, DESCRIBING THE
ADOPTION OF THE COMPREHENSIVE CLAIMS POLICY

The present statement is concerned with claims and proposals for the settlement of long-standing grievances. These claims come from groups of Indian people who have not entered into Treaty relationship with the Crown. They find their basis in what is variously described as "Indian Title", "Aboriginal Title", "Original Title, "Native Title", or "Usufructuary Rights". In essence, these claims relate to the loss of traditional use and occupancy of lands in certain parts of Canada where Indian Title was never extinguished by treaty or superseded by law.

The Government has been fully aware that the claims are not only for money and land, but involve the loss of a way of life. Any settlement, therefore, must contribute positively to a lasting solution of cultural, social and economic problems that for too long have kept the Indian and Inuit people in a disadvantaged position within the larger Canadian society.

It is basic to the position of the Government that these claims must be settled and that the most promising avenue to settlement is through negotiation. It is envisaged that by this means agreements will be reached with groups of the Indian and Inuit people concerned and that these agreements will be enshrined in legislation, enacted by Parliament, so that they will have the finality and binding force of law.

The Government is now ready to negotiate with authorized representatives of these native peoples on the basis that where their traditional interest in the lands concerned can be established, an agreed form of compensation or benefit will be provided to native peoples in return for their interest. . . .

The Government views this claims policy in the context of other policies intended and designed to remove the sense of grievance and injustice which impedes the relationship of the Indian and Inuit peoples with the governments concerned and with their fellow Canadians.[100]

FRANK CALDER, DESCRIBING THE NISGA'A TREATY

Under the [Nisga'a] Treaty, we will no longer be wards of the state. We will no longer be beggars in our own lands. We will own our own lands, which now far exceed the postage stamp reserves that were begrudgingly set aside for us by colonial governments. We will once again govern ourselves by our institutions, in the context of Canadian law. We will be allowed to make our own mistakes, to savour our own victories, to stand on our own feet.[101]

The government's perpetual focus on studies regarding the conditions of Indigenous Peoples, and seeking new policies, would continue. Some earlier reports after the Second World War, such as the Hawthorn-Tremblay Report [102]—which looked at the contemporary situation of the Indians of Canada with a view to understanding the difficulties they faced in overcoming some pressing problems—introduced the idea of Indigenous Peoples being "citizens plus," in the face of continuing and growing Indigenous advocacy for recognition of their rights and self-government.

In 1969, Prime Minister Pierre Elliott Trudeau took a different approach, issuing the "White Paper," which called for an end to Indian status. The White Paper created an immediate and harsh backlash and deepened the bitter and ongoing legacy of intense suspicion and questioning of the federal government's true policy agenda.

PRIME MINISTER PIERRE ELLIOTT TRUDEAU, DESCRIBING THE WHITE PAPER

We have set the Indians apart as a race. We've set them apart in our laws. We've set them apart in the ways the governments will deal with them. They're not citizens of the province as the rest of us are. They are wards of the federal government. They get their services from the federal government rather than from the provincial or municipal governments. They have been set apart in law. They have been set apart in the relations with government and they've been set apart socially too . . .

We can go on treating the Indians as having a special status. We can go on adding bricks of discrimination around the ghetto in which they live and at the same time perhaps helping them preserve certain cultural traits and certain ancestral rights. Or we can say you're at a crossroads—the time is now to decide whether the Indians will be a race apart in Canada or whether [they] will be Canadians of full status.

. . . well one of the things the Indian bands often refer to are their aboriginal rights and in our policy, the way we propose it, we say we won't recognize aboriginal rights. We will recognize treaty rights. We will recognize forms of contract which have been made with the Indian people by the Crown and we will try to bring justice in that area and this will mean that perhaps the treaties shouldn't go on forever. It's inconceivable, I think, that in a given society one section of the society to have a treaty with the other section of the society. We must be all equal under the law and we must not sign treaties among ourselves and many of these treaties, indeed, would have less and less significance in the future anyhow but things that in the past were covered by the treaties like things like [*sic*] so much twine or so much gun powder and which haven't been paid this must be paid. But I don't think that we should encourage Indians to feel these treaties should last forever within Canada so that they be able to receive their twine or their gun powder. They should become Canadians as all other Canadians. . . .[103]

JEAN CHRÉTIEN, MINISTER OF INDIAN AFFAIRS AND NORTHERN DEVELOPMENT, IN THE STATEMENT OF THE GOVERNMENT OF CANADA ON INDIAN POLICY (THE WHITE PAPER)

... Indian relations with other Canadians began with special treatment by government and society, and special treatment has been the rule since Europeans first settled in Canada. Special treatment has made the Indians a community disadvantaged and apart.

Obviously, the course of history must be changed.[104]

STATEMENT OF THE GOVERNMENT OF CANADA ON INDIAN POLICY (THE WHITE PAPER)

The policies proposed recognize the simple reality that the separate legal status of Indians and the policies which have flowed from it have kept the Indian people apart from and behind other Canadians. The Indian people have not been full citizens of the communities and provinces in which they live and have not enjoyed the equality and benefits that such participation offers.

[A] separate road cannot lead to full participation, to equality in practice as well as theory. ... [T]he Government has outlined a number of measures and a policy which it is convinced will offer another road for Indians, a road that would lead gradually away from different status to full social, economic and political participation in Canadian life. This is the choice. Indian people must be persuaded, must persuade themselves, that this path will lead them to a fuller and richer life.[105]

GEORGE MANUEL, FIRST PRESIDENT OF THE WORLD COUNCIL OF INDIGENOUS PEOPLES, ON AGENDA INDIGENOUS PEOPLES SHOULD FOLLOW

Organize and unify around a clear set of objectives. Battle against all the forces of assimilation and try to build your nations economically, culturally and politically. Consult the people, politicize the people and never get too far ahead of them, because when all is said and done, they are your masters.[106]

EXCHANGE BETWEEN "GRANDMOTHER FROM SIX NATIONS RESERVE" AND JEAN CHRÉTIEN

[Grandmother:] When did we lose our identity?
[Jean Chrétien:] When you signed treaties.
[Grandmother:] How can you come here and ask us to become citizens when we were here long before you? [107]

HAROLD CARDINAL, CREE WRITER AND LEADER, IN RESPONSE TO THE WHITE PAPER

[The White paper is] a thinly disguised programme of extermination through assimilation.

In spite of all government attempts to convince Indians to accept the white paper, their efforts will fail, because Indians understand that the path outlined by the Department of Indian Affairs through its mouthpiece, the Honourable Mr. Chrétien, leads directly to cultural genocide. We will not walk this path. [108]

✳

We do not want the Indian Act retained because it is a good piece of legislation. It isn't. It is discriminatory from start to finish. But it is a lever in our hands and an embarrassment to the government, as it should be. No just society and no society with even pretensions to being just can long tolerate such a piece of legislation, but we would rather continue to live in bondage under the inequitable Indian Act than surrender our sacred rights. Any time the government wants to honour its obligations to us we are more than ready to help devise new Indian legislation. [109]

PRIME MINISTER PIERRE ELLIOTT TRUDEAU, IN
RESPONSE TO CRITICISMS OF THE WHITE PAPER

We'll keep them in the ghetto as long as they want.[110]

The 1960s saw the emergence of new national Indigenous political organizations—and for many of them the White Paper became a rallying cry. While there had been efforts to establish such organizations as far back as 1919, and various initiatives in this direction over the years, it was in 1961 that the National Indian Council (NIC) was formed. In 1968, the NIC split into the National Indian Brotherhood and the Canadian Métis Society (which became the Native Council of Canada [NCC] in 1971—established to represent the interests of Métis and non-status people). In 1971, the Inuit Tapirisat of Canada (ITC) created a united advocacy voice for the Inuit.

The Native Indian Brotherhood became the Assembly of First Nations in 1982. The Métis National Council (MNC) was formed in 1983. The ITC changed its name to the Inuit Tapiriit Kanatami in 2001. In 1993, the NCC was reorganized and renamed the Congress of Aboriginal Peoples, representing urban and non-status Indians. All of these organizations continue today as national political advocacy bodies for Indigenous Peoples.

CHARTER OF THE ASSEMBLY OF FIRST NATIONS

SO, WE HAVE RESOLVED TO CONFINE OUR EFFORTS TO ACCOMPLISH COMMON AIMS.

ACCORDINGLY, our respective Governments, through their Chiefs assembled in the City of Penticton in 1982, agreed to establish a national organization known as the Assembly of First Nations (AFN) and now agree in the City of Vancouver in 1985 to the Charter of the Assembly of First Nations.[111]

INUIT TAPIRIIT KANATAMI, DESCRIBING THEIR FOUNDING

Inuit Tapiriit Kanatami, formerly the Inuit Tapirisat of Canada, was founded at a meeting in Toronto in February 1971 by seven Inuit community leaders. The impetus to form a national Inuit organization evolved from shared concern among Inuit leaders about the status of land and resource ownership in Inuit Nunangat. Industrial encroachment into Inuit Nunangat from projects such as the then proposed Mackenzie Valley pipeline in the Northwest Territories and the James Bay Project in Northern Québec, spurred community leaders to action.

They agreed that forming a national Inuit organization was necessary to voice their concerns about these and related issues, choosing the name Inuit Tapirisat of Canada ("Inuit will be united") for the new organization. The first ITC conference was held in Ottawa later that year.[112]

MÉTIS NATIONAL COUNCIL, DESCRIBING THEIR HISTORY

Since 1983, the MNC has represented the Métis Nation nationally and internationally. It receives its mandate and direction from the democratically elected leadership of Métis governments in Ontario, Saskatchewan, Alberta, and British Columbia, the MNC Governing Members. Specifically, the MNC reflects and moves forward on the desires and aspirations of these Métis governments at the national and international levels.[113]

The increasing focus on the North proceeded unabated into the 1970s as resource development continued to grow, including proposals for a natural gas pipeline in the Mackenzie Valley. To examine these proposals, the federal government launched a commission of inquiry chaired by politician and jurist Thomas Berger. The Berger Commission assessed the impacts of the potential pipelines. A tragedy underlined the importance of the inquiry—two days after testifying, Nelson Small Legs Jr. committed suicide, leaving a note that condemned the treatment of Indigenous Peoples. Berger would end up recommending a ten-year ban on any pipeline development until land claims were settled. The federal government accepted the recommendation.

DENE CHIEF FRANK T'SELEIE TO THE BERGER
COMMISSION, DESCRIBING OPPOSITION TO
PIPELINE DEVELOPMENT, 1974

You are coming to destroy a people that have a history of
thirty thousand years. Why? For twenty years of gas? Are
you really that insane? The original General Custer was
exactly that insane. You still have a chance to learn. A chance
to be remembered by history as something other than a fool
bent on destroying everything he touched. You still have a
chance, you have a choice. Are you a strong enough man to
really exercise your freedom and make that choice. You can
destroy my nation, Mr. Blair [a prominent Calgary oilman
whose company had applied for pipeline rights as a part
of a consortium, who attended the hearings], or you could
be a great help to give us our freedom. Which choice do
you make, Mr. Blair? Which choice do you make for your
children and mine?

It seems to me that the whole point in living is to
become as human as possible. To learn to understand the
world and to live in it. To be part of it. To learn to understand the animals, for they are our brothers and they have
much to teach us. We are a part of this world. We are like
the river that flows and changes, yet is always the same.
The river cannot flow too slow and it cannot flow too fast.
It is a river and it will always be a river, for that is what it
was meant to be. We are like the river, but we are not the
river. We are human. That is what we were meant to be.

We were not meant to be destroyed and we were not meant to take over other parts of the world. We were meant to be ourselves. To be what it is our nature to be.

Our Dene Nation is like this great river. It has been flowing before any of us can remember. We take our strength and our wisdom and our ways from the flow and direction that has been established for us by ancestors we never knew, ancestors of a thousand years ago. Their wisdom flows through us to our children and our grandchildren to generations we will never know. We will live out our lives as we must and we will die in peace because we will know that our people and this river will flow on after us.

We know that our grandchildren will speak a language that is their heritage, that has been passed on from before time. We know they will share their wealth and not hoard it, or keep it to themselves. We know they will look after their old people and respect them for their wisdom.

We know they will look after this land and protect it and that five hundred years from now someone with skin my colour and moccasins on his feet will climb up the Ramparts and rest and look over the river and feel that he too has a place in the universe, and he will thank the same spirits that I thank, that his ancestors have looked after his land well and he will be proud to be a Dene.

It is for this unborn child, Mr. Berger, that my nation will stop the pipeline. It is so that this unborn child can know the freedom of this land that I am willing to lay down my life.[114]

GEORGE ERASMUS, DESCRIBING TESTIMONY
AT THE BERGER COMMISSION

We were simply stating the same position that our people have always had. Our people have never given up the right to govern themselves. Our people have never given up the right to this land.[115]

THOMAS BERGER, DESCRIBING
THE COMMISSION FINDINGS

It is my conviction that the social impact on the native people will be devastating. I think the economic benefits, to northerners generally, will be limited.

The North is a frontier, but it is a homeland too. . . . And it is a heritage, a unique environment that we are called upon to preserve for all Canadians.

The decisions we have to make are not, therefore, simply about northern pipelines. They are decisions about the protection of the northern environment and the future of northern peoples.[116]

Since the 1920s, there has been dialogue and debate about repatriating and amending the Constitution. This focus intensified in the late 1970s, leading to formal efforts in this regard by the Trudeau government in the early 1980s. Major issues being considered were the potential inclusion of a Charter of Rights and Freedoms, and the ongoing threat of Quebec separation. There was a range of reactions from Indigenous Peoples regarding this development. Some had fears about severing ties with Great Britain and what constitutional repatriation would mean for treaties signed with the Crown , as well as other rights. These concerns increased in 1980 when Indigenous leaders learned that the proposed constitutional amendments would not include a reference to Indigenous Peoples or protection of their treaties, title, and rights. A legal case was brought forward by Indigenous Peoples of Alberta, New Brunswick, and Nova Scotia seeking responsibility to be left with the British Crown. Direct action was also taken by Indigenous Peoples, including what was called the "Constitution Express"—a movement in the early 1980s to protest the lack of recognition of Aboriginal rights in the proposed repatriation of the Canadian Constitution.

UNION OF BRITISH COLUMBIA INDIAN CHIEFS (UBCIC), DESCRIBING THE POSITION OF THE CHIEFS OF BRITISH COLUMBIA ON CONSTITUTIONAL REFORM

[T]he convention gives full mandate to the UBCIC to take the necessary steps to ensure that Indian Governments, Indian Lands, Aboriginal Rights and Treaty Rights are entrenched in the Canadian Constitution.[117]

LORD DENNING ON ABORIGINAL RIGHTS AND THE CONSTITUTION ACT, 1982

The Indian peoples of Canada have been there from the beginning of time. So they are called the "aboriginal peoples." . . . They had their chiefs and headmen to regulate their simple society and to enforce their customs. I say "to enforce their customs," because in early societies custom is the basis of law. Once a custom is established it gives rise to rights and obligations which the chiefs and headmen will enforce. These customary laws are not written down. They are handed down by tradition from one generation to another. Yet beyond doubt they are well established and have the force of law within the community.

In England we still have laws which are derived from customs from time immemorial. Such as rights of villagers to play on the green: or to graze their cattle on the common . . . These rights belong to members of the community: and take priority over the ownership of the soil.[118]

GEORGE MANUEL, PRESIDENT OF THE UNION OF BRITISH COLUMBIA INDIAN CHIEFS, DESCRIBING CONCERNS WITH CONSTITUTIONAL REFORM

I would rather pass on to my grandchildren the legitimacy of the struggle than to leave them with a settlement they can't live with.[119]

ACTIVISTS ERIC ROBINSON AND HENRY BIRD QUINNEY, DESCRIBING HOW CONSTITUTIONAL REFORM THREATENS SELF-DETERMINATION AND SELF-GOVERNMENT

During early colonialism, infested blankets were used to wipe out entire Tribes and Nations of the Original Peoples of this land now called Canada . . . Today in a 1980's style of colonialism, Canada is trying to blanket the First Nations with the 1982 Canada Act. It is infested with colonialism and the death of Indian Nationhood. Today, Indian Nations must not trade off our Sovereign Nationhood for this modern form of genocide.[120]

The Constitution was repatriated in 1982 and included provisions—section 35—regarding the collective rights of Indigenous Peoples.

CONSTITUTION ACT, 1982

35 (1) The existing aboriginal and treaty rights of the aboriginal peoples of Canada are hereby recognized and affirmed. (2) In this Act, "aboriginal peoples of Canada" includes the Indian, Inuit and Métis peoples of Canada.[121]

It was unclear what the protections of Indigenous rights in section 35(1) meant. Studies and reports continued, including one in 1983 on Indian self-government, which recommended that First Nations be recognized as a distinct order of government, and that processes leading to self-government be established. There was a promise to hold constitutional conferences to address the matter. Four conferences did occur—in 1983, 1984, 1985, and 1987—and while some amendments were made to the Constitution in 1983 regarding modern land claims agreements and gender equality, the conferences did not address the core issues about the protection of Indigenous rights. The result of this inaction was an intensification of Indigenous Peoples turning to the courts for answers. In court, and effectively in law, policy, and practice, the federal and provincial governments adopted a position in court that section 35(1) meant very little: those Indigenous rights had been largely extinguished or surrendered. The courts clearly and consistently disagreed with the Crown, and affirmed that Indigenous rights are real, meaningful, and must be upheld.

EXCHANGE BETWEEN CHIEF JAMES GOSNELL
(NISGA'A) AND PRIME MINISTER PIERRE ELLIOTT
TRUDEAU AT THE FEDERAL-PROVINCIAL
CONFERENCE OF FIRST MINISTERS ON
ABORIGINAL CONSTITUTIONAL MATTERS, 1983

[Gosnell:] It has always been our belief, Mr. Chairman, that
when God created this whole world he gave pieces of land
to all races of people throughout this world, the Chinese
people, Germans and you name them, including Indians.
So at one time our land was this whole continent right from
the tip of South America to the North Pole . . . It has always
been our belief that God gave us the land . . . and we say
that no one can take our title away except He who gave it to
us to begin with. . . .

[Trudeau:] Going back to the Creator doesn't really help
very much. So He gave you title, but you know, did He draw
on the land where your mountains stopped and somebody
else's began . . . ? God never said that the frontier of France
runs along the Rhine or somewhere west of Alsace-Lorraine
where the German-speaking people of France live. . . .
I don't know any part of the world where history isn't constantly rewritten by migrations and immigrants and fights
between countries changing frontiers and I don't think you
can expect North America or the whole of the Western
Hemisphere to settle things differently than they have been
settled everywhere else, hopefully peacefully here.[122]

[Trudeau:] [Y]ou have to sit down and discuss with someone what that [Aboriginal] title is.
[Gosnell:] [W]e are the true owners of the land, lock, stock
and barrel.[123]

Debates continued through the Meech Lake and Charlottetown Accord processes to amend the Constitution. Both processes were divisive for Indigenous Peoples and, ultimately, neither was ratified. First Nations leader Elijah Harper was a central force in the defeat of the Meech Lake Accord. The Charlottetown Accord would have included provisions regarding self-government.

ELIJAH HARPER, DESCRIBING HIS OPPOSITION TO THE MEECH LAKE ACCORD

Well I was opposed to the Meech Lake Accord because we weren't included in the Constitution. We were to recognize Quebec as a distinct society, whereas we as Aboriginal people were completely left out. We were the First Peoples here—First Nations of Canada—we were the ones that made treaties with the settlers that came from Europe. These settler people and their governments didn't recognize us as a Nation, as a government and that is why we opposed the Meech Lake Accord.[124]

✳

We need to let Canadians know... that we have been shoved aside. We're saying that Aboriginal issues... should be put on the priority list. We want to be a part of the Canadian society... and to contribute toward... the development of this Country.[125]

PRIME MINISTER BRIAN MULRONEY, IN
REFERENCE TO ELIJAH HARPER'S OPPOSITION

Aboriginals are not to blame for Meech Lake's failure despite Elijah Harper's stupidity ... He turned down a sweetheart deal.[126]

LOUIS "SMOKEY" BRUYERE, PRESIDENT OF
THE NATIVE COUNCIL OF CANADA, DESCRIBING
ATTITUDES TO THE MEECH LAKE ACCORD

Aboriginal peoples' view on the [Meech Lake] Accord can be summarized in four words: It abandons aboriginal peoples. It does this by being silent about the uniqueness and distinctiveness of aboriginal peoples.[127]

PHIL FONTAINE, DESCRIBING THE STOPPING
OF THE MEECH LAKE ACCORD

[Meech Lake] was a turning point in history for indigenous people. . . . We came to the realization very quickly that our voice mattered. We could make history, we could change the course of history. We knew and understood what was possible.[128]

CHARLOTTETOWN ACCORD, FINAL TEXT

2. (1) The Constitution of Canada, including the Canadian Charter of Rights and Freedoms, shall be interpreted in a manner consistent with the following characteristics:

     (b) the Aboriginal peoples of Canada, being the first peoples to govern this land, have the right to promote their languages, cultures and traditions and to ensure the integrity of their societies, and their governments constitute one of the three orders of government in Canada.

. . .

41. The Inherent Right of Self-Government
    The Constitution should be amended to recognize that the Aboriginal peoples of Canada have the inherent right of self-government within Canada. This right should be placed in a new section of the Constitution Act, 1982, section 35.1(1).

The recognition of the inherent right of self-government should be interpreted in light of the recognition of Aboriginal governments as one of three orders of government in Canada.

A contextual statement should be inserted in the Constitution, as follows:

The exercise of the right of self-government includes authority of the duly constituted legislative bodies of the Aboriginal peoples, each within its own jurisdiction:

(a) to safeguard and develop their languages, cultures, economies, identities, institutions and traditions; and,

(b) to develop, maintain and strengthen their relationship with their lands, waters and environment so as to determine and control their developments as peoples according to their own values and priorities and ensure the integrity of their societies.

Before making any final determination of an issue arising from the inherent right of self-government, a court or tribunal should take into account the contextual statement referred to above, should enquire into the efforts that have been made to resolve the issue through negotiations and should be empowered to order the parties to take such steps as are appropriate in the circumstances to effect a negotiated resolution.

. . .

60. Aboriginal Consent

There should be Aboriginal consent to future constitutional amendments that directly refer to the Aboriginal peoples. Discussions are continuing on the mechanism by which this consent would be expressed with a view to agreeing on a mechanism prior to the introduction in Parliament of formal resolutions amending the Constitution.[129]

With the constitutional issues still at the forefront, in 1990, the so-called Oka Crisis took place between the Mohawk People of Kanesatake and the town of Oka, northwest of Montreal. This seventy-eight-day conflict was triggered by the proposed expansion of a golf course onto Mohawk lands, which a court had allowed to proceed. Some members of the Mohawks erected a barricade, and eventually tensions escalated as police advanced on them and a police officer was killed. The blockade expanded. The RCMP and the armed forces—some four thousand soldiers— were deployed, and the blockades were removed.

GEORGES ERASMUS, NATIONAL CHIEF OF THE
ASSEMBLY OF FIRST NATIONS, ON SELF-GOVERNMENT
AND IN RESPONSE TO OKA, 1990

The time is here. We must now be sincere. Native people are not a threat to this country. We are not a threat to the sovereignty of Canada. We actually want to reinforce the sovereignty of Canada. We want to walk away from the negotiating table with an agreement that Canada feels good about and Native people feel good about, where we can say that we have strengthened the sovereignty of Canada . . . we're not a threat. We are only a threat if we continue to be ignored and taken lightly. We are only a threat if people don't understand that it is impossible for people to maintain the frustration level without the kind of actions that we've seen this summer [at Oka] . . .

We're not trying to get out of Confederation. We never were a part of it. We're still knocking on the door. Let's hope we get a wonderful reception when the door is open.[130]

PRIME MINISTER BRIAN MULRONEY,
IN RESPONSE TO OKA, 1990

The summer's events must not be allowed to over-shadow the commitment that my government has made to address-ing the concerns of aboriginal people. . . . These grievances raise issues that deeply affect all Canadians and therefore must be resolved by all Canadians working together . . . . The government's agenda responds to the demands of aboriginal peoples and has four parts: resolving land claims; improving the economic and social conditions on reserves; defining a new relationship between aboriginal peoples and governments; and addressing the concerns of Canada's aboriginal peoples in contemporary Canadian life. Consultation with aboriginal peoples and respect for the fiduciary responsibilities of the Crown are integral parts of the process. The federal government is determined to create a new relationship among aboriginal and non-aboriginal Canadians based on dignity, trust and respect.[131]

One of the responses to the Oka Crisis and the failure of the Meech Lake Accord was the formation of the Royal Commission on Aboriginal Peoples in 1991. The commission undertook the most comprehensive study ever completed on the state of Indigenous Peoples in this country. Its identification of the challenges to be addressed, and the solutions to be implemented, was clear, compelling, and specific. Nonetheless, to this day its recommendations remain almost completely unimplemented by successive governments.

ROYAL COMMISSION ON ABORIGINAL PEOPLES, STATING SOME OF ITS RECOMMENDATIONS, 1996

Our vision of a renewed relationship is based on four principles: mutual recognition, mutual respect, sharing and mutual responsibility.

These principles define a process that can provide solutions to many of the difficulties afflicting relations among Aboriginal and non-Aboriginal peoples. Again, we have chosen a circle to represent this process because a circle has no beginning and no end; the process is continuous. As we move through the cycle represented by the four principles, a better understanding is gradually achieved. As the cycle is repeated, the meanings associated with each principle change subtly to reflect this deeper level of understanding. In other words, no single, all-encompassing definition can be assigned to any of these principles. They take on different meanings, depending on the stage we have reached in the process. When taken in sequence, the four principles form a complete whole, each playing an equal role in developing a balanced societal relationship. Relations that embody these principles are, in the broadest sense of the word, partnerships.

. . . The Commission recommends that a renewed relationship between Aboriginal and non-Aboriginal people in Canada be established on the basis of justice and fairness.

The Commission recommends that

1.16.1 To begin the process, the federal, provincial and territorial governments, on behalf of the people of Canada, and national Aboriginal organizations, on behalf of the Aboriginal peoples of Canada, commit themselves to building a renewed relationship based on the principles of mutual recognition, mutual respect, sharing and mutual responsibility; these principles to form the ethical basis of relations between Aboriginal and non-Aboriginal societies in the future and to be enshrined in a new Royal Proclamation and its companion legislation. . . .

2.3.2 All governments in Canada recognize that Aboriginal peoples are nations vested with the right of self-determination.[132]

The use of the courts by Indigenous Peoples continued to expand, and the courts continued to uphold Indigenous rights. Dozens upon dozens of cases have reached the Supreme Court of Canada, with a large majority of them confirming the existence of Indigenous rights, clarifying constitutional obligations of the Crown, and highlighting the need for governments to negotiate and address issues of Indigenous rights. There are core themes in these court decisions: that a just reconciliation is required between Indigenous Peoples and the Crown; that Indigenous title and rights are inherent—meaning they exist because Indigenous Peoples were here, had governments, and were sovereigns before the arrival of Europeans; that the Crown must act honourably in all dealings with Indigenous Peoples; that acting honourably imposes many legal obligations on the Crown, including to consult and accommodate; and that treaties must be diligently implemented. These decisions also encouraged the necessity of political negotiations to resolve these matters.

CHIEF JUSTICE ANTONIO LAMER, IN
DELGAMUUKW V. BRITISH COLUMBIA, 1997

Finally, this litigation has been both long and expensive, not only in economic but in human terms as well. By ordering a new trial, I do not necessarily encourage the parties to proceed to litigation and to settle their dispute through the courts. As was said in Sparrow, at p. 1105, s. 35(1) "provides a solid constitutional base upon which subsequent negotiations can take place". Those negotiations should also include other aboriginal nations which have a stake in the territory claimed. Moreover, the Crown is under a moral, if not a legal, duty to enter into and conduct those negotiations in good faith. Ultimately, it is through negotiated settlements, with good faith and give and take on all sides, reinforced by the judgments of this Court, that we will achieve what I stated in Van der Peet, supra, at para. 31, to be a basic purpose of s. 35(1)—"the reconciliation of the pre-existence of aboriginal societies with the sovereignty of the Crown". Let us face it, we are all here to stay.[133]

CHIEF JUSTICE BEVERLEY MCLACHLIN,
IN *HAIDA NATION V. BRITISH COLUMBIA*
(MINISTER OF FORESTS), 2004

The government's duty to consult with Aboriginal peoples and accommodate their interests is grounded in the principle of the honour of the Crown, which must be understood generously. While the asserted but unproven Aboriginal rights and title are insufficiently specific for the honour of the Crown to mandate that the Crown act as a fiduciary, the Crown, acting honourably, cannot cavalierly run roughshod over Aboriginal interests where claims affecting these interests are being seriously pursued in the process of treaty negotiation and proof. The duty to consult and accommodate is part of a process of fair dealing and reconciliation that begins with the assertion of sovereignty and continues beyond formal claims resolution. The foundation of the duty in the Crown's honour and the goal of reconciliation suggest that the duty arises when the Crown has knowledge, real or constructive, of the potential existence of the Aboriginal right or title and contemplates conduct that might adversely affect it. Consultation and accommodation before final claims resolution preserve the Aboriginal interest and are an essential corollary to the honourable process of reconciliation that s. 35 of the Constitution Act, 1982, demands.[134]

JUSTICE IAN BINNIE, IN *MIKISEW*
CREE FIRST NATION V. CANADA
(*MINISTER OF CANADIAN HERITAGE*), 2005

The fundamental objective of the modern law of aboriginal and treaty rights is the reconciliation of aboriginal peoples and non-aboriginal peoples and their respective claims, interests and ambitions. The management of these relationships takes place in the shadow of a long history of grievances and misunderstanding. The multitude of smaller grievances created by the indifference of some government officials to aboriginal people's concerns, and the lack of respect inherent in that indifference has been as destructive of the process of reconciliation as some of the larger and more explosive controversies.[135]

Contrary to hopes that the resolution of issues regarding Indigenous rights and settling claims would accelerate, progress remained slow. Even with the advances made by Indigenous Peoples in the courts, which included strong encouragement to negotiate and settle these issues; the climate of growing conflict; and the insights and guidance of the Royal Commission on Aboriginal Peoples, it would take decades for a number of land claims agreements to finally be reached in the North, including the founding of Nunavut in 1999. In British Columbia, the tripartite treaty process began in 1993 among many Indigenous Peoples and the federal and provincial governments, with the vision of settling the "Indian Land Question" across the province in five years. Approximately three decades later, only three Final Agreements (modern treaties) have been completed through this process.[136] The Nisga'a Final Agreement was negotiated outside of the BC treaty process.

JOHN AMAGOALIK, INUIT LEADER SOMETIMES CALLED THE "FATHER OF NUNAVUT," DESCRIBING SOME OF THE PROCESS OF CREATING NUNAVUT

When we first presented our Nunavut proposal to the Government of Canada, they indicated that they did not want to deal with political development at the land claims table. They very much wanted to negotiate land claims and to leave political development on "another track." Those were their words. The Inuit wanted to keep the two things together. We made it very clear that we could not sign any agreement that did not include the commitment to create

Nunavut. At that point we agreed to disagree. But we agreed to start negotiating the details of the land claims agreement while we were pursuing Nunavut through the political arena. We made it clear that when the land claims agreement was ready to be signed, the creation of Nunavut would have to be brought in, if it was ready to be part of the land claims agreement. In the twenty years that it took to negotiate the land claims settlement, the two went along parallel lines. We were negotiating the claims here, and we were pursuing Nunavut through other means.[137]

CHIEF JOE MATHIAS OF THE SQUAMISH NATION AT THE FOUNDING OF THE BRITISH COLUMBIA TREATY PROCESS

Negotiations, in our view, will not be based on that tired old notion of extinguishment. We will not tolerate the extinguishment of our collective Aboriginal rights.[138]

DOUGLAS EYFORD, IN A REVIEW OF THE MODERN TREATY NEGOTIATIONS ON BEHALF OF THE FEDERAL GOVERNMENT, 2015

There is a conspicuous lack of urgency in negotiations and in many cases there are sharp differences between the parties about the core elements of a modern treaty.[139]

As awareness of the need for transformative shifts to address the enduring and harsh social, economic, and cultural reality of Indigenous Peoples grew, non-Indigenous governments began contemplating possible responses. One initiative was the Kelowna Accord in 2002, which was led by Prime Minister Paul Martin, the provinces and territories, and Indigenous leaders. The accord would have included $5 billion in the first five years to improve Indigenous health care and education, and another $5 billion in the subsequent five years. Five days after the Kelowna Accord was signed, Martin's minority Liberal government fell. The new Conservative government of Stephen Harper did not follow through on the mandates laid out in the accord, providing only a fraction of the funding committed.

PRIME MINISTER PAUL MARTIN, REFLECTING ON HIS APPROACH TO THE KELOWNA ACCORD

The position that I took [with Indigenous leaders] was to say to them, look, I'm going to call a federal-provincial conference and we are going to work with you.

You tell us what you believe the issues are, so it's going to be your agenda. And they said to us the issues are health care, education, and those things which follow, child welfare being one of them. . . .

Ultimately my goal was the elimination of the Indian Act and its replacement by self-government dealing with all of these issues, beginning with health care and education, and child welfare.[140]

PRESIDENT CLÉMENT CHARTIER, MÉTIS NATIONAL
COUNCIL, DESCRIBING THE IMPORTANCE OF
THE KELOWNA ACCORD

The Kelowna Accord will mean the difference between
continuing the cycle of poverty and desperation to one
of real hope. The agreement will help to bring our people
out of poverty by creating jobs, securing health care and
education opportunities.[141]

*Although the Kelowna Accord was killed, momentum continued
over addressing one specific expression of colonialism—the impacts
of residential schools. These efforts resulted in the 2006 financial
settlement agreement, an apology from Prime Minister Stephen
Harper in the House of Commons in 2008, and the creation of
the Truth and Reconciliation Commission.*

INDIAN RESIDENTIAL SCHOOLS SETTLEMENT,
SCHEDULE N, 2006

There is an emerging and compelling desire to put the
events of the past behind us so that we can work towards
a stronger and healthier future. The truth telling and reconciliation process as part of an overall holistic and comprehensive response to the Indian Residential School legacy is
a sincere indication and acknowledgement of the injustices

and harms experienced by Aboriginal people and the need for continued healing. This is a profound commitment to establishing new relationships embedded in mutual recognition and respect that will forge a brighter future. The trust of our common experiences will help set our spirits free and pave the way to reconciliation.[142]

PRIME MINISTER STEPHEN HARPER,
IN HIS APOLOGY FOR THE RESIDENTIAL
SCHOOL SYSTEM, 2008

I stand before you today to offer an apology to former students of Indian residential schools. The treatment of children in these schools is a sad chapter in our history. . . .

Two primary objectives of the residential school system were to remove and isolate children from the influence of their homes, families, traditions and cultures, and to assimilate them into the dominant culture.

These objectives were based on the assumption that aboriginal cultures and spiritual beliefs were inferior and unequal.

Indeed, some sought, as was infamously said, "to kill the Indian in the child". . . .

The government now recognizes that the consequences of the Indian residential schools policy were profoundly negative and that this policy has had a lasting and damaging impact on aboriginal culture, heritage and language. . . .

The government recognizes that the absence of an apology has been an impediment to healing and reconciliation. . . .

The burden of this experience has been on your shoulders for far too long. The burden is properly ours as a government, and as a country. There is no place in Canada for the attitudes that inspired the Indian residential schools system to ever again prevail. . . .

You have been working on recovering from this experience for a long time, and in a very real sense we are now joining you on this journey. The Government of Canada sincerely apologizes and asks the forgiveness of the aboriginal peoples of this country for failing them so profoundly.

We are sorry.[143]

NATIONAL CHIEF PHIL FONTAINE, ASSEMBLY OF FIRST NATIONS, IN RESPONSE TO THE APOLOGY, 2008

[F]or all of the generations which have preceded us, this day testifies to nothing less than the achievement of the impossible. . . . [T]he significance of this day is not just about what has been but, equally important, what is to come. Never again will this House consider us the Indian problem just for being who we are.

We heard the Government of Canada take full responsibility for this dreadful chapter in our shared history. We heard the Prime Minister declare that this will never happen again. Finally, we heard Canada say it is sorry.

Brave survivors, through the telling of their painful stories, have stripped white supremacy of its authority and legitimacy. The irresistibility of speaking truth to power is real. . . .

The memories of residential schools sometimes cut like merciless knives at our souls. This day will help us to put that pain behind us.

But it signifies something even more important: a respectful and, therefore, liberating relationship between us and the rest of Canada. . . .

I reach out to all Canadians today in this spirit of reconciliation.

Meegwetch [thank you].[144]

WILLIE BLACKWATER, A SURVIVOR AND LEADER
OF LEGAL ACTION ABOUT THE RESIDENTIAL
SCHOOLS, IN RESPONSE TO THE APOLOGY, 2008

The apology makes a huge difference for me, because it will help . . . the pain and suffering I inflicted not only on my wife and daughter but also to my son . . . and his mother, because they felt the pain and they felt the atrocities too.[145]

CHARLIE THOMPSON, SURVIVOR,
IN RESPONSE TO THE APOLOGY, 2008

Today I feel relief. I feel good. For me, this is a historical day.[146]

PRESIDENT MARY SIMON OF THE INUIT TAPIRIIT
KANATAMI, IN RESPONSE TO THE APOLOGY, 2008

I am one of these people that have dreamed for this day and there have been times in this long journey when I despaired that this would never happen. I am filled with hope and compassion for my fellow aboriginal Canadians. There is much hard work to be done. We need the help and support of all thoughtful Canadians and our governments to rebuild strong healthy families and communities. This can only be achieved when dignity, confidence and respect for traditional values and human rights once again become part of our daily lives and are mirrored in our relationships with governments and other Canadians.

I am also filled with optimism that this action by the Government of Canada and the generosity in the words chosen to convey this apology will help all of us mark the end of this dark period in our collective history as a nation. . . . Let us now join forces with the common goal of working together to ensure that this apology opens the door to a new chapter in our lives as aboriginal peoples and in our place in Canada. . . . I stand here today ready to

work with you, as Inuit have always done, to craft new solutions and new arrangements based on mutual respect and
mutual responsibility.[147]

PRESIDENT BEVERLEY JACOBS OF THE
NATIVE WOMEN'S ASSOCIATION OF CANADA,
IN RESPONSE TO THE APOLOGY, 2008

Prior to the residential schools system, prior to colonization,
the women in our communities were very well respected and
honoured for the role that they have in our communities as
being the life givers, being the caretakers of the spirit that
we bring to mother earth. We have been given those responsibilities to look after our children and to bring that spirit
into this physical world.

Residential schools caused so much harm to that respect
and to that honour. There were ceremonies for young men
and for young women that were taken away for generations in
residential schools. Now we have our language still, we have
our ceremonies, we have our elders, and we have to revitalize
those ceremonies and the respect for our people not only
within Canadian society but even within our own peoples . . .
it is about making sure that we have strong nations again.

We have given thanks to you for your apology. I have to
also give you credit for standing up. I did not see any other
governments before today come forward and apologize,
so I do thank you for that.[148]

The findings of the Truth and Reconciliation Commission in 2015 and the National Inquiry into Missing and Murdered Indigenous Women and Girls in 2019 brought vital awareness and education to the Canadian public about the depth of colonialism's impacts on children, families, women, and the LGBTQ+ community. It also made clear the pressing need for urgent change, and the various and far-reaching solutions that needed to be implemented.

TRUTH AND RECONCILIATION COMMISSION, DESCRIBING WHAT RECONCILIATION REQUIRES, 2015

For over a century, the central goals of Canada's Aboriginal policy were to eliminate Aboriginal governments; ignore Aboriginal rights; terminate the Treaties; and, through a process of assimilation, cause Aboriginal peoples to cease to exist as distinct legal, social, cultural, religious, and racial entities in Canada. The establishment and operation of residential schools were a central element of this policy, which can best be described as "cultural genocide."

. . . *Cultural genocide* is the destruction of those structures and practices that allow the group to continue as a group. States that engage in cultural genocide set out to destroy the political and social institutions of the targeted group. Land is seized, and populations are forcibly transferred and their movement is restricted. Languages are banned.

Spiritual leaders are persecuted, spiritual practices are forbidden, and objects of spiritual value are confiscated and destroyed. And, most significantly to the issue at hand, families are disrupted to prevent the transmission of cultural values and identity from one generation to the next.

In its dealing with Aboriginal people, Canada did all these things. . . .

We invite you to search in your own traditions and beliefs, and those of your ancestors, to find these core values that create a peaceful harmonious society and a healthy earth.

Reconciliation is going to take hard work. People of all walks of life and at all levels of society will need to be willingly engaged.

Reconciliation calls for personal action. People need to get to know each other. They need to learn how to speak to, and about, each other respectfully. They need to learn how to speak knowledgeably about the history of this country. And they need to ensure that their children learn how to do so as well.

Reconciliation calls for group action. The 2010 Vancouver Olympics Organizing Committee recognized, paid tribute to, and honoured the Four Host First Nations at all public events it organized. Clubs, sports teams, artists, musicians, writers, teachers, doctors, lawyers, judges, and politicians need to learn from that example of how to be more inclusive and more respectful, and how to engage more fully in the dialogue about reconciliation.

Reconciliation calls for community action. The City of Vancouver, British Columbia, proclaimed itself the City of Reconciliation. The City of Halifax, Nova Scotia, holds an annual parade and procession commemorating the 1761 Treaty of Peace and Friendship. Speeches are delivered and everyone who attends is feasted. The City of Wetaskiwin, Alberta, erected a sign at its outskirts with the city's name written in Cree syllabics. Other communities can do similar things.

Reconciliation calls for federal, provincial, and territorial government action.

Reconciliation calls for national action.

The way we govern ourselves must change.

Laws must change.

Policies and programs must change.

The way we educate our children and ourselves must change. The way we do business must change.

Thinking must change.

The way we talk to, and about, each other must change.

All Canadians must make a firm and lasting commitment to reconciliation to ensure that Canada is a country where our children and grandchildren can thrive.[149]

NATIONAL INQUIRY INTO MISSING AND
MURDERED INDIGENOUS WOMEN AND GIRLS,
DESCRIBING THE TRUTHS FROM THEIR INQUIRY

The truths shared in these National Inquiry hearings tell
the story—or, more accurately, thousands of stories—of
acts of genocide against First Nations, Inuit and Métis
women, girls, and 2SLGBTQQIA people. This violence
amounts to a race-based genocide of Indigenous Peoples,
including First Nations, Inuit, and Métis, which especially
targets women, evidenced notably by the *Indian Act*, the
Sixties Scoop, residential schools, and breaches of human
and Inuit, Métis and First Nations rights, leading directly to
the current increased rates of violence, death, and suicide in
Indigenous populations.

. . . These abuses and violations have resulted in the
denial of safety, security, and human dignity. They are
the root causes of the violence against Indigenous women,
girls, and 2SLGBTQQIA people that generate and maintain a world within which Indigenous women, girls, and
2SLGBTQQIA people are forced to confront violence on
a daily basis, and where perpetrators act with impunity.[150]

International developments also begin to influence Canada's policy towards Indigenous Peoples.

In 2007, after approximately twenty-five years of efforts to draft a specific instrument dealing with the protection of the human rights of Indigenous Peoples around the world, the United Nations Declaration on the Rights of Indigenous Peoples was adopted. The declaration expresses established international human rights norms as applied in the specific context of Indigenous Peoples. The forty-six articles of the UN Declaration are understood to be the minimum standards for the "survival, dignity, and well-being" of Indigenous Peoples. Canada was one of four countries—the others being the United States, New Zealand, and Australia—that voted against the adoption of the UN Declaration. Canada reversed its position and expressed support for the declaration, with "reservations," in November 2010. In 2016, Canada removed these reservations and fully endorsed the UN Declaration.

UNITED NATIONS GENERAL ASSEMBLY PRESIDENT SHEIKHA HAYA RASHED AL KHALIFA, ON THE ADOPTION OF THE UN DECLARATION, 2007

The General Assembly today overwhelmingly backed protections for the human rights of indigenous peoples, adopting a landmark declaration that brought to an end nearly 25 years of contentious negotiations over the rights of native people to protect their lands and resources, and to maintain their unique cultures and traditions. By a vote of

143 in favour to 4 against (Australia, Canada, New Zealand and the United States), with 11 abstentions, the Assembly adopted the United Nations Declaration on the Rights of Indigenous Peoples, which sets out the individual and collective rights of the world's 370 million native peoples, calls for the maintenance and strengthening of their cultural identities, and emphasizes their right to pursue development in keeping with their own needs and aspirations.

The importance of this document for indigenous peoples and, more broadly, for the human rights agenda, cannot be underestimated.[151]

PRIME MINISTER STEPHEN HARPER, ON THE
ADOPTION OF THE UN DECLARATION BY
THE UNITED NATIONS GENERAL ASSEMBLY, 2007

We shouldn't vote for things on the basis of political correctness; we should actually vote on the basis of what's in the document.[152]

NATIONAL CHIEF PHIL FONTAINE, ASSEMBLY OF
FIRST NATIONS, ON CANADA'S VOTE AGAINST
THE UN DECLARATION, 2007

In our view, it's a stain on Canada's reputation internationally. . . . In this case, Canada is blowing against the very consistent position it has taken in the last few decades. . . .

When they decided to go against the thing that they
had supported for so long, it was inexplicable. . . . It's an
aspirational document, neither convention nor treaty . . .
We're talking here about minimum standards that relate
to our right to self-rule of our territories.[153]

MINISTER CAROLYN BENNETT, EXPRESSING CANADA'S FULL ENDORSEMENT OF THE UN DECLARATION, 2016

Today, we honour all of their work as we continue the
journey. As the Minister of Justice indicated yesterday, our
Prime Minister [Justin Trudeau] wrote to every Minister
and indicated in their mandate letters, and I quote: "No
relationship is more important to me and to Canada than
the one with Indigenous peoples. It is time for a renewed
relationship with Indigenous peoples based on recognition
of rights, respect, cooperation and partnership."

All of these mandate letters were made public, and by
doing so, the Prime Minister spoke to all Canadians. Today,
we are addressing Canada's position on the UN Declaration
on the Rights of Indigenous Peoples. I'm here to announce,
on behalf of Canada, that we are now a full supporter of the
Declaration without qualification.

We intend nothing less than to adopt and implement the
declaration in accordance with the Canadian Constitution.
Canada is in a unique position to move forward.[154]

Even prior to the adoption of the UN Declaration, Indigenous
advocacy was also evolving as women, young people, and grassroots
community members increasingly and publicly pressed for change.
In 2012, the Idle No More movement caught fire and captured
the attention of Canadians for weeks. Thousands of Indigenous
people and supporters called for change on the streets of Ottawa
and around the country. At the same time, after expansive efforts
to draw attention to the dire circumstances in her community,
Attawapiskat Chief Theresa Spence went on a hunger strike on
Victoria Island, near the Parliament Buildings in Ottawa.

CHIEF THERESA SPENCE, SENDING A MESSAGE TO INDIGENOUS PEOPLES, CANADIANS, AND GOVERNMENTS, 2011

We must go together and tell the government: This is our
land, this is our life. We need to say enough is enough.[155]

SYLVIA MCADAM, ONE OF THE FOUNDERS OF IDLE NO MORE, ON THE ROOTS OF THE IDLE NO MORE MOVEMENT, 2013

After I graduated from law school, I returned to my father's
traditional land near the Whitefish reserve and to the waters
that I had been to when I was a child, and they were gone.
The waters had dried up! It was a terrible thing to witness.

168

When my father and I went back to his traditional hunting lands, his cabin was gone. There was just a huge burn mark on the ground. When my father saw it, he just stood there, so quiet, so upset. It was terrible to watch.

I started investigating, and I learned that the conservation officers had blocked hunting roads to keep the traditional indigenous hunters away, and the lands were being logged. I felt intensely protective of the land and the water, so I went around nailing boards on trees, saying, "No Trespassing. Treaty 6 Territory!"

When I read Bill C-45 [156], I was horrified. I got into a chat on Facebook with Jessica [Gordon] and Nina [Wilson], and I started explaining to them the implications of C-45 for the environment, for the waters. I told them there's something in law called acquiescence. That means that if you're silent, then your silence is taken as consent. All of us agreed that we couldn't be silent, that grassroots people have a right to know.[157]

NATIONAL CHIEF SHAWN ATLEO, ASSEMBLY
OF FIRST NATIONS, SPEAKING DURING
IDLE NO MORE PROTESTS, 2013

This is a powerful moment. Unlike anything we have ever experienced. . . . There is no going back to the way it was before. This country will be forever changed because of what is happening and there are decisions that must be made at this crucial juncture, by the Prime Minister and by extension, all parliamentarians, but make no mistake, every single Canadian now. . . .

This is not something that we created as First Nations. It was thrust on us. The unilateral actions of others. . . .

As I'm standing right here our spirit is not broken. Our spirit is strong. Our people are proud. The young people are leading the way. And, Chiefs we better make sure we follow the young people. Because they are not the leaders, not of tomorrow, they are the leaders of right now . . .

We will not silently suffer without protest.[158]

The Supreme Court of Canada continued to issue critical rulings in favour of the rights of Indigenous Peoples, and to urge crown governments to take action that effects real change. These included the Haida decision in 2004, which affirmed the duty to consult and accommodate, and the Tsilhqot'in Nation decision in 2014, which for all intents and purposes settled the core legal issues related to the outstanding "Indian Land Question." In Tsilhqot'in, the court declared title existed on a territorial basis—in this instance more than 1,750 square kilometres—and confirmed that wherever Title exists, Indigenous consent is the standard, and that the Crown has no beneficial or economic interest in the lands and resources subject to Indigenous title. In other words, the Crown has been infringing on Indigenous title throughout the history of Canada; it continues to do so today, and the risks and costs of continuing this pattern are high.

CHIEF JUSTICE BEVERLEY MCLACHLIN, IN *HAIDA NATION V. BRITISH COLUMBIA (MINISTER OF FORESTS)*, 2004

Where treaties remain to be concluded, the honour of the Crown requires negotiations leading to a just settlement of Aboriginal claims . . . . Treaties serve to reconcile pre-existing Aboriginal sovereignty with assumed Crown sovereignty, and to define Aboriginal rights guaranteed by s. 35 of the Constitution Act, 1982. Section 35 represents a promise of rights recognition, and "[i]t is always assumed that the Crown intends to fulfil its promises". . . . This promise is realized and sovereignty claims reconciled through the process of honourable negotiation. It is a corollary of s. 35 that the Crown act honourably in defining the rights it guarantees and in reconciling them with other rights and interests. This, in turn, implies a duty to consult and, if appropriate, accommodate.[159]

CHIEF JUSTICE BEVERLEY MCLACHLIN, IN *TSILHQOT'IN NATION V. BRITISH COLUMBIA*, 2014

With the declaration of title, the Tsilhqot'in have now established Aboriginal title to the portion of the lands designated by the trial judge. . . . This gives them the right to determine, subject to the inherent limits of group title held for future generations, the uses to which the land is put and to enjoy its economic fruits. As we have seen, this is not merely a right of first refusal with respect to Crown land management or usage plans. Rather, it is the right to proactively use and manage the land.

. . .

I add this. Governments and individuals proposing to use or exploit land, whether before or after a declaration of Aboriginal title, can avoid a charge of infringement or failure to adequately consult by obtaining the consent of the interested Aboriginal group.[160]

In 2015, Justin Trudeau became prime minister, promising transformative change based on recognition of rights, respect, co-operation, and partnership. Three years later, he announced in the House of Commons that his government would enact a "Recognition and Implementation of Indigenous Rights Framework" involving new laws, policies, and practices by the end of 2018.

PRIME MINISTER JUSTIN TRUDEAU, COMMITTING CANADA TO THE ESTABLISHMENT OF A NEW RECOGNITION AND IMPLEMENTATION OF INDIGENOUS RIGHTS FRAMEWORK, 2018

Last September, at the United Nations, I spoke to delegations from around the world and told some hard truths about Canada's long and complicated relationship with First Nations, Inuit, and Métis peoples.

I talked about the colonial approach that led to the discriminatory and paternalistic *Indian Act*.

A colonial approach that systematically ignored the history of the Métis Nation, and denied its peoples their rights.

And that, in the name of Canadian sovereignty, forced the relocation of entire Inuit communities—starving individuals, uprooting families, and causing generations of harm.

. . .

It's clear, Mr. Speaker, that Indigenous Peoples and all Canadians know it is past time for change.

At the same time, some view our government's commitments with some degree of scepticism—and if you look at how things have been handled in the past, it's hard to say that that scepticism is misplaced.

After all, it's not like we are the first government to recognize the need for change, and promise that we'd do things differently.

It's been more than 20 years since the Royal Commission on Aboriginal Peoples called for "the recognition of Aboriginal Peoples as self-governing nations with a unique place in Canada."

More than 30 years have passed since the Penner Report and the First Ministers' Conferences on the Rights of Aboriginal Peoples.

And last year marked 35 years since Aboriginal and treaty rights were recognized and affirmed through Section 35 of the *Constitution Act*.

You might recall . . . that the government of the day—led by my father—did not intend to include these rights at the outset.

It was the outspoken advocacy of First Nations, Inuit, and Métis peoples, supported by non-Indigenous Canadians, that forced the government to reconsider.

Imagine what that must have felt like, Mr. Speaker.

To have fought so hard, for so long, against colonialism. Rallying your communities, reaching out to Canadians, riding the "Constitution Express." And in the end, to finally be recognized and included. To see your rights enshrined and protected in the foundational document on which Canada's democracy rests.

Now imagine the mounting disappointment—the unsurprising and familiar heartache, and the rising tide of anger—when governments that had promised so much did so little to keep their word.

You see . . . the challenge—then and now—is that while Section 35 recognizes and affirms Aboriginal and treaty rights, those rights have not been implemented by our governments.

The work to give life to Section 35 was supposed to be done together with First Nations, Inuit, and Métis Peoples. And while there has been some success, progress has not been sustained, or carried out.

And so over time, it too often fell to the courts to pick up the pieces, and fill in the gaps.

More precisely, instead of outright recognizing and affirming Indigenous rights—as we promised we would—Indigenous Peoples were forced to prove, time and time again, through costly and drawn-out court challenges, that their rights existed, must be recognized and implemented.

Indigenous Peoples, like all Canadians, know this must change.

We know it, too.

. . .

And so today, I am pleased to announce that the government will develop—in full partnership with First Nations, Inuit, and Métis people—a new Recognition and Implementation of Indigenous Rights Framework that will include new ways to recognize and implement Indigenous Rights.

This will include new recognition and implementation of rights legislation.

Going forward, recognition of rights will guide all government relations with Indigenous Peoples.[161]

Despite these promises, the pace of change remains slow. The Recognition and Implementation of Indigenous Rights Framework has not materialized. There have been some shifts in legislative and policy change—most notably the passage of the Declaration on the Rights of Indigenous Peoples Act in British Columbia and the passage of the United Nations Declaration on the Rights of Indigenous Peoples Act by Canada—but these remain modest and fall short of what was promised or is needed. At the same time, the colonial Indian Act remains in place.

Public attention and awareness of the situation of Indigenous Peoples and the urgent need for change has steadily increased, reaching a place it has never been in the history of Canada. A number of events have served as signposts that the country now recognizes how real the need for change is. Three examples are the conflict over pipeline development—particularly in Wet'suwet'en territory; the discovery of unmarked graves at the sites of former residential schools; and systemic racism in society, including in child and family services for Indigenous children, the health care system, and policing.

Our work continues . . .

JUSTICE MURRAY SINCLAIR, DESCRIBING THE
ONGOING WORK OF RECONCILIATION, 2012

The road we travel is equal in importance to the destination we seek. There are no shortcuts. When it comes to truth and reconciliation we are forced to go the distance.[162]

GOVERNOR GENERAL MARY SIMON, REFLECTING
ON THE ONE-YEAR ANNIVERSARY OF THE
IDENTIFICATION OF UNMARKED GRAVES
AT TK'EMLÚPS TE SECWÉPEMC, 2022

We, as Indigenous peoples, grow up with legends and myths, of creation and family. Eventually, we make our own stories, which we pass down to the next generation.

At this residential school and others like it across the country, churches and governments eradicated Indigenous languages and identity through corrupt policies. They took away our stories.

Over the years, too much of our culture, language and people have been lost because of residential schools, colonization and assimilation policies.

We still feel its impact today. We still experience trauma today.

For these children, their stories were cut short, but you won't let it end like this. By speaking up, you strip away the anonymity forced upon them by this school.

These were young boys and girls, with hopes and dreams, love in their hearts and their lives ahead of them. They had families and friends and were integral to their community and culture.

And it's up to all of us, across the country, to tell the stories of these kids, no different than any other child, no different than our children. To say in one voice: we failed them, and you.

We can never let that happen again.

The time for "we didn't know" is over. To all Canadians, I deliver this message. Indigenous families didn't know what happened to their children and many still don't. Most Canadians didn't know about residential schools. Now they do.

How, then, do we move forward from the shadows to the light and begin to heal?

Wherever I go in Canada or around the world, I vow to take your stories with me. I will share your stories and the stories of these children. I will do my part to bring their memories into the light.

I consider this a sacred responsibility, as governor general, as an honorary witness of the Truth and Reconciliation Commission, as a mother and a grandmother.

This is a responsibility all Canadians share. We all need to listen. We all need to understand.[163]

I THINK IT IS CLEAR from our history that while we are continuing to move forward, there are patterns of thought, action, and circumstance that are deeply entrenched as part of the legacy of colonialism. We see this in how slow tangible change is to take root, in how we study things endlessly, and in how governments still fail to follow through.

To break these patterns, we all have a responsibility, and we must all play a role. We must recognize that the story this oral history tells is not over. We are still midstream.

So what comes next? When this story is told again in five years, or ten years, or fifty years, whose voices should we hear? And what should they be saying?

I firmly believe that this story will increasingly be "our" story. Of change that is increasingly advanced together, with increasingly common visions and goals. Of change that reflects not only true reconciliation, but a revitalized vision of Canada. And the predominant voices in the story will be of Canadians from all walks of life and backgrounds, expressing how they asked what they could do and came to understand what action they can take, and illustrating how they acted and had an impact.

Will your voice be part of that story?

ADVANCING OUR LEARNING

At the heart of learning is listening to and telling new stories. In particular, we need to tell a new story about how we arrived at this moment in history in the relationship between Indigenous and non-Indigenous peoples in Canada. This story needs to be reflective and inclusive of all of the experiences that have shaped the Canada of today, and it needs to transform the narrative of exclusion that has been predominant.

A vital aspect of learning and telling new stories is recognizing that different peoples tell their stories in different ways, and that it matters who is telling the story. The predominant stories of Canada continue to be stories told by non-Indigenous peoples, told in ways that do not reflect Indigenous Peoples and their cultures. As you have seen, Indigenous Peoples have long traditions of storytelling, and ways of understanding and sharing their histories. These traditions existed before the arrival of Europeans, and they have continued to exist since.

We need to listen, learn, and share in these traditions. Learning in this way is a foundation of true reconciliation. It is like a compass that ensures we are pointing in the direction we need to go—towards a future based on knowledge of our past and present. Without following that compass, we can become easily lost, trying very hard, even tirelessly, but not actually moving in the direction we intend.

PART 2

Understand

Understand

Consider these words:

"We are as much alive as we keep the earth alive" and
"One thing to remember is to talk to the animals. If you do,
they will talk back to you. But if you don't talk to the animals,
they won't talk back to you, then you won't understand, and
when you don't understand you will fear, and when you fear
you will destroy the animals, and if you destroy the animals,
you will destroy yourself."[1]

*

"We carry the life stories and experiences of our ancestors . . . so that our generations can live life in a good way.
Our stories carry in the land, in the rock, in the rivers in
the whole environment co-existing so that there is harmony
between all beings."[2]

✳

"With all things and in all things, we are relatives."[3]

How do you understand these words? Do you agree with
them? Do they reflect how you think about the world and
your place within it?

One thing you may have taken from these quotes is that
they emphasize relationships, connections, and understanding—between human beings, between human beings and
the natural world, and between all things past, present, and
future. When people speak about reconciliation they often
do so with relationships in mind. And that is important. The
word *reconciliation* itself is about those who are in conflict
moving out of conflict. For example, one typical dictionary
definition of *reconciliation* is "a situation in which two people
or groups of people become friendly again after they have
argued."[4] Another defines it as "the act of bringing people
together to be friendly again or coming to an agreement."[5]
Notice the word *again*—and remember what was said earlier
about why the term *reconciliation* is controversial for many
Indigenous people.

Yes, part of reconciliation is building better relationships and finding connections between and among people who are in conflict. Yes, we need to have kind, constructive, and respectful relations with each other that recognize how we are interconnected. And, yes, we must always be striving to improve our interpersonal skills and build better interpersonal dynamics, through empathy, respect, and trust, in our work together.

But relationships are not enough.

Colonialism did not occur because people had bad relationships (though there were, and are, many frayed and destructive relationships because of colonization). To say it another way, if we want to talk about the history of colonialism in Canada truthfully or coherently—as we did in part 1—we can't reduce it to a story about people who had trouble in their relationships and, therefore, need to re-establish patterns of good relations. As we saw, colonialism was a practice based on beliefs about cultural and racial superiority, the taking of lands and resources, and the domination of some peoples by another.

This is all to say that true reconciliation, and addressing the legacy of colonialism, will not occur just through better relationships (though we do need lots of those). There is a lot more involved.

What true reconciliation requires, in addition to new relationships, are changes in how society is structured and organized, how we collectively live with each other, and the ways we make decisions, including about governance, economics, culture, and the environment. And being an agent of true reconciliation means understanding how we all need to contribute and support these larger societal shifts through our conduct and choices in our daily lives.

But how do we gain that understanding? What are the key understandings that will allow our actions to be most impactful in the ways we desire?

In part 1, I talked about the silos that have been built up because of our history. These silos have prevented us from gaining the knowledge of our true history, and from building a shared story of this country. Silos also hinder us when it comes to seeing and understanding how we have constructed patterns in our lives that reflect certain peoples and their traditions, and that feel comfortable and familiar for people from certain backgrounds but feel alienating and marginalizing for others. True reconciliation requires us to see these patterns and how we built them, and to envision what new ones may look like.

The reality that social structures and processes will be reflective and familiar for some, and marginalizing and even oppressive for others, is related to what is often called *privilege*. *Privilege* is a widely used term these days. It can be defined in many ways, but at its core it refers to an advantage, typically unearned, that those in one group of people hold and those in other groups do not. Privilege is also a sense of entitlement to advantages above others that are not earned.[6]

Often, our privilege is unconscious—people do not realize they are gaining benefit and advantage because of a characteristic they have or a group they are part of, while others are disadvantaged because they do not share in those things. Also often "unconscious" are implicit biases that we may hold about peoples or groups—negative attitudes that can play a role in sustaining racism. As has been explained: "It is the casual, insidious forms of racism that people are often blind to that play such a pivotal role in upholding racism. People don't see it because these attitudes are often so deeply ingrained that it takes the ability to be deeply self-critical to examine and challenge those attitudes."[7]

As the author and scholar Ibram X. Kendi writes: "the only way to undo racism is to consistently identify and describe it—and then dismantle it"—to be anti-racist.[8]

True reconciliation requires a transformative shift. It requires us to see past the silos that have been created and recognize the roles of privilege and bias in our own ways of thinking. And it requires us to envision fundamental changes in how we structure and organize aspects of our collective life to be inclusive and recognize new connections. *Understanding* is about how we do that, with a focus on two sets of connections that I think are critical, and that we typically do not see clearly enough: (1) the connection between our worldviews and the world we create; and (2) the connection between Indigenous rights and the social and economic reality of Indigenous Peoples.

OUR WORLDVIEWS AND THE WORLD WE CREATE

Let's return to the quotations that opened this part of the book. As I said, these powerful statements speak to the importance of relationships. But they also express a particular way of perceiving the world—what is often called a *worldview*.

A worldview is the lens through which we see the world around us. It is like a pair of glasses that may focus, or tint, what we see in certain ways.

The term has been defined in countless ways, across many fields of study, including anthropology, sociology, and psychology. While there are different definitions of *worldview*, generally the term is used to refer to how people comprehend—see meaning and order in the world—and make sense of the world within which they exist.

Here is a good summary of some of the different definitions of *worldview*:

Worldviews reflect the way an individual or group perceives reality, human nature, the purpose of human life and the laws governing human relationships. For the most part, we are only partially conscious of the worldviews we hold. Nevertheless, worldview determines where we see ourselves going, what we understand to be the processes taking place around us, and what we believe our role in these processes can and should be.

Worldviews develop in the contexts of family, religion, culture, and school; and are additionally shaped by the political environment, the media and our life experiences. Discussed in their various aspects as "social representations," "dispositions," "cultural fabric" and "collective narratives and beliefs," worldviews "are constructed, transmitted, confirmed, and reconstructed in social interactions, and they mediate social action." In other words, worldviews influence everything we think, feel and do.[9]

We are not born with our worldviews. They are constructed and shaped during our lives, particularly in childhood. Our culture and the people we come from, our parents and families, what we are taught, and the experiences we have in life are all powerful forces in shaping how we look at the world around us and make sense of our existence.

Our worldviews are both our own and are shared. We are all individuals, living our own lives, and we will each express our worldviews in unique ways. But core aspects of ourselves are reflected in the worldviews shared with others—grounded in our cultures and teachings. We share these aspects with those who have come before us, and pass it down to the generations to come. Worldviews survive over time and are a source of strength, identity, and resilience in the face of life's challenges. Worldviews help let us know who "we" are, and who "I" am.

For example, at the core of my Kwakwaka'wakw worldview is the belief that all things are in their greatest state of well-being when there is balance. This includes balance between humans and the natural world, between genders, between groups of peoples, within a family or community, or in how we live and organize our own lives. Balance is viewed as the proper state of things, where conditions of harmony and justice flourish, while imbalance is what gives rise to conflict, contention, and harm. So, in all aspects of our social organization and life, balance needs to be sought out. In my worldview—which animates the Kwakwaka'wakw system of government, our laws, and legal order—if women are not playing their needed roles in leadership in all aspects of society, there is an imbalance, and all suffer. A society imbalanced in this way is like a bird with an injured wing. It cannot fly, its purpose and potential cannot be met, and all are held back.

I am very lucky to have been raised knowing my Kwakwaka'wakw worldview. Many have not been so lucky. I know how much sacrifice generations of people had to make—in the face of colonialism—to ensure that my people's worldview survived and thrived. I also know our worldview was a source of strength that helped those sacrifices to be made, just as my worldview is a source of strength for me today that guides me through hardships. In my life, as a reflection of my worldview, the principle of balance is a predominant guiding direction in all of my personal and professional relationships.

It is also important to realize that in some ways our worldviews are dynamic, not static. While core elements of our worldview are shaped when we are young, and we share it with our family and the culture of which we are a part, throughout our lives we have new experiences, and gain new insights and understandings. As this happens, our understanding of our own worldview shifts or deepens.

Think about it: As human beings, we all naturally grow and change throughout our life. Aspects of our worldview will be expressed differently at different stages of our life—as infants, children, adolescents, adults, or elders. This is because at different stages of our journey we will be faced with various psychological, intellectual, or biological realities that can influence what we are aware of in the world around us, and within ourselves. Just imagine for a moment how an infant perceives the world around them, as distinct from a child or adolescent. An infant, because of their cognitive development, is focused on basic forms of survival and comfort. As they move into childhood, this focus changes because a child perceives and understands more of the world.

Why are worldviews important?

Worldviews help determine the actions we choose to take and the worlds we create. They heavily influence us when we act as individuals, and they shape the society we build, our laws, institutions, and systems of government.

Here is a simple example: Imagine if someone has a worldview that primarily sees the world as a dangerous, hostile, and harsh place—a place where there are constant threats to one's well-being. In such a worldview, one will act in a certain way. Most likely one will try to establish control and dominance so that there is safety and an ability to survive, and, through that, alleviate fear. One will also be quite self-focused, centred on the well-being of oneself and those close to you, sometimes at the expense of, and with fear or hostility towards, others.

Now think about such a worldview being shared among people. What kind of society will they strive to create? It will have elements that might be called authoritarian and oppressive. It will be a society in which there is rigidity and control—so that what threatens us can be kept in check, and we can be safe and thrive through domination.

Do you know individuals who seem to have such a worldview? Or aspects of it? Have you been in contexts—such as families or workplaces—that reflect such a worldview?

You've probably figured out that in describing such a worldview and the type of society it creates, I am very simplistically describing aspects (though not all) of the ways of thinking that lead to patterns of injustice and oppression in society. Like colonialism. But more on that later.

There is one other important point to keep in mind when striving to understanding worldviews: they are often hidden to us. We do not move through life consciously thinking about our worldviews, or talking about how they shape our actions. Yes, there are times when we reflect on them, but those are the exceptions and not the rule. And, similarly, while there are times when we may recognize how our worldview has shaped the ways we have chosen to act, those times are also more the exception than the rule.

Now, I know that this last paragraph conflicts somewhat with what I said earlier, when I described my own worldview and noted how I often share it when speaking. That's because I make a conscious choice to acknowledge my worldview when given the chance to do so. I do this, in part, as a response to the legacy of colonialism in this country. Furthermore, I also believe it is part of advancing true reconciliation.

One of the realities of colonialism is that it sought to assimilate Indigenous Peoples so that they would be forced to abandon their own worldviews and adopt ones from European traditions. Because Indigenous Peoples were removed from public life, decision-making, and governance—as we discussed in part 1—the foundations of Canadian society have been largely built around patterns that ignore and marginalize Indigenous worldviews.

Let me give you an example: The residential school system can be thought of as one part of the effort to eradicate Indigenous worldviews and impose a different one. This is one way to interpret the infamous and hideous statement that the purpose of the schools was to "take the Indian out of the child."[10] The goal was to stop Indigenous children from being raised to understand their worldview, express it, and live it— and try to force them to adopt another worldview. By doing this, it was believed that what was "Indigenous" in Indigenous Peoples would go away. Our identities. Our languages. Our ways of life. It was believed that by eradicating our worldview, one could eradicate who we are. It was even considered benevolent at the time, perhaps by some even now; that it was in the best interest of Indigenous Peoples to "civilize" us—to impart to us a European worldview and way of life—as we were "savage" and would benefit both spiritually and materially by becoming, even through force, more European.

As described earlier, Indigenous Peoples, for thousands of years, have had their own sophisticated systems of government. These systems are diverse—different First Nations have different governing traditions—but they have always existed in one form or another. While these governing systems are different in many ways from, for example, contemporary models of liberal democracy (like our parliamentary system) or European monarchies, at their core Indigenous systems of governance have always played the same roles and upheld the same responsibilities as any other governing system. In essence, these systems are how a society makes decisions on behalf of the collective, to provide for well-being, safety, and order. Decisions are made in accordance with certain practices, protocols, and laws. Individuals, and groups of individuals, hold certain authorities and responsibilities, which they must fulfil in particular ways. There are also established mechanisms and processes through which those in leadership positions may be replaced.

For many Indigenous Peoples, traditional systems of governance have a "hereditary" dimension, meaning that certain roles and responsibilities are carried forward over time through different families and groups. Many of our Indigenous systems also operate through communal forms of decision-making, meaning that rarely do individuals possess much "power" themselves. Decisions typically require consensus among many. As well, many traditional Indigenous systems are grounded in a worldview that emphasizes balance, including between men and women. While men and women have different governing roles, all of these roles are essential, critical, and valued.

After Canadian Confederation, there was a deliberate effort to destroy these traditional Indigenous systems of governance, mainly through the Indian Act. It outlawed our systems of governance and imposed a system of Band Council governance that was totally different from how decisions had been made in the past—including what decisions could be made about, who made them, and how leaders were chosen. The Big House, for example, was banned, and replaced by a decision-making structure devised in accordance with a statute, written in Ottawa and based on common-law administrative practices, that reflected European modes of decision-making.

The results of these efforts to destroy our governance system remains with us in very real ways today. Take, for example, the conflict in Wet'suwet'en territory—the Wet'suwet'en Yintah—in central British Columbia about pipeline development. The roots of this conflict are often portrayed as a struggle within the Wet'suwet'en between "hereditary" and "elected" forms of government. But whatever internal conflict there may be among the Wet'suwet'en is a symptom—not the root—of the challenge. There was one governing system for the Wet'suwet'en People for countless generations prior to contact with Europeans. Canada outlawed that system, divided the nation and its people into smaller units, and created and imposed multiple governing bodies. Now, the Wet'suwet'en, like First Nations across the country, are in midst of the hard work of rebuilding their governing system for all their people after more than a century of colonial division and control. That does not happen overnight. It will not be easy. And we should not be confused about how we ended up in this position—it is because of the Crown, the Indian Act, and its racist attack on First Nations governments.

This colonial practice of "divide and conquer" is also the source of what is often called the "challenge of overlapping territories"—the idea that many First Nations say they have title and rights to the same land. As is the case with any peoples and governments, for thousands of years First Nations had protocols and practices with their neighbours that confirmed their relationships to lands, where they were shared (and not), and how disputes about those lands would be settled. When Canada divided First Nations into smaller units, imposed the reserve and Band Council system, and moved them off their lands, it threw these traditional systems of land governance into chaos. As First Nations rebuild their governments and nations, these issues of territory and land relationship will also be resolved through revitalizing these protocols and expressing them in tangible and workable ways in the contemporary world. But again, as with the confusion over governance systems playing out in Wet'suwet'en, we should have no illusions or confusion about how we got here.

While Canada attacked our governments to control our people, these actions were also driven by a belief that Indigenous Peoples did not actually have a system of government. From a European worldview, our Indigenous systems were not really seen or recognized, and certainly not viewed as governments, so part of "civilizing" us, and assimilating us, was to impose on us a European system of governance, controlled by Europeans in Ottawa. This, of course, was because we did not yet know how to govern ourselves. We had to learn the right ways, the European ways.

Today, as with the residential school system, we recognize more and more the fallacies, harms, and destruction caused by this attitude and attack on Indigenous governing systems. We also recognize more and more the chaos it has created and that must be addressed as part of the work of true reconciliation, such as the example we discussed earlier about "hereditary" and "elected" leaders within First Nations. This confusion and conflict is because of the reality I just described: Indigenous Peoples have always had systems of government. Canada ignored this reality, and imposed a system based on its own worldview and traditions. Indigenous systems never went away; they were maintained and kept—even when this had to be done in the shadows. And so today, when we recognize the wrongs of colonialism and the change that is needed, we experience a complicated reality in which there are multiple governing systems and sets of laws operating at once.

A related issue is the focus on Indigenous self-determination and the inherent right of self-government that is so often emphasized when we talk about Indigenous rights and the United Nations Declaration on the Rights of Indigenous Peoples. While colonization involved imposing on Indigenous Peoples a governing system that was grounded in a European worldview and was considered "civilized," reconciliation necessarily involves ensuring there is recognition, support, and space for Indigenous Peoples to rebuild their governing systems on their own terms, in ways that reflect their own worldviews. Self-determination by Indigenous Peoples is a vital and necessary antidote to the continuing disempowerment caused by colonialism.

So, when I speak publicly of my worldview, like many Indigenous people do, it is part of a response to the legacy of colonialism that sought to cut us off from our cultures, people, and systems of governance and social organization. By speaking it and sharing it, we are pushing back against and responding to what colonialism sought to eradicate. It is a way of demonstrating that what was tried, failed.

But speaking of worldviews is not just about Indigenous Peoples standing up for who they are. Recognizing the relationships between worldviews and the world we create is fundamental to true reconciliation. True reconciliation involves seeing how Canada has been constructed in ways that exclude or marginalize Indigenous worldviews, and imagining social patterns that respect and have space for those world-views and what they mean for our collective life.

True reconciliation requires understanding Indigenous worldviews, how they are different from other worldviews, and how, unlike in much of our history, we can live together respecting and recognizing these differences.

Understanding Indigenous Worldviews

There is, to be clear, no single "Indigenous worldview." There are many. Indigenous worldviews reflect the distinctiveness and diversity between and among Indigenous Peoples, though they do share certain features. As has been said: "There are many Indigenous peoples, and therefore many Indigenous worldviews. They share, however, a relational worldview emphasizing spirit and spirituality and, in turn, a sense of community and respect for the individual."[11]

And there is another critically important point we must always remember: All of us exist and have experiences and realities that are at the intersection of many different peoples, cultures, traditions, and worldviews. None of us has a worldview that is completely reflective of one people or culture or another—each of us has been influenced and shaped by many forces. For Indigenous people, it is challenging to figure out how much our worldviews have been shaped by our Indigenous culture, and how much they have been impacted by colonization. As Leroy Little Bear, a Blackfoot scholar and leader, has stated: "No one has a pure worldview that is 100 percent Indigenous or Eurocentric; rather, everyone has an integrated mind, a fluxing and ambidextrous consciousness, a precolonized consciousness that flows into a colonized consciousness and back again. It is this clash of worldviews that is at the heart of many current difficulties."[12]

So as we talk about Indigenous and Eurocentric worldviews, we are talking about the predominant perspectives and orientations individuals may have, but also the ones that are not fixed or uniform or somehow shut out from each other. We are talking about how individuals will always have their own ways of expressing their worldviews—ways that reflect their particular experiences, including the experience of colonization.

How do we understand the dimensions and aspects of Indigenous worldviews? By listening to people share them. I shared aspects of my Kwakwaka'wakw worldview earlier on. Here are some other Indigenous voices sharing aspects of their worldviews. Think about what strikes you as you read them. Do they feel familiar? Do you identify with them? Are they confusing or foreign? Consider also how you would describe your worldview if you were asked to share it.

"What is life? It is the flash of a firefly in the night. It is the breath of a buffalo in the wintertime. It is the little shadow which runs across the grass and loses itself in the sunset."[13]

✳

"So we asked our Elders: who are we as Indian thinkers? Our Creation stories; what do they say? And a lot of our stories said that humans were created as equal to all creation. And the concept of being equal defined our thinking and understanding. So I was equal to the animals and plants, the air and the water; the stars were equal to me, and I was equal to all human beings, and even to bugs.

Now the concept of being created equally was the basis of all our practices—our forms of governance, and social relations. We are all created together, and all are sacred. So our Piikani Blackfoot language and oral system are based in ceremonial practices; a ceremonial circle structure was our way of communicating and working in a group."[14]

✳

"The four directions, North, East, South and West, are represented respectively by the colours white, red, yellow and black. Within these colours are the four races of Man: the White Man, the Red Man, the Yellow Race, and the Black Race; the four Life-givers: air, food, sun, and water; the four seasons: winter, spring, summer, and fall; the four vices: greed, apathy, jealousy, and resentment; the four moral principles: caring, vision, patience, and reasoning. The North gives us the rocks, which speak to us of strength. The East gives us the animals, which talk to us about sharing. From the South we get the trees, which teach us about honesty, and from the West we are given the grasses, which teach us about kindness. All things in this Life were, and are, given to us by the Mother of us all. Our Mother the Earth . . . "[15]

❋

"All things and all people, though we have our own individual gifts and special place, are dependent on and share in the growth and work of everything and everyone else. We believe that beings thrive when there is a web of interconnectedness between the individual and the community, and between the community and nature.

Everything we do, every decision we make, affects our family, our community, it affects the air we breathe, the animals, the plants, the water in some way. Each of us is totally dependent on everything else."[16]

✷

"Indigenous worldviews are generally holistic in perspective
and encompass interconnections amongst all aspects of life
and place. From this interconnected view of the universe,
a sense of cultural identity, collective purpose and belonging is derived. Cultural wellbeing relies on the individual
becoming situated within a cultural worldview. For Inuit,
being grounded in *Inuit Qaujimajatuqangit* supports personal wellness, but also contributes to a collective cultural
sense of health and wellness which has sustained Inuit
over generations. Inuit Elders in Nunavut are documenting
Inuit worldview so that the strengths which have always
sustained them will still be available to future generations."[17]

Of course, language is vital to expressing and capturing
elements of a worldview. As a result, some meanings are lost
when we translate into English. Often, one word can reflect
a whole people and their worldview. For example, the word
otipemisiwak, which has Cree origins, means "those that rule
themselves." *Otipemisiwak* is often used by Métis to describe
themselves, their culture, and worldview. It evokes the distinctiveness of the Métis way of life, and acknowledges that they
have systems of governance, knowledge, and kinship grounded
in their own identity. Central to this way of life is a worldview that is grounded in "parallel notions of individual independence and communal independence."[18] Community and
family are core to this worldview:

To Métis people, the words community and family are almost interchangeable. Métis people view not only their relations as family, but friends, neighbours and workmates can all be a part of what a Métis person considers part of the family. In Métis culture, children are not solely the responsibility of their parents. The whole community traditionally shares in the task of raising the next generation. Elders, grandparents, aunts, uncles, trusted friends, leaders and other community members all have their vital role to play in shaping the future of our Nation.[19]

You likely noticed some differences not only between these worldviews but also in how they are expressed. Different Indigenous Peoples will express their worldviews through different imagery, describing relations with differing aspects of the natural world, and through emphasizing different types of connections and relationships. And, of course, this also reflects the different languages that Indigenous Peoples use, that inform and shape distinct identities and modes of expression.

While there are distinctions and diversity among Indigenous worldviews, it is also the case, as mentioned briefly earlier, that many of them share certain elements. One of these is that Indigenous worldviews are often said to be "integrative" or "interconnected." They emphasize and see how everything in existence is interdependent and indivisible. Another way to describe this is that they are "holistic" or "relational." For this reason, in Indigenous culture and art, Indigenous worldviews are often reflected in a "circle" that emphasizes the connection between things.

One way that this perspective that all things are connected is expressed is through the importance of responsibilities: "In the Aboriginal view, all of creation is a circle in which there are only responsibilities inherent in the nature of each being, human and non-human, born and unborn, living and not living. Since all things are related and part of creation, they all have a responsibility to maintain the harmonious relations that were established in the beginning."[20]

Another central theme shared in many Indigenous worldviews is how all things in creation are understood to be animated by spirit, and are viewed as having a sacred dimension. It is vital, in determining how we act in our lives, to recognize this spiritual dimension to all things, respect it, and see our connection to it. One expression of this is the "belief in the power of creating a positive shared mind with all of creation. This is best defined as 'power with,' as opposed to 'power over.'"[21]

Related to this are Indigenous ways of knowing and learning. Indigenous knowledge refers to the learning that has been gained over countless generations through their ways of surviving, living, and stewarding their relationship with the natural world and other peoples. Historically, as part of colonization, this knowledge has been ignored, devalued, and denigrated, particularly because it was dismissed as unscientific, or at least not developed in the same way as the European model of the scientific method.

For example, *Inuit Qaujimajatuqangit* is the term used to describe Indigenous knowledge of the Inuit. *Inuit Qaujimajatuqangit* has been described in the following way: "The term translates directly as 'that which Inuit have always known to be true.' It is the foundation upon which social/emotional, spiritual, cognitive and physical well-being is built."[22]

Indigenous knowledge is also communicated in particular forms and modes. As I shared earlier, oral traditions of story-telling as a means of communicating and passing on knowl-edge are also integral to Indigenous worldviews. Storytelling practices reflect and re-enforce the collective and communal nature of life, relationships across time, and the connections that we must always keep in the forefront of how we live our life. Consider these descriptions of Indigenous storytelling practices:

"The Elders would serve as mnemonic pegs to each other. They will be speaking individually uninterrupted in a circle one after another. When each Elder spoke they were conscious that other Elders would serve as 'peer reviewer' [and so] they did not delve into subject matter that would be questionable. They did joke with each other and they told stories, some true and some a bit exaggerated but in the end the result was a collective memory. This is the part which is exciting because when each Elder arrived they brought with them a piece of the knowledge puzzle. They had to reach back to the teachings of their parents, grandparents and even great-grandparents. These teachings were shared in the circle and these constituted a reconnaissance of collective memory and knowledge. In the end the Elders left with a knowledge that was built by the collectivity."[23]

❋

"Through oral tradition, our Métis worldview, history, and cultural teachings are preserved for future generations. Our stories give us our identity and a sense of belonging."[24]

❋

"There are different ways of telling stories. Some people would get up and they would recite really long stories; they would almost sing or chant them. Then there were stories that people played with fiddles and were part of fiddle dances. There were the stories that were told in the evening in the winter—and there were stories that had laws and taught us how to live good lives."[25]

In addition to storytelling, many artistic and ceremonial forms of expression are used to transmit knowledge:

Traditionally, Aboriginal cultural knowledge is transmitted and documented primarily through the oral tradition, but also through such things as dramatic productions, dance performances, and they are documented on such artifacts as wampum belts, birch bark scrolls, totem poles, petroglyphs and masks. This is the Aboriginal way of transmitting knowledge and of recording information and history.[26]

Another central feature of many Indigenous worldviews is that they are communal or collective, meaning they emphasize the group as the central foundation of culture and society, as distinct from the individual. As such, spiritual, cultural, social, economic, and political values and practices emphasize communal processes and well-being. Leroy Little Bear describes how this communal ethic exists at all levels: "The value of wholeness speaks to the totality of creation, the group as opposed to the individual, the forest as opposed to the individual trees. It focuses on the totality of constant flux rather than on individual patterns. This value is reflected in the customs and organization of Plains Indian tribes, where the locus of social organization is the extended family, not the immediate, biological family. Several extended families combine to form a band. Several bands combine to form a tribe or nation; several tribes or nations combine to form confederacies . . ."[27]

With all these aspects of Indigenous worldviews, a uniting theme is "respect." Respect for the past, present, and future; the dead, the living, and the unborn; all things in creation; the spirit and the material; and for an essential relationship between all things. Respect is also an overarching principle in different Indigenous legal orders. For example, the following has been described in the context of Treaty 6, which stretches from parts of Alberta, through Saskatchewan, to Manitoba: "Powerful laws were established to protect and to nurture the foundations of strong, vibrant nations. Foremost amongst these laws are those related to human bonds and relationships known as the laws relating to *miyo-wicehtowin* include those

laws encircling the bonds of human relationships in the ways
in which they are created, nourished, reaffirmed, and recreated
as a means of strengthening the unity among First Nations
people and of the nation itself."[28]

Indigenous worldviews are seen to be different from those
considered to be "Western" or "European." Again, we have
to be careful with such general and all-encompassing terms.
Indigenous Peoples are diverse, with plural traditions, realities,
and experiences. The same can be said about what is meant
by "Western" or "European." As such, when people study and
speak of "Indigenous" and "European" worldviews (and many
do—just google the words), they are generalizing about different sets of diverse cultures and peoples who happen to share
certain aspects of their worldviews.

Here is one summary description of differences between
"Indigenous" and "Western" worldviews:

> Worldviews emerge from the totality of peoples' social,
> political, economic, cultural and spiritual perceptions and
> beliefs. [Willie J.] Ermine defines Aboriginal and Western
> worldviews as "diametric trajectories in the realm of know-
> ledge." He describes Aboriginal worldviews as founded on a
> search for meaning from a metaphysical, implicit, subjective
> journey for knowledge based on the premises of "skills that
> promote personal and social transformation; a vision of
> social change that leads to harmony with rather than control
> over the environment; and the attribution of a spiritual
> dimension to the environment." He contrasts it with the

Western worldview of the physical, explicit, scientific and objective journey for knowledge. Ermine draws upon Engels' false consciousness concept and says: "the Western world has capitulated to a dogmatic fixation on power and control at the expense of authentic insights into the nature and origin of knowledge as truth." It is not surprising that the two worldviews often clash with one another.

"At a fundamental cultural level, the difference between traditional Aboriginal and Western thought is the difference in the perception of one's relationship with the universe and the Creator." Euro-Christian Canadians believed that they were meant to dominate the Earth and its creatures. The Aboriginal peoples believed that they were the least important creatures of the universe and that they were dependent upon the four elements (fire, water, earth and air) and all of creation for survival. For many Aboriginal peoples today, this belief system continues to be the framework from which they live their lives. Others do not accept traditional worldviews any longer, and some are returning to traditional ways seeking meaning and harmony in their lives.[29]

Let's return to some of the questions I asked earlier: Do you identify with these statements of Indigenous worldview, and the elements described? Do you think they reflect aspects of your worldview? Do you agree with the distinctions that are drawn between Indigenous and European worldviews? How would you describe your worldview or elements of it?

Worldviews and the Canada We Have Created

One of the realities of Canada—due to how its history has unfolded and the reality of colonialism—is that it has been predominately shaped by European worldviews. And while there have been ways in which Indigenous worldviews have shaped what Canada means, and what it means to be Canadian, we often do not recognize those.

Let me you give some examples from the sphere of politics.

When I was in Ottawa serving as minister of justice and attorney general of Canada, I observed a lot about how decisions are made, nowhere more so than around the Cabinet table.

Reflecting European worldviews, our approach to political decision-making in the parliamentary system is both individualistic and competitive. Yes, Cabinet makes decisions, but in this system, there are layers upon layers—from top to bottom—of individual decision-makers. The prime minister is the ultimate decision-maker. Each minister is a decision-maker. Legislation appoints hundreds of individuals as statutory decision-makers. In theory, there is a democratic logic to this: we diffuse power among many individuals, and have them govern by the rule of law (also, in theory!). Unlike in Indigenous systems, though, this method of decision-making is not communally grounded in recognition that the decision-maker is a collective operating through consensus.

Of course, we also have structures in our political system where multiple individuals make decisions together—like Cabinet. But Cabinet decision-making is not the same as collective decision-making. It is true that Cabinet is meant to be a place for open debate and dialogue, and where, if needed, majority decisions can be made, sometimes by voting, and advanced. In my experience, Cabinet today is often an arena in which decisions that have effectively already been made, and that reflect the will of the prime minister and the Prime Minister's Office (PMO), are affirmed. As I described previously in *Indian in the Cabinet*, when reflecting on whether I found being in Cabinet different than what I had expected:

> . . . it was different than what I was used to in Indigenous politics, where consensus building is so central. I had thought there would be more of a search for truth and a building of consensus around the best decision at the Cabinet table. I had thought our work around that table would include genuinely caring about what each other thought and the diverse perspectives we shared, and that we would build the best decisions by drawing on all the bits of wisdom we each contributed. I reflected that it was not this way; it was not about forging consensus, and that was different for me and a surprise. A surprise that was at once sad and maddening.
>
> So many times after Cabinet meetings ministers would groan about how everything was staged and how their opinions did not matter. Or they'd grumble about how they did not want to say anything because they knew how the PM or the PMO felt about an issue.[30]

In both theory and practice, Canada's mode of political decision-making is starkly different than the communal decision-making processes that are reflected in Indigenous worldviews. A communal decision-making process recognizes that the decision must come from the collective—that it is the whole that has the responsibility and authority to make a decision, and it is from the collective that the best decisions arise. As such, the process of decision-making is focused on a process where everyone is seeking to reach a common outcome.

In such a communal model, a primary goal is to reach consensus. By its very nature this involves individuals coming into the process recognizing that their views are perhaps incomplete and may be wrong, being ready to change their views as appropriate, and having a willingness to accept that the collective decision, and maintaining the unity of the collective, is paramount to one's individual views and perspectives.

This extends to our whole political system. When a political system reflects a collective and communal worldview, organizing into political teams—different teams that are opposed to one another—makes no sense. The goal is not to "win" over the other team because there are no other teams in that sense; there is only the collective, with everyone having a responsibility to contribute. In a collective and communal political system, we do not evaluate ideas based on partisanship—something which is, unfortunately, a cornerstone of how federal and provincial governments operate today—but rather aim to base ideas on their merit. "Politics" is less a process of competition between parties and more a process of building cohesion. So many of the things we take for granted in our Canadian political system—the idea of a "loyal opposition," whose role it is to challenge and criticize the decisions that are made; or the emphasis on public debate through Question Period; or the way in which politics is talked and thought about as competition—is almost completely foreign to political systems based on Indigenous worldviews.

A good illustration of this is from the governance rebuilding that has taken place by the Inuit. The governments of Nunavut and the Northwest Territories both function through a system of "consensus government," as distinct from one based on political parties. Nunatsiavut, an autonomous area in Newfoundland and Labrador, also functions through a consensus model. One thing all three of these areas share is a majority Indigenous population.

While this model of consensus government has many elements that are based on the parliamentary system that is seen in our federal and provincial governments, it also, as has been said in relation to Nunavut, is "more in keeping with the way that Inuit have traditionally made decisions."[31]

A critical feature of consensus government is that everyone is elected as an independent and does not run as a member of a political party. The premier and members of Cabinet in Nunavut are then chosen from those who are elected, by those who are elected. There is no Official Opposition. Further, the number of individuals in Cabinet cannot be a majority of those in the legislature—so the executive must be responsible to the legislature, where members are sitting independently.

Writing with respect to Nunavut, some have suggested that "the absence of parties is simply a sign of our lack of political 'maturity' and that once we have reached the proper stage of political development, we will acquire parties."[32] But as one former Speaker of the Legislative Assembly of Nunavut describes, there are advantages to this non-partisan system: "Our Legislative Assembly simply is not as adversarial as party-dominated Houses"; "debate is civil. MLAs [members of the Legislative Assembly] listen to each other and do not often interrupt"; "Heated political battles occur behind the scenes but the norms of civility and respect are powerful."[33]

From time to time there remains discussion about how those with consensus government should shift to the more common party-based model. But, regardless of where one comes down on the matter, consideration should be given to what jurisdictions with political parties can learn from those with consensus government, including the value of increased independence and less adversarial discourse. Indeed, I am of the view that there is much to be learned about how we could be governing Canada not only from the model of consensus government in the Northwest Territories, Nunavut, and Nunatsiavut but also from traditional Indigenous models of government that have existed for countless generations, such as the Potlatch of my people.

Now, it is important not to idealize what politics based on aspects of Indigenous worldviews might look like. Indigenous politics struggles with all sorts of division and dysfunction. Just like politics anywhere, including in Canada, it struggles to live up to its ideals. But that is just the human way. We are not perfect translations of what we aspire to be. We all imagine the "ideal" that we strive to make "real." And there is always a gap between our ideal vision and what is real. Striving to make the real more ideal is core to what motivates us and drives us to make progress in life. But, of course, we are imperfect. In certain contexts, and for occasional periods of time, we do better. In others, we struggle more. And we have to factor in the realities of colonialization, which has been a very destructive force in Indigenous politics and governing systems.

The point, however, is that the visions and ideals we aspire to are reflections of our worldviews. And they are different because worldviews are different.

Let me contrast an experience I had when I was Regional Chief of British Columbia with one from when I was the minister of justice and attorney general of Canada; the exercise will illustrate the core differences between Indigenous and European worldviews, and how the latter dominates our system.

In 2014, the Supreme Court of Canada issued the decision in *Tsilhqot'in Nation v. British Columbia*, which, as I noted earlier, effectively settled the "Indian Land Question." One of the follow-ups to that decision was the establishment of a new political process between all First Nations in British Columbia and the Government of British Columbia, in which all Chiefs would meet with the premier and the entire Cabinet to discuss critical issues. The inaugural BC Cabinet and First Nations Leadership Gathering was planned for September 11, 2014.

Two days prior to the gathering, I held an All-Chiefs meeting involving the Chiefs of all First Nations in British Columbia. There were leadership representatives from the vast majority of First Nations in attendance—close to two hundred people. The focus of the meeting was our preparation for the gathering with the BC Cabinet and, in particular, to see if a common strategy and approach could be reached. In our First Nations way, the goal was to reach consensus and make decisions collectively. Everyone had the opportunity to say their piece and respectfully listen to the ideas of each other. No one was excluded and, as always, it was recognized that everyone's input and perspective was important.

As we went around the room, shared ideas began to emerge. We wanted to go into the meeting with a set of principles about how relations should be reset. Those principles were to be concise, short, and clear. We started writing together up on the screen. A set of principles took shape for all to see. As we got closer to consensus, some nations still had concerns about specific wording, such as how historic treaties were to be referenced or economic matters addressed. So we kept working, and making edits together. And then there was a moment in which we all simply knew: we had consensus. We formally adopted the "Four Principles," as they came to be known, and they became the basis for how we collectively approached the forthcoming gathering. The principles also became the basis for other important political processes and initiatives that continue today in British Columbia.

Now contrast that way of making decisions with what happens in the federal government. When I became minister of justice and attorney general of Canada in 2015, I immediately began encouraging and pushing Cabinet to adopt a set of principles to guide how Canada conducts itself in the work of reconciliation. In effect, it was the same work as the Chiefs were trying to advance through the Four Principles—to lay proper foundations for relations and reorient how policy is developed together. Well, perhaps needless to say, the process of getting Cabinet to agree to a set of principles was very different.

For one thing, the process took almost two years. While the idea of adopting a set of principles was endorsed very early by the prime minister and Cabinet, the work just went in endless cycles. Drafts of the principles were completed by early 2016, but Cabinet, ministers, and their offices just kept spinning their wheels about them. Sometimes you would seek comment and hear nothing for months. Other times there would be a flurry of activity and then nothing. No real forum seemed to exist to build consensus on an approach, so one had to be created—a new "Working Group of Ministers." But the Working Group was never really supported in its work, and it was short-lived.

Ultimately, the Principles Respecting the Government of Canada's Relationship with Indigenous Peoples (often referred to as the "10 Principles") was released on July 14, 2017. This occurred only after a number of weeks of it being held up by a few ministers because they still didn't like a certain word or had fears over how the principles would be used.

And throughout the process, even at the end of it, some made it clear they were against the principles, although they failed to ever articulate what their issues were. Because of the nature of this process, which was never focused on reaching consensus, I could not say with much confidence that there was a shared understanding or sense of commitment or ownership over the principles. Indeed, many ministries never took concrete steps to implement them—except for perhaps hanging them on the wall of government offices, where they continue to hang today.

Of course, the ways in which a European worldview has been dominant in structuring Canada is not limited to any one sector of our society. It is widespread.

Let's look at a more historical example, one that our children may read about when studying Canadian history. It is about economics. In general terms, First Nations economies prior to the arrival of Europeans were often described as subsistence economies. There was typically a high degree of economic independence of families and individuals, within which there was the exchange and sharing of resources. Basically, you procured your own food. Made your own tools and clothes. Built your home. It was a local economy and everyone had a role to play, with no real accumulation of individual wealth, though everyone was cared for. Indeed, in some First Nations cultures, including my own, the individual accumulation of wealth was considered wrong. As such, one function of our Potlatch was to redistribute wealth to make sure everyone had what they needed and was cared for, and no one was accumulating too much.

At the same time, there were many cultural and economic resources that, in various ways, were communally owned and used for the benefit of the collective. This could include fishing sites, for example, which certain families may have had particular responsibilities and authorities for, but which also were communal in purpose and function.

In this system we see a complex network of individual, community, and tribal economic interconnection and interdependence. Individuals did not possess "capital" or hold deeds to property, such as in Europe. Rather, ownership was of the intangible—such as names, songs, and dances. This form of ownership illustrated one's connection to a group, territory, and resource, and identified, among other things, what economic relations, opportunities, and responsibilities existed. Within this complex network, there was what we would characterize today as commercial and trade relations, but these were based on communal and collective understandings of prosperity and wealth rather than ideas of individual ownership.

Now imagine the discordance when Europeans brought with them to North America their economic perspectives and approach—of which the fur trade was an early focus. While there was nothing foreign about the idea of trade, the values around wealth were significantly different. While trade for First Nations was focused on acquiring what was needed, for Europeans the focus was on accumulating wealth—for the Hudson's Bay Company, the Crown, and the individuals involved.

The impacts of this distinction were massive. For example, the economic focus of Europeans meant they required the labour of Indigenous people to trap and produce furs. Such conceptions of labour were different from the economic practices among First Nations for generations, and thus resulted in changes to the social dynamics for men and women. As well, the different economic understandings, grounded in wholly different worldviews, established a context for economic exploitation of First Nations, as Europeans pursued resource acquisition and ownership, while First Nations sought to maintain and respect a network of connections to territory and the collective.

Consider the following story from a Hudson's Bay post during the 1720s. The Hudson's Bay Company had been trading one gun for fourteen pelts. At the time, other trading goods had different pelt values, but the gun was far and away the most expensive. Presumably, the company needed, or desired, more pelts, and so they wanted the Indigenous trappers to work harder to bring more of them in. In contemporary language, they wanted to incentivize the First Nations trappers. So, what did they do? They offered two guns for fourteen pelts, effectively a raise. What happened? The Indigenous trappers didn't need two guns, so some brought in seven pelts to get one gun. Under the Indigenous worldview, you take and use only what you need. If you need only one gun, then why trap fourteen pelts to get two?[34]

Another aspect of our history of colonialism and the dominance of European worldviews is how the influence and impact of Indigenous worldviews on Canada has been rendered nearly invisible. It exists, but we often don't recognize it.

It is invisible to us; and that invisibility is another example of how the history of Canada has excluded Indigenous Peoples.

As we explored in part 1, Indigenous Peoples have indeed been out of sight and out of mind for much of Canada's history, including at our founding. The ways in which we don't *see* how Indigenous worldviews have shaped parts of Canada reflects the need to make the invisible visible as part of true reconciliation. Let me give you some examples of how Indigenous worldviews have shaped and influenced Canada and our Canadian identity. If these examples seems familiar, it may be that you have read the book *A Fair Country* by John Ralston Saul, the Canadian writer and philosopher. Saul writes: "What we are today has been inspired as much by four centuries of life with the indigenous civilizations as by four centuries of immigration. Perhaps more. Today we are the outcome of that experience. As have Métis people, Canadians in general have been heavily influenced and shaped by the First Nations. We still are. We increasingly are. This influencing, this shaping is deep within us."[35]

In describing elements of how Canada imagines itself that have been influenced and shaped by Indigenous Peoples, Saul emphasizes things like Canada's "obsession with egalitarianism," our "desire to maintain a balance between individuals and groups," and "our tendency to try to run society as an ongoing negotiation." He points to how we place a value on balance, consensus, and equilibrium that is perhaps uniquely Canadian.[36]

In other words, aspects of Indigenous worldviews, cultures, and ways of life have shaped the predominant worldview and understanding of what it means to be Canadian. We just tend not to recognize that; indeed, in some ways the Indigenous influence on what Canada means is denied. Saul even suggests that there is some elite denial of this reality because there is fear of how it requires us to reach back into our history. After all, "if the great and timeless West Coast epic poem Raven Travelling or one of the creation myths from the same area is central to Canadian culture, then that culture is not simply derivative of great foreign empires. If our elites could admit that that was so, they would have to deal with what it means to think of themselves as actually being from here."[37]

It is not just Saul who has shared this idea. Lots of leaders, authors, and experts, including Indigenous ones, have identified the often unseen and unrecognized ways Indigenous worldviews, cultures, and peoples have influenced and shaped Canada and beyond, and the costs of not seeing or acknowledging this reality. This reflects what we explored in part 1 about the need to continue retelling our stories. Here are examples of this thinking from Bev Sellars, a Xat'sull leader and author, and Cora Voyageur, a scholar from the Athabasca Chipewyan First Nation:

"As 'Indian givers,' Aboriginal people have provided to the world many everyday things we now take for granted. Once you know the many contributions of Aboriginal people, you will realize the genius of our Aboriginal ancestors.

. . .

When the newcomers came to the Americas, we freely and generously shared what we knew of the land to help the newly arrived adapt to and overcome the hardships of life here. We shared a wealth of intelligence that was returned to Europe with the explorers who 'discovered' America. Today people around the world enjoy certain foods, languages, and medicines without being aware of their origin. Aboriginal people have contributed to the world economy, introduced new sports, improved transportation, strengthened military strategy and government, and inspired art and architecture."[38]

❋

" . . . history consists of the stories that we tell ourselves about past events. But what happens when a story is incorrectly told or missing altogether? When significant parts are missing, then the story is incomplete and understanding is skewed. If the story is incorrectly told, then our understanding of ourselves is erroneous. However, if there is no story at all, then humanity is denied. We do have opportunities and, we believe, responsibilities to fill in omitted story segments, to correct the stories that are inaccurate, and to include missing stories. In doing so, we acknowledge the humanity of Aboriginal peoples."[39]

The critical point in these perspectives is that the role of Indigenous Peoples has been largely hidden. Unrecognized.

Unconscious. Unnamed. In failing to see this influence, we are failing to see and understand in the ways we must if we are going to be agents of true reconciliation. It is another act of leaving Indigenous Peoples out of sight and out of mind, and of taking without acknowledging. That must stop.

True reconciliation requires building a vision of a Canada in which Indigenous worldviews are reflected and play a role in how we govern and organize our collective lives, and in how Indigenous Peoples can choose to live their lives. This is essential to responding to discrimination, systemic racism, and privilege. The exclusion and marginalization of Indigenous worldviews is at the core of racism and privilege. It means that social patterns and institutions are built in ways that exclude Indigenous Peoples, make it harder for them to participate, and create environments that are not culturally supportive or safe.

The depths of this marginalization has been well-documented. We see more and more studies and reports that illustrate the challenges Indigenous Peoples face because of it.

Here is just one example, from the health care system.

You are probably aware of the tragic death of Joyce Echaquan, an Atikamekw woman who died on September 28, 2020, at the age of thirty-seven. She was a mother of seven and had a history of health problems. On September 26, she was hospitalized in Quebec with stomach pains. Two days later she was given morphine, even though she expressed concerns she would have an adverse reaction. As she had in the past, she used Facebook Live to have a cousin help translate her medical discussions. The livestreamed video shows Joyce screaming in pain. It also shows her being insulted. She is asked by an employee if she is "done acting stupid." She is told she is only "good for sex," and that she is "stupid as hell."[40]

She died later that day. Her family has said she was allergic to morphine.

This disgusting and tragic episode is, unfortunately, not an exception. In 2020, the BC government conducted an investigation into allegations of racism in the BC health care system. The investigation was expansive and comprehensive, hearing from almost nine thousand people and analyzing 185,000 health utilizations and health outcomes of Indigenous Peoples. The core finding was clear:

> The results are disturbing. Through listening to thousands of voices—via survey results, direct submissions, health care data and interviews with Indigenous people who have been impacted by the health system, health care practitioners and leaders—a picture is presented of a B.C. health care system with widespread systemic racism against Indigenous peoples. This racism results in a range of negative impacts, harm, and even death.
>
> The Review also found that this widespread racism has long been known by many within the health care system, including those in positions of authority, and is widely acknowledged by many who work in the system.[41]

The investigation identified a number of racist stereotypes that are active throughout the health care system, including that Indigenous people are less worthy of care; drinkers/alcoholics; drug-seeking; bad parents; and are even unfairly advantaged. The result of this is inequitable and discriminatory health care, including: poorer care and even death; unacceptable personal interactions; longer wait times and denial of service; as well as not being believed or experiencing a minimization of concern.[42]

Of course, this mistreatment in health care is not new. It is part of a colonial legacy that includes inferior and segregated Indian hospitals "established primarily to allay white settler fears associated with the communicability of tuberculosis"[43] and to save money; and "Indigenous peoples being used for medical research and experimentation, again primarily to aid in the discovery of treatments for the settler population."[44]

If we want to tangibly address these examples—and so many others—of how the Canada we have created marginalizes Indigenous Peoples, we must understand that one of the foundations of the problem has been the exclusion and oppression of Indigenous worldviews in shaping our society. As we understand this and see the connection between worldviews and the challenge of true reconciliation we face, we make progress.

INDIGENOUS RIGHTS AND THE SOCIAL AND
ECONOMIC REALITY OF INDIGENOUS PEOPLES

I began this part of the book by saying it was about seeing connections. I have spent a lot of time talking about one connection that is vitally important—the connection between worldviews and the world we create. In doing this, I have encouraged you to think about how you (and we) think about the world around us.

But there is another vital and, in a way, more immediately tangible connection I want you to see—that between the social and economic inequalities in our society that are disproportionately faced by Indigenous Peoples, and the recognition and implementation of Indigenous rights. I am focusing on this particular connection for an important reason: because while we often think and talk about Indigenous rights and about the social and economic challenges facing Indigenous Peoples, we rarely talk about them *together*, or in the ways we need to.

Let's zoom out for a second. Consider all the news you come across every day about Indigenous matters in this country. Much of this news—I would reckon to say nearly all of it—falls into one of two types.

The first is news about social and economic disparities—whether it is lack of clean drinking water, lack of access to education or employment, poverty, violence, addiction, suicide, and so on. Sometimes, though not nearly as often as we need, there is a success story about addressing these disparities in certain places, or perhaps about how they are being overcome in new ways. But my point remains: at their root, these stories are about the existence of these inequalities.

The second type is news about Indigenous rights. These stories involve court cases, the Constitution, consultation and accommodation, the United Nations Declaration on the Rights of Indigenous Peoples, treaties and agreements, and so on. Typically, these stories will be about how rights are not being fully upheld and implemented. Sometimes, though again not nearly as often as we need, they are about successes in rights recognition and implementation, such as a new agreement being reached, or how an Indigenous nation is advancing its self-government.

Here is the issue: social and economic disparities and Indigenous rights are completely intertwined and interconnected. They are indivisible. We will not, and cannot, address social and economic disparities without addressing the recognition and implementation of Indigenous rights. They are two tracks that criss-cross in countless ways and do not run parallel and separate from each other. We must move down both tracks in a conscious, coherent, and consistent way if we want to effect true reconciliation.

Track 1 is closing the gap on socio-economic issues—such as ensuring clean drinking water and access to quality education, and addressing issues of children and family and the unacceptable rate of kids in care.

Track 2 is the foundation and transformational piece of rights recognition. This track involves making changes to laws, policies, and practices, and doing the work of nation and government rebuilding—by replacing denial of rights with recognition as the very base of our relations. Central to this is supporting Indigenous nations in rebuilding their governing systems and implementing their right of self-government, including so that they can lead and hold the responsibility and authority to fix the challenges of Track 1.

Think about it this way: Colonization featured the disempowerment of Indigenous Peoples and governments, through the Crown imposing and taking control. Addressing this legacy, which is at its heart what reconciliation is about, must involve removing Crown control and respecting the autonomy, authority, and jurisdiction of Indigenous Peoples and their governments.

The United Nations Declaration on the Rights of Indigenous Peoples

With the increasing focus on the United Nations Declaration on the Rights of Indigenous Peoples as the "framework for reconciliation" in Canada, there has also been a lot of confusion about what the UN Declaration is, and what it means.

The United Nations Declaration on the Rights of Indigenous Peoples was adopted by the General Assembly of the United Nations in 2007. Work on the UN Declaration had begun decades before, in the early 1980s, as part of efforts to respond to the specific forms of discrimination faced by Indigenous Peoples around the world. The first draft was produced in 1994.

The work of completing the UN Declaration was slow for a range of reasons, most significantly resistance by some members to provisions regarding Indigenous self-determination and the relationship of Indigenous Peoples to their lands and resources. An open-ended process was begun involving member states, as well as representatives of Indigenous Peoples, to complete the declaration. After more than a decade of effort, debate, and deliberation, the UN Declaration was completed.

At the time of its adoption by the General Assembly, 144 countries voted in favour of the UN Declaration, and four countries voted against it: Australia, Canada, New Zealand, and the United States. Canada eventually endorsed the UN Declaration with reservations in 2010, and removed all reservations in 2016. Similarly, Australia, New Zealand, and the United States have now endorsed the declaration.

There is ambiguity by the public as to what the UN Declaration is and is not. A "declaration" in international law is a statement that affirms and recognizes a universally valid principle. A declaration is not a binding agreement between nations, such as a convention. However, the principles in a declaration can be binding on states through other means—such as if a principle is understood to be part of "customary international law." Nation-states may also bind themselves to principles through the use of their own domestic law.

The forty-six articles and twenty-six preambular statements of the UN Declaration constitute "the most comprehensive international instrument on the rights of indigenous peoples. It establishes a universal framework of minimum standards for the survival, dignity and well-being of the indigenous peoples of the world and it elaborates on existing human rights standards and fundamental freedoms as they apply to the specific situation of indigenous peoples."[45]

The standards in the UN Declaration are not new. They express established human rights norms—such as those in the milestone and historic Universal Declaration on Human Rights adopted in 1948—in the specific context of Indigenous Peoples. The content of these standards has been summarized as follows:

> The Declaration addresses both individual and collective rights, cultural rights and identity, rights to education, health, employment, language, and others. The text says indigenous peoples have the right to fully enjoy as a collective or as individuals, all human rights and fundamental freedoms as recognized in the Charter of the United Nations, the Universal Declaration of Human Rights and international human rights law. Indigenous peoples and individuals are free and equal to all other peoples and individuals and have the right to be free from any kind of discrimination, in the exercise of their rights, in particular that based on their indigenous origin or identity. Indigenous peoples have the right to self-determination. By that right they can freely determine their political status and pursue their economic, social and cultural development. They have the right to maintain and strengthen their distinct political, legal, economic, social and cultural institutions, while retaining their rights to participate fully, if they choose to, in the political, economic, social and cultural life of the state.[46]

There is an interpretive principle of the UN Declaration that it must be read as a whole—that all of the articles are interdependent and should be read in conjunction with the others. We often ignore this principle in our public debates and dialogue about the UN Declaration—focusing on words and phrases such as *self-determination, self-government,* or *free, prior, and informed consent* without reading these in conjunction with the limits and balancing provisions of the UN Declaration, such as those in article 46.

The following "Ten Facts on the *Declaration*" is a helpful reminder of some of the basics of the UN Declaration as we continue to work together to meet its standards in Canada:

Ten Facts on the *Declaration*

1. The *Declaration* was adopted by a vote of the overwhelming majority of the UN General Assembly.
2. The only four states that voted against the Declaration have all reversed their positions and endorsed the *Declaration.*
3. The *Declaration* affirms collective rights of Indigenous Nations or Peoples and the individual rights of Indigenous persons.
4. All rights in the *Declaration* are inherent: governments cannot give or take away these rights.
5. All governments have a responsibility to respect, protect and fulfill these rights.

6. The *Declaration* builds on decades of expert interpretation of existing international human rights laws and standards. It does not create new rights.

7. International human rights declarations have diverse legal effects.

8. Canadian courts and Tribunals have already applied the *Declaration* in the interpretation of Canadian law.

9. Indigenous Peoples' representatives worked for more than two decades to achieve the *Declaration*. It is the first international instrument where the rights holders themselves participated equally with states in the drafting.

10. The *Declaration* constitutes a principled framework for justice, reconciliation, healing and peace.[47]

Both tracks are needed and are interrelated, and the first will never be fully realized—the gaps closed—until and unless the second is made real. Thinking that good intentions, tinkering around the edges of the Indian Act, or making increased financial investments—however significant and unprecedented—will in themselves close the gaps, is naive. Transformative change and new directions are required, changes and directions that see Indigenous governments in charge of the well-being of citizens under their own laws, traditions, and approaches.

When I speak of these tracks, I sometimes use the analogy of a tree: if the roots of a tree are dead, the tree will not grow—even if we water it. And while the trunk may stand for years, at some point it begins rotting and falls over. The patterns governments have been locked in on Indigenous issues are akin to watering dead roots, hoping that the tree will grow. Seeking to address Track 1 by making greater and greater expenditures, but without tackling Track 2 in any coherent or meaningful way, will not work. It cannot work. It will never work.

And here is the thing: We have known this for a long time. We have studied the issues endlessly. There is no excuse of ignorance available to us. There is only the reality of inaction.

In 1996, it was estimated that in the period between 1965 and 1996, a span of thirty years, almost nine hundred reports on Indigenous policy were completed, with well over one hundred considered "major." I would guess that the number of studies and reports has kept up a similar pace in the years since 1996. In other words, there are thousands of studies and reports about the state of Indigenous Peoples in Canada.[48]

The most comprehensive was the Royal Commission on Aboriginal Peoples. It was formed in response to a number of forces, including the armed confrontation, in the summer of 1990, between Mohawks and the police and military at Kanesatake (Oka), as well as the ongoing failure of the constitutional amendment processes, including the Meech Lake Accord. The Royal Commission was asked to do a lot: to investigate the evolution of the relationship among Indigenous Peoples, the Canadian government, and Canadian society as a whole, and to offer solutions. The commission did its job and in 1996 issued a final report including 440 wide-ranging recommendations for change and a twenty-year timeline for implementation. The commission, in its own words, effectively laid out the two interconnected tracks I referenced above— emphasizing that addressing the urgent social and economic conditions of Indigenous Peoples (Track 1) required rights recognition, support for self-government, addressing the Indian Act, and transformation of laws, policies, and practices to make these shifts a reality (Track 2). Almost all of the recommendations have been ignored by successive governments.

More recently, two of the largest and most well-known studies and reports have been tabled: the Truth and Reconciliation Commission and the National Inquiry into Missing and Murdered Indigenous Women and Girls. The Truth and Reconciliation Commission released its report in 2015, summarizing the tragic experiences of approximately 150,000 residential school students in Canada, and provided "calls to action" to "redress the legacy of residential schools and advance the process of Canadian reconciliation." The calls to action continue to be a rallying cry for change on the ground and within governments. Again, we see the two tracks at the core of how we move forward. The calls to action identify how the UN Declaration must be adopted and implemented as the "framework for reconciliation," including through new legislation (Track 2), as part of addressing the urgent social and economic crises that are part of the legacy of the residential schools.[49]

We heard the same message in 2019 in the report of the National Inquiry into Missing and Murdered Indigenous Women and Girls. The report shared the experiences and truths of 2,380 family members, survivors of violence, experts, and Knowledge Keepers, and included "calls for justice" directed at governments, institutions, social service providers, industries, and all Canadians. The inquiry revealed "that persistent and deliberate human and Indigenous rights violations and abuses are the root cause behind Canada's staggering rates of violence against Indigenous women, girls and 2SLGBTQQIA people."[50] To say it another way, the failure to implement rights (Track 2) is at the foundation of the urgent social and economic crises we see today (Track 1).

Implementation of Studies about Indigenous Peoples

While there have been countless studies regarding Indigenous Peoples in Canada, there has always been significant concern about the lack of implementation of those studies. For example, the recommendations of the Royal Commission on Aboriginal Peoples were almost all ignored. This pattern continues with more recent studies and inquiries.

Justice Murray Sinclair, chief commissioner of the Truth and Reconciliation Commission, has repeatedly said, "Truth is hard. Reconciliation is harder." He has spoken to how much work

non-Indigenous people need to do to effect reconciliation, including implementing the calls to action:

> I think there is a growing body of reasonable people out there
> who are trying to figure out what to do and what they can do to
> contribute to the process of reconciliation but the difficulty they
> face, the difficulty that Canada faces generally is that there is a
> group of very vocal, very influential people in Canada who hold
> significant positions of power who are working hard against rec-
> onciliation. People who are holding positions of privilege, who
> are benefitting from the riches of this country that have been
> taken away from Indigenous people. The people who have
> been taught to believe that they are superior to Indigenous
> people and don't want to think they are not. I said at the end of
> the TRC report getting to the truth was hard but getting to rec-
> onciliation will be harder because I knew that there would be
> people working very hard, very forcefully, even violently against
> reconciliation.
>
> And so one of the things I make sure non-Indigenous people
> understand is we don't need you to help heal us, we need you to
> fix yourselves. We need you to get those people out there who are
> perpetrating this process of working against reconciliation under
> control. We need you to straighten yourselves out, we don't need
> you to just step forward and say well here is what we can do for
> you because my question is always, what are you doing for your-
> self? What are you doing to get rid of that violent vocal force that
> is holding us all back, holding us all, holding this country back?
> Because that is what's going to stop reconciliation.[51]

As another commissioner, Dr. Wilton Littlechild, stated in 2020, "We're collectively quite concerned that it's been moving too slow and it's a matter of urgency that we have another look at our Calls to Action and maybe get a fresh start in terms of some of the changes that you've seen over the past five years."[52]

There are also concerns about the lack of implementation of the calls for justice of the Inquiry into MMIWG. As Chief Commissioner Justice Marion Buller stated in 2022: "The federal government was not at all ready for the work that we had to do and to help us do it." She referred also to the "lack of priority given to the national inquiry," and suggested that "the federal government has fallen flat on its face. We don't have an implementation plan. There hasn't been any sort of cohesive statement on the part of the federal government about what it plans to do. . . ."[53]

At its core, the message is always the same. We need to dig up the dead roots, plant something new, and then properly water and fertilize it. Track 2—the recognition and implementation of Indigenous rights through changes in federal and provincial laws, policies, and practices and the active work of nations rebuilding their governments—is the soil for the new healthy roots.

This is the only way the new tree will grow.

But here is our problem: For the longest time, federal and provincial governments have failed to see the connection between the two tracks. And the way government has conducted itself on these tracks—treating them as separate and different—has reinforced the idea for Canadian society that they are somehow distinct and separate in the work of reconciliation. But the reality is that true reconciliation can only occur when we are moving down both tracks at once—when we see the connection between them, and act based on that.

Worse than this, governments have often worked at cross-purposes. They have invested more and more in Track 1, only to see that the challenges remain, and, in some instances, even get worse. At the same time, governments have fought against Track 2, litigating and negotiating endlessly without much progress.

The government's approach to reconciliation over the last four decades can be summed up with a very simple story. It starts with the government recognizing—often because of shame and public outcry—that a particular social and economic inequality faced by Indigenous Peoples needs to be addressed. So, it dedicates some new money to try to fix it. By and large, these efforts are ineffective, and the cycle continues: of human suffering, public outcry, and the throwing of more money at the issue.

At the same time, governments have been systematically denying the existence of Indigenous rights, actively fighting against those rights every day, even today, in court. This is a deliberate choice—and one we touched on in the first part of this book. It is helpful to look a little closer at that legal history and practice of governments, especially since the adoption of section 35(1) of the Constitution in 1982 that recognized and affirmed existing Indigenous rights.

Section 35(1) was vigorously debated by Indigenous Peoples and governments before it was adopted. Indigenous Peoples were divided about whether to include this provision in the Constitution because of mistrust of government, and because of concern that it might negatively impact the inherent rights and treaty rights of Indigenous Peoples.

When section 35(1) was finally agreed to, Crown governments clearly thought it meant very little, if anything. Indeed, Indigenous leaders know from stories that we have been told by federal and provincial leaders at the time that governments were clear among themselves that section 35(1) meant nothing—that there were no "existing" Indigenous rights. As such, it was not surprising that the political conferences held in the 1980s (as was required by the Constitution) to provide more definition and specificity to section 35(1) largely failed. Nor was it a surprise that the courts were turned to as a venue to interpret what section 35(1) meant. Governments argued that Indigenous rights do not exist—that they never existed or have been extinguished or abandoned. They argued that section 35(1) was "empty," just words on the page with no meaning. They still often make these arguments today. Indigenous Peoples, on the other hand, argued that section 35(1) is a "full box" of rights and proceeded to use the courts to support comprehensive recognition of inherent rights and treaty rights.

Consider for a second the hypocrisy and racism in the governments' position. Section 35(1) was adopted at the same time as the Charter of Rights and Freedoms. But they were treated very differently. When we think or speak about Charter rights—freedom of expression, freedom of religion, equality—we have a deep sense that these rights are part of what makes us uniquely Canadian. We do not question the existence of these rights. Rather, we celebrate them and organize governments to respect them. This is what governments did after 1982. They changed laws, policies, and practices to align with the Charter, and relied on the courts for the hard questions where disagreements might arise about the scope and extent of a particular right.

Conversely, Indigenous rights in section 35(1) were simply denied. No rights exist. If you think you have a right, go prove it in court and then we might talk to you. The burden—hugely expensive, time-consuming, and complicated—was put on Indigenous Peoples.

So we went to court. Hundreds of times. And time and again, the courts affirmed our rights. Section 35(1) is not empty. It has always been full. Courts have continually affirmed the existence of specific rights. The courts have shown how Indigenous rights exist, are broad and extensive, and take many different forms and expressions across all spheres of political, economic, and social life. Time and again, the courts have also urged governments to stop fighting over the existence of rights and focus on how we respect and implement them.

Sure, the courts have done a lot of things that Indigenous people do not like and have disagreed with. And there are also many issues that will require legal guidance to be sorted out.

But the courts have helped get us to a place where we have more than enough direction and impetus to be making real progress involving Indigenous rights. In areas where we are not making progress today, the challenge, more than anything, is one of political will.

There have been so many legal decisions, and the courts have said so much on this issue, that it is sometimes hard to see the forest for the trees. The bottom line is that Indigenous rights exist because Indigenous Peoples were here—we've always been here—and governed and "owned" the lands that now make up Canada. Europeans, and ultimately the British Crown, arrived and asserted sovereignty. The only proper way to address relations between the pre-existing sovereignty of Indigenous Peoples and governments and the assertion of sovereignty by the Crown is by agreement—such as by a treaty. Some of these were entered into historically, but treaties also have to be honoured and fully implemented, and typically the Crown has not done so. In other places, in almost all of British Columbia, in particular, treaties were never entered into. As such, there was no legal basis for land to be taken up or assumed by the Crown.

We have a lot of work to do to sort out the violation of historic treaties, and to complete agreements about lands and governance where treaties do not exist. But to be clear, this is the same work that has existed since before Canada was formed; it is what the common law always said needed to be done, as we saw in part 1, for example, in the Royal Proclamation of 1763.

The courts continue to issue rulings that support driving this work forward. They affirm the existence of Indigenous title. They affirm the existence of many forms of fishing, hunting, gathering, forestry, and governing rights. They instruct how treaties must be interpreted. They implore governments to take action to settle these issues and sort this stuff out. They talk time and again about "reconciliation" and what this work is about.

They even created a body of law, often identified with the *Haida* decision in 2004, that put pressure on governments to accelerate the work of sorting these things out. The law of "consultation and accommodation" says to government that while you are doing the real work of reconciliation between pre-existing sovereignty of Indigenous Peoples and asserted Crown sovereignty, you still have to *do* things. You can't just delay settling these issues, and, in the meantime, continue to undermine or erode the connection of Indigenous Peoples to their lands and resources through government decision-making. The Haida people saw their lands and resources being increasingly used—especially their forests—without an existing treaty or resolution of their land rights with the Crown. So, they went to the courts and asked a basic question: Before we properly resolve the details about jurisdiction and ownership of lands and resources between the Crown and the Haida governments, such as through a treaty, is the Crown simply allowed to use and take everything from our territory? The Supreme Court of Canada's answer was simple and straightforward: No. The Crown cannot just use and take everything. They must always act honourably with Indigenous Peoples, and that means they are limited in what they can do before these issues of Indigenous rights are sorted out. For example, they must consult and accommodate before making any decision that may impact, even minimally, an Indigenous right.

But again, consultation and accommodation is just an interim obligation on the Crown. While proper consultation is important, it is not the outcome or end-goal that Indigenous Peoples are focused on. Simply being consulted is not what we are trying to achieve, though it is one means to an end. What we need and want is for our peoples, governments, laws, cultures, traditions, and ways of life—which are reflected and supported in various ways through our rights—to be able to survive, thrive, and be respected. This is what the Constitution and the law ultimately requires.

This is the work of Track 2.

Again, instead of seeing the inextricable connection between Track 1 and Track 2, governments have for far too long treated them as largely disconnected. By doing this— by fighting against recognition and implementation of Indigenous title and rights while trying (somewhat, not enough) to address social and economic disparities—they are undermining their own efforts. Trying to empower people by alleviating social and economic obstacles, while at the same time actively working to keep them disempowered by argu- ing against their rights, and against the authority and role of their own Indigenous governments to care for them, is, well, short-sighted at best, certainly ignorant, and, in some instances, cruel.

I suggested in part 1 that some of this is changing. The relationship between the two tracks is beginning to be understood. But we are not yet where we need to be. Patterns of behaviour and old practices and ways of looking at issues are hard to shift. It is a mindset.

For example, when I was minister of justice, the federal government started to affirm the need to make a shift based on seeing the connection between the two tracks. This is what the Recognition and Implementation of Indigenous Rights Framework was about. Prime Minister Justin Trudeau announced the framework in that historic speech in the House of Commons on Valentine's Day in 2018. As you read in the oral history in part 1, he explained the framework as a fundamental shift away from decades of inaction and unmet promises to uphold Indigenous rights, and toward a new approach that would address the social and economic challenges faced by Indigenous Peoples.

The details of what the framework was to do were well established. They were based on the findings of the Royal Commission on Aboriginal Peoples. For a few years before the prime minister's 2018 speech, there had been several dialogues and engagements with Indigenous Peoples and experts about what might be in such a framework. Here is one summary of what I called, at the time, the minimum elements of new relations based on the recognition of rights:

- Harmony between the laws of Canada and UNDRIP;
- The replacement of the *Comprehensive Claims Policy* and *Inherent Right of Self-Government Policy, and Consultation and Accommodation* approaches with policies based on true recognition;
- Legislated, binding standards on all public officials to ensure they act in all matters with Indigenous Peoples based on recognition of title and rights;
- Legislative, binding obligations on the Crown to take action in partnership with Indigenous nations to implement models of self-government that are self-determined by Indigenous peoples;
- Accountable, independent oversight of the conduct of government respecting Indigenous rights—as well as new methods of dispute resolution that include applications of Indigenous laws and processes;
- New institutions—that are independent of government, and designed in partnership with communities—that support the work of rebuilding their nations and governments; and,
- Development of proper processes and structures between Canada and Indigenous governments for decision-making, including in order to obtain free, prior, and informed consent.[54]

Yet despite all of this advocacy by Indigenous Peoples, years of discussing a framework, and a commitment by government to enact it, it did not happen. Once again, the prime minister's own words proved true: "Now imagine the mounting disappointment—the unsurprising and familiar heartache, and the rising tide of anger—when governments that had promised so much did so little to keep their word."[55]

Truly, there has been an intractable refusal by governments to make the legal changes required to uphold Indigenous rights. Let's look at just one manifestation of this. I have talked a lot about the Indian Act in the pages of this book. The reason for this is that even though the Indian Act is a racist and colonial statute that is well over a century old, it remains the statute—the law—that governs the lives of almost all First Nations people in Canada. This is a remarkable fact: that in 2022 we still have a law that says because an individual is part of a particular racial group, their lives will be more controlled by government in certain ways, and that one of the largest departments of the federal government, with an annual budget in the billions of dollars (Indigenous Services Canada), exists to exercise this control—with the minister being the top Indian agent in charge of those lives. Further, the Indian Act, through one specific section—section 88—also allows provincial governments to apply their laws to Indigenous Peoples and lands in various ways, including over Indigenous children and families.

And remember that at the root of this legislative reality is the system of federalism that was created at Confederation and that left Indigenous Peoples and governments out. This system was created on the fiction that Indigenous laws and governments did not exist and had no roles to play, and, as such, all jurisdiction, authority, and power was allocated between the federal and provincial governments. The tragic results of this are many: that Indigenous Peoples are often an object of a jurisdictional struggle between the federal and provincial governments, and suffer the consequences of neither level of government wanting to take responsibility (or pay) for necessary services and care; that Indigenous governments and laws are viewed as illegitimate, and not having any powers or authority other than those granted by the Crown; that Indigenous governments are in many ways effectively barred from doing the work they have always done of caring for their citizens and stewarding their lands and resources. In the face of this, our political and legal systems have been very slow to recognize and accept that all power does not, and cannot, lie with Crown governments, and that there must be fundamental structural change to address the fact that Indigenous governments were ignored when Canada was founded.

There is yet another remarkable fact in this legislative reality, which is that there are so few other laws in Canada that consider the reality and the rights of Indigenous Peoples. Indeed, legislation in Canada has two purposes with respect to Indigenous Peoples: to control us, such as through the Indian Act; or to ignore us, such as through the land and resource statutes that have been enacted by the federal and provincial governments as if Indigenous Peoples and rights do not exist.

The Inherent Right of Self-Government

Prior to colonization, Indigenous Peoples had their own governments and legal orders through which decisions were made, lands were stewarded, and society was organized.

After colonization, the Crown imposed governing systems on Indigenous Peoples and sought to break up and destroy Indigenous governance systems. It was believed that doing this was necessary to effect assimilation. With respect to First Nations, the Indian Act was the main legislative tool used to accomplish this.

Indigenous Peoples resisted these efforts, often moving their governing institutions underground. In other words, they maintained their traditional systems of government, while also having to operate through those that were imposed on them.

Given this, Indigenous governance rights have always been one of the central focuses of efforts at decolonization and the recognition and implementation of Indigenous rights. The term most often used for this is the "inherent right of self-government," which reflects the idea that all distinct "peoples" have an inalienable right to govern themselves. The term is now used in both international and Canadian law, and self-government is upheld in multiple articles of the UN Declaration, including articles 3 and 4.

Self-government is also emphasized because it is recognized that societies that govern well, including those of Indigenous Peoples, simply do better in meeting the needs of their populations economically, socially, and politically. Strong and appropriate governance increases a society's chances of effectively meeting the needs of its people.

While self-government is generally affirmed as a centrepiece of decolonization, its recognition and implementation has been slow—like many aspects of Track 2 work. The federal government has a policy for negotiating self-government, but it has always been understood by Indigenous Peoples as being limited in scope and application and requiring change. As well, the federal government is very slow in negotiating under the policy. As such, today there are still only thirty First Nation groups that are recognized as self-governing, and who have moved out of the Indian Act. The Inuit also address governance through their land claims agreements, and there are some agreements that address Métis governance. This means the vast majority of First Nations remain subject to the Indian Act.

Today, Indigenous Peoples are rebuilding their governing institutions in their own ways, at their own paces. But the speed and scale of this work needs to increase—and for that to happen, new laws, policies, and practices need to be put in place by Crown governments that support Indigenous Peoples as they lead and do this work. Until this work accelerates in greater ways, we will continue to face ongoing reconciliation challenges, including: understanding which Indigenous government speaks for which people; understanding the division of powers between all orders of government (federal, provincial/territorial, and Indigenous), and whose laws apply, how and where; and, more generally, ensuring the good governance necessary to provide programs and services to address the colonial legacy in communities and move forward (for example, lack of clean water, child apprehensions, policing, education, etc.).

> Simply stated, true reconciliation is unlikely to occur until a critical mass of Indigenous Peoples are self-governing. Those populations must, through their own institutions of good governance, make the decisions, or participate directly in decision-making, on matters that affect them.

This is in stark contrast, for example, to the United States. Yes, there is a legacy of harm, racism, and colonialism perpetrated against Indigenous Peoples in the United States, just as there is in Canada. At the same time, however, there are many distinctions between the United States and Canada regarding the history and contemporary reality of Indigenous Peoples, and in our governing structures. Some of the distinctions include the roles of war in settlement of the United States; the ways that federal and state power and jurisdiction are allocated; the constitutional tradition regarding Indigenous Peoples and their rights; and the ways in which treaties have been understood and "reserves" are defined. One result of these distinctions is that in the United States there has been a steady development of federal legislation designed in partnership with Indigenous Peoples with the goal of facilitating aspects of Indigenous control and self-determination. This work began in 1970, when President Richard Nixon officially "renounced past practices that attempted to 'terminate' tribes and undermine Indigenous self-determination," and announced a national policy goal of "strengthening the Indian's sense of autonomy

without threatening his sense of community."⁵⁶ The result
has been statute after statute that has helped facilitate some
expressions of Indigenous self-determination and control.
As Professor John Borrows summarizes:

> When these initiatives began in the early 1970's [*sic*], tribes
> only controlled 1.5% of the delivery and administration of
> federal services to Indian people, whereas today they control
> over 50% of this sector. While there is much work ahead,
> Indian control of Indian services has made a significant
> difference in the United States because it has strengthened
> the economic, social, and cultural health of Indian tribes.⁵⁷

On this measure—Indigenous government control over
government services—Canada lags far behind the United
States.

Obviously, in Canada, where the Indian Act remains predominant, there is no history of legislation that recognizes
and upholds Indigenous rights, including rights related to
lands and resources. As we saw, even with the passage of section 35(1) in 1982, and hundreds of court decisions that uphold
Indigenous rights, there has been almost no legislative change.

Very recently—since around 2019—this has begun to
change. We see legislation beginning to be passed that is different and reflects the idea of upholding Indigenous rights.
The two pieces of legislation that are the furthest reaching,
and that have gotten the most public attention, are British
Columbia's Declaration on the Rights of Indigenous Peoples

Act and the federal government's United Nations Declaration on the Rights of Indigenous Peoples Act. In effect, these statutes are the same, and both are based on models of legislation that have been advocated for since 2007.

These statutes are high-level and require further work to be done. Specifically, they require Crown governments, with Indigenous Peoples, to create action plans to meet the objectives of the UN Declaration and to take all measures necessary to ensure consistency between legislation and regulations and the UN Declaration. Requiring these things to happen is, of course, important. But what is far more important and impactful is actually doing them. It is unfortunate that a statute—a law—is needed to get governments to move on upholding the human rights of Indigenous Peoples, even after constitutional reform and hundreds of court cases. Indeed, one might see these statutes as admissions of failure. Can you imagine, for example, that forty years after the adoption of the Charter, governments had to pass a statute saying they will make sure their laws are consistent with the Charter and have an action plan to meet the objective of respecting Charter rights? But that is where we are.

What these statutes do not do is create the actual, practical mechanisms of change. For example, the federal statute does nothing practical to facilitate the implementation of the inherent right of self-government or the movement out of the Indian Act for First Nations. It also does not create any tangible supports—whether new Indigenous institutions, capacity, or processes—for Indigenous Peoples to rebuild their governments and exercise their jurisdiction. Similarly, the statutes do not create new structures or processes to resolve disputes, and, as such, do not tangibly shift us away from long, expensive, and adversarial court proceedings. We have also seen throughout this book how colonialism has been reinforced by a lack of accountability when it comes to governments not living up to their own standards or following through on processes to change. There is no mechanism with any teeth for accountability in these statutes; all they require is for government to report annually.

This is all to say that we are only at the beginning of the legislative change that will be needed. The legislative actions that have been taken thus far with respect to the UN Declaration are merely a first step. Specifically, these changes are not impactful in tangible and needed ways on the ground like, for example, the changes we have seen in the United States, where the jurisdiction of Indigenous Peoples over caring for their own citizens is recognized, implemented, facilitated, and supported in a principled manner. (It's worth noting that the changes here will have to look different in order to respect Indigenous Peoples as well as our governing and legal frameworks.)

Free, Prior, and Informed Consent

The standard of the UN Declaration that gets the most attention is "free, prior, and informed consent." Free, prior, and informed consent appears in many articles of the document, including in relation to decisions about the use of lands and resources.

I think a lot of the discussion and debate about consent is filled with confusion and fear. Too often, "consent" is used as a rhetorical device in the context of potential conflict, or for political purposes. Too rarely do we actually have a discussion about how to pragmatically operationalize and implement it. Here are three things I think we need to focus on in order to understand and implement consent.

First, we need to be clear that the issue of consent is not "new," and that it has not somehow arisen because of the UN Declaration. Consent has been noted as a matter to be addressed in Crown-Indigenous relations by the courts for many years. For example, in *Tsilhqot'in Nation v. British Columbia*, the Supreme Court of Canada speaks of the necessity of the Crown to obtain consent as the standard for decision-making where title exists. The court also urged the Crown and proponents to obtain consent regardless of whether a court has ruled on title and rights, or an agreement requires it. The rationale for doing this is that it would remove the likelihood of conflict, legal struggles, and uncertainty about a project or decision.

Second, we have tended to view consent through the wrong lens. Many people talk about consent as the extension of a process of "consultation," where government is seeking the views and information of Indigenous Peoples about a particular decision. This is not a helpful way of thinking about consent. Consent is not simply an extension of a process of government consultation. Rather, we need to see consent as part and parcel of the new relationship we seek to build with Indigenous Peoples, who are reconstituting and rebuilding their political, economic, and social structures.

Viewed this way, consent is analogous to the types of relations we typically see, and are familiar with, between governments. In such relations, where governments must work together, there is a range of mechanisms used to ensure that the authority and autonomy of both governments is respected, and decisions are made in a way that is consistent and coherent and does not often lead to regular or substantial disagreement. These mechanisms are diverse, and can range from shared bodies and structures, to utilizing the same information and standards, to agreeing on long-term plans or arrangements that will give clarity to how all decisions will be made on a certain matter or in a certain area over time. Enacting these mechanisms is achieved through a multiplicity of tools, including legislation, policy, and agreements.

The structures and mechanisms for achieving this consent, once established, are also consistent over time and across types of decisions; they are known and transparent. Roles and responsibilities are defined, and they are ready to be implemented when needed. One result of this is significant certainty. Moving to consent-based decision-making is about building these structures and mechanisms of consistent, collaborative decision-making.

Third, for consent to be fully operationalized as part of a relationship between governments, significant work has to be done by

Indigenous Peoples, in addition to the federal and provincial governments. In particular, Indigenous Peoples need to reconstitute their nations and governments as part of exercising their right of self-government. This is part of Indigenous Peoples ensuring that their jurisdiction and authority, including the giving of consent, is being properly granted and exercised consistent with the right to self-determination. One implication is that consent will not be operationalized in a linear or uniform manner. It will occur in a diversity of ways, with various steps and stages being taken in different contexts and relationships at different times.

In this way, implementing consent is, as I have emphasized throughout this book, work in which many have roles and responsibilities, and all must play their part.

A final point, which may already be clear. We need to see more than just the connection between the two tracks. We also need to be clear that moving down the two tracks—and accomplishing the work of true reconciliation—is indivisible from the well-being of Canada as a whole. There are no significant challenges Canada faces, whether economic, social, or political, that can be adequately addressed or responded to without moving down the two tracks in a coherent way.

I have talked about political and governance realities a lot, and social ones as well. Let me now speak about our economic reality as a country, and how it is indivisible from the work of moving down these tracks.

Earlier, we examined the differences between the economic systems of Indigenous Peoples and Europeans, which include conceptions about land and property. Among these differences was the emphasis in European capitalist systems on individual ownership and possession of land, while in Indigenous systems such an idea of individual ownership of land is fundamentally foreign.

In the British system of land ownership, the Crown holds underlying title to all land, while individuals can own an interest in land—most typically a "fee simple interest." This is the system in Canada today, and how Canadians own their homes. Of course, British common law reflected this capitalist vision of ownership, and so, as the British colonized North America, the common law dictated that any interest in land held by Indigenous Peoples had to be dealt with in order for the Crown to acquire it and, ultimately, for Europeans to own it. At once, Britain declared the land as theirs, reflecting the racist doctrine of *terra nullius*. In other words, Britain asserted, or assumed, sovereignty—while at the same time stating that interests in land had to be acquired from Indigenous Peoples, such as was stated in the Royal Proclamation of 1763, with treaty-making being the vehicle for doing this.

This approach led to massive problems—problems that are at the root of the economic challenges and liabilities in Canada to this day. Presently, we are the inheritors of a history of economic injustice towards Indigenous Peoples that affects everything from our investment climate to resource development, taxation regimes, and land development. That economic injustice, which is about land rights—and which is the core of Track 2—must be rectified as part of addressing the socio-cultural disparities that we see on Track 1.

What are some of the problems with how the Indigenous interest in lands was dealt with historically?

First, the Crown rarely demonstrated that they took the Indigenous interest in land seriously, or that they really believed Indigenous Peoples owned or had rights to the land, because there was no system of titles and deeds like under the common law. And, of course, there were racist attitudes about Indigenous Peoples not being fully human, more likely "savages." So how could they own the land? This is the thinking that justified Britain's assertion of sovereignty in the first place.

Second, while at times the Crown took treaty-making seriously—as a means of establishing relations between sovereigns—this attitude was not consistent or maintained for long periods of history. Indigenous Peoples, reflecting their worldviews as well as what they were told when historic treaties were entered into, understood treaties as fundamentally establishing how Indigenous Peoples and the Crown would share the land. The idea that they were transferring ownership was a foreign one, because the very concept of "ownership" was foreign. The Crown, on the other hand, predominately has interpreted treaties as ending any Indigenous interest in the land and confirming the Crown's right to fully govern the land.

Third, the Crown never really took treaty implementation seriously enough. Where historic treaties were signed, they have and continue to be systemically violated, even when one interprets the treaties in the ways the Crown does. For example, much of the lands that were affirmed by treaties for First Nations were not set aside—they were taken up by settlers anyway—and today we are left with significant treaty land entitlement disputes and settlement negotiations, lawsuits, and conflicts across the country because treaties were not implemented.

Fourth, the Crown did not sign treaties covering significant parts of the country, such as in British Columbia. In other words, the First Nations' interests in the land and resources were simply not addressed—and have still not been addressed over most of the province. In the words of the law, Aboriginal title exists and encumbers any claim to Crown title.

What is the economic impact of this?

The bottom line is that the impact is massive—and far worse than our political leaders have let on. Of course, the failure of our political leaders to resolve these issues over generations has compounded the problem. Which is another reason why they do not own up to it.

We have all witnessed the economic impacts in relation to resource development, and the associated investment climate. Some projects that in the past would have been easily approved and built are unable to proceed today. Sometimes they are stopped by the courts, sometimes by active opposition, and sometimes—most often—by the early realization that pursuing them is too risky and a waste of the money, time, and effort it requires. But the underlying reason they are unable to proceed is fundamentally the same: because the Indigenous interest in the land has not been addressed—including the decision-making authority that comes with an interest in land—there is no clear path forward.

Today, the projects that do proceed without much conflict and risk are the ones that have de facto consent, most often expressed through agreements with the Crown and/or companies. But, of course, achieving consent and agreement is never easy—especially because we are still dealing with the impacts of the imposition of the Indian Act, which divided First Nations and their governments into many smaller units. As such, agreements are now typically needed with multiple governments and nations. This will change as the work of nation and government rebuilding is supported properly and accelerates. But again, this is the heart of Track 2—the work that governments have ignored and avoided for so long.

The massive economic impact has been felt in another way as well: in the accruing of liability by Crown governments due to the use of lands and resources without Indigenous consent or accommodation when they were required to have it. This is actually very straightforward and simple. Under the common law, we call the pre-existing Indigenous interest in land Aboriginal title. The Supreme Court of Canada has been clear: Aboriginal title is a property interest. While it is a distinct, or *sui generis,* type of property interest and has many unique aspects, it also shares many characteristics with, for example, fee simple property interests. As the Court states:

Aboriginal title confers ownership rights similar to those associated with fee simple, including: the right to decide how the land will be used; the right of enjoyment and occupancy of the land; the right to possess the land; the right to the economic benefits of the land; and the right to pro-actively use and manage the land.[58]

We all have a pretty good understanding of this. Somebody cannot use your land without your permission or consent. Somebody cannot build something, or take something from your land, without your permission. Similarly, they are not allowed to damage your property. If they do any of these things, they are liable and have to compensate you. Well, guess what? In this regard, the First Nations interest in land—Aboriginal title—is no different. This is precisely what the Supreme Court confirmed in the *Tsilhqot'in Nation* decision, reiterating what they had said in *Delgamuukw v. British Columbia.*

Here is the problem: Governments have been using lands subject to Aboriginal title without permission, and without providing compensation, for generations. Treaties are the main vehicle through which permission would have been granted. As we know already, in some areas of the country, there are very few treaties. In other places, the treaties that were entered into have been breached, and their meaning is disputed. By not resolving the "Indian land question"—by not doing the Track 2 work—we have been building up liabilities, while even more so perpetuating harms to Indigenous Peoples and communities.

Today, you can feel this long, unresolved reality coming to a head. One response is #landback. Return lands, support Indigenous Peoples to rebuild their communities and economies, and stop accruing liabilities. Another response is in the growing conflict we see with almost any form of resource development. Another is in companies realizing they must work with Indigenous Peoples and nations as governments, and agreeing that they will not proceed without consent. And yet another, but still the slowest response, is Crown governments realizing they must do the long overdue Track 2 work that they have avoided for so long.

ADVANCING OUR UNDERSTANDING

At the heart of *Understanding* is seeing things in ways we have not seen before. Specifically, it is about seeing connections where we might not have previously realized they exist. In this section, I have highlighted two connections in particular.

The first connection is the one between our worldviews and the world we create. Understanding this connection helps us realize that true reconciliation requires examining how Indigenous worldviews are distinct and how they must inform the ways in which we organize Canada and our communities and society.

The second connection is between the recognition and implementation of Indigenous rights and the addressing of social and economic inequalities. Understanding this connection helps us realize that true reconciliation requires shifting away from existing patterns and practices that have been at cross-purposes, leading us to think we are pursuing reconciliation while in actuality we are simultaneously acting in opposition to it. Making these connections is important work, and in opening our minds and hearts to seeing them, we are taking the steps needed to break with the past and advance true reconciliation.

PART 3

Act

Act

"Be the change you wish to see in the world." [1]

To be a force for change—to contribute to addressing the challenges that are a result of Canada's legacy of colonialism— we must know about our history and current reality *(Learn)* and be able to envision what true reconciliation looks like *(Understand)*.

And we need to *Act*.

We can all be the change we wish to see in this country when it comes to true reconciliation.

We need to act in ways that are consistent with true reconciliation in our daily lives, in our own context—our own spaces. In how we spend our time, use our resources, and relate to others. Whether as individuals, communities, organizations, or governments, we need to each play our part, fulfil our responsibilities, and be forces of change.

As each of us acts towards a goal of true reconciliation, our collective capacity to drive the needed change increases, and the pace of actual change that helps the lives of individuals and communities accelerates. We influence policy-makers in government. And captains of industry.

But not all actions are the same. Some are important, and some are not. Some are impactful, and some are not. Some are wise, and some are not. Some are easy, and some are hard. Some can be quick, while others take time, even a generation or two.

This part of the book is about sorting through which actions for true reconciliation are most impactful and appropriate in your own lives and contexts. Your spaces. *Act* is also about making clear the distinct actions that need to be taken by governments, organizations, communities, and individuals for true reconciliation to occur. In this way, we will know who has responsibility to do what, and we can challenge those who are not meeting those responsibilities.

TRUE RECONCILIATION IS A MARATHON, NOT A SPRINT

True reconciliation is not an event. There is not a moment of time when it happens, and after which we can say "we are done" and move onto something else. It is ongoing, a long-term undertaking of creating new patterns of social, cultural, and economic relations as individuals, peoples, communities, and governments. It is about building a vision of the future that both addresses, and breaks away from, the legacy of colonialism.

Achieving this takes endurance, resilience, and consistent effort. It also means recognizing from the beginning that it requires staying the course, even when it feels incredibly hard.

With that in mind, I have come to think of true reconciliation as a marathon, though not one with a medal at the finish that signals the end. To run a marathon requires seeing how far you have to go, through learning and understanding, and setting out with determination to get there. At times you will go faster, and at other times slower, but you must keep moving and stay on the course. In this marathon that we are all running, it's important to adjust along the way, and certainly to recognize and understand how far we have come. It's also important to recognize that not everyone has to actually run or walk the marathon. People can participate in diverse ways—by supporting, training, motivating, and organizing. Everyone can play a part.

But here is the thing: True reconciliation is often treated as a sprint. A momentary burst of energy, followed by a short period of intense effort, that then reaches an (illusory) finish line.

We have seen a lot of reconciliation sprints in our history. We keep running them. But that is not what we need. What we need is more people running, walking, or supporting a marathon.

Let me explain by using government as an example.

You will recall that in part 2 we spoke of the two interrelated but distinct tracks of necessary government action. Track 1 is to tackle the day-to-day states of poverty, marginalization, and crisis that many Indigenous Peoples and communities find themselves facing—whether it be inadequate housing, food insecurity, lack of access to health and education supports, or children and youth at risk. Track 2 is to end the denial of Indigenous rights and shift to relations based on the recognition of rights—including Indigenous self-determination and the inherent right of self-government—that is part of the political, legal, and governance dimensions of reconciliation. This track involves removing the legal and policy foundations that were put in place, and that helped perpetuate colonial relationships in which Indigenous nations were divided, governments dismantled, laws and jurisdictions encroached upon, and title and rights, including those enshrined in historic treaties, systematically ignored and infringed.

Moving down these two tracks is a marathon, not a sprint. It is about creating mechanisms—through changes to laws, policies, and practices—that support Indigenous governments to rebuild and take control over the well-being of their own communities. As that occurs, the root causes of the symptoms of colonialism—lack of clean drinking water, homelessness, suicide, food insecurity, addiction, violence—can be addressed. At the same time, we need to invest in ways to mitigate the urgent pressures of these symptoms and alleviate human suffering now, as best we can.

But governments are prone to being sprinters, not marathoners. They will publicly proclaim and commit to big steps, often with lofty rhetoric. And sometimes they will even take those steps. But more often than not, within a relatively short time frame, the energy recedes. They slow down. And effectively stop. And for them, reconciliation fades somewhat into the background. Until the next sprint. And the next one. With very little change being accomplished in either the long or short term.

Governments do this because, while some may indeed have good intentions (although many historically have had the opposite of good intentions), they do not generally have the will to run the marathon. The nature of our political system always focuses governments on the shorter term, on prioritizing what can be done, to public acclaim, usually on the timelines of electoral cycles. The sprint is over within the life of the government that needs to get re-elected. But the marathon of true reconciliation is longer than the life of any one government. There are few, if any, immediate political benefits. So, governments choose to sprint rather than run the marathon. Political expedience makes it so.

I know this might sound cynical, but I can tell you it is true. I saw it constantly while in the federal Cabinet. I described in part 2 how government was going to create a Recognition and Implementation of Indigenous Rights Framework but failed to follow through. Why? Because that work was never viewed as politically expedient. It would never produce a partisan advantage or demonstrate near-term, on-the-ground benefits that could impact the next election.

While the government proclaimed it was ready for the marathon, the choice was made to just keep sprinting. What that amounted to was focusing on one, or a few, of the symptoms of colonialism—the urgent crises on Track 1, such as clean drinking water on reserves.

Yes, it is vitally important and urgently necessary to get clean drinking water to First Nations communities. It must happen. It is shameful that in a country such as Canada, in 2022, thousands of people and communities do not have access to clean drinking water. But one very large reason this issue was chosen as a focus of government efforts was because it was viewed as politically viable, effective, and expedient—it was tangible; the public understood it and wanted to see it done; and it could be done in an election cycle. And it polled well. The government would be cheered when it reached this particular finish line. But of course, it never got there. The government failed to meet its commitment to deliver clean drinking water. This became political fodder for the opposition, and was hugely frustrating to Indigenous leaders, not to mention those on reserves without clean drinking water. But why was this promise not kept? What prevented the government from following through on its commitment? The answer to that question can be found in our two inextricably linked tracks—and the government's failure to recognize them as such. They thought getting clean drinking water to First Nations communities was a sprint, but it is actually one part of the marathon, and must be understood and addressed as such.

Massive amounts of energy and money was—and continues to be—targeted to addressing clean water on reserves. It became the primary personal focus of the prime minister when it came to Indigenous issues, the thing he would talk to me about more than any other aspect of reconciliation. And yet, not only did the government fail to cross its self-imposed finish line in this particular sprint, but it has still not completed the race. In 2015, Prime Minister Trudeau committed to end all long-term water advisories by March 2021. It is now estimated it will take until 2025. The original funding of more than $2 billion in 2016 to achieve this goal had to be supplemented by an additional $1.5 billion in 2020. As of September 2021, forty-five drinking water advisories were still in effect.[2]

Just remind yourselves for a moment what we are talking about. In 2022, we are spending billions of dollars to try to address one social issue—how to provide something as basic and fundamental as clean drinking water—on reserves that were created under a racist colonial statute, the Indian Act, that is more than a century old. And we still can't achieve it, even at the cost of billions of dollars and with the personal commitment of the prime minister himself. At the same time, there are many other pressing, and even more complex, expensive, and intractable social issues on reserves.

If we choose to keep focusing on sprinting, we will continually be running the same hundred-metre track—and not getting anywhere new, or different, as a result of work on reconciliation. We will burn lots of energy with little to show for it. Rather than advancing in the marathon, we will have lost our direction.

The metaphor of a marathon versus a sprint does not only apply to governments. It also is relevant to us individually and collectively. We sometimes see very well-intentioned bursts of desire to act by individuals, communities, and organizations as a result of events that occur. We see a push for change—a push for true reconciliation to take place.

Take, for example, what happened in the aftermath of the first reports of unmarked graves on the grounds of the former Kamloops Indian Residential School at Tk'emlúps te Secwépemc. The amount of public attention, the heartfelt response, and the desire for change was, in many ways, unparalleled. It was a moment of real learning and understanding and, as such, it inspired many to want to act. To do something. And we did see action. We saw people gather in groups to reflect, learn, and understand. We saw demonstrations of love and support. We saw creative works, such as the placement of children's shoes in many prominent locations, that honoured those that did not return. We saw people motivated to reach out to their Indigenous neighbours in ways that they had not done before, to help support individuals, families, and communities. We saw advocacy and pressure on our governments to take more tangible action.

But let's also continue to challenge ourselves. Has that moment resulted in enough tangible action? If so, how much? For you individually? For your community or organization? Has it resulted in the scope of actions that you think it should?

How have you responded to other reports of unmarked graves, such as at Cowessess First Nation, or to reports of First Nations commencing searches? Have you witnessed a decrease in the will to act? Or an increase in the sowing of seeds of doubt and denial about the facts surrounding the impacts of residential schools and the reality of unmarked graves?

I imagine you can see where I am going with this—which is that as individuals and collectives, we too can be prone to treating reconciliation as a sprint rather than a marathon. Reacting to particular events or news with a burst of energy, only to have that energy and the action it brings subside.

This needs to change. True reconciliation is about taking the sixty thousand steps required to run the marathon and not just repeating, from time to time, the fifty steps required to run the hundred-metre dash.

True reconciliation requires marathoners. Slow, fast, walking, running, cheering, and supporting. It doesn't matter. We need everyone and all of us. But we need to be on the course for the long haul.

Learning and understanding are the foundation for preparing for the marathon. They are the training. They are the infrastructure for true reconciliation, the work that will maintain our will to persevere and keep taking the necessary steps. That is why I put such emphasis on them in the first two parts of this book.

Having and maintaining the consistency of will to stay in the marathon is also about courage. Having the courage to reject the status quo and to call out limited practices that will not be conducive to the true work of reconciliation. And having the courage to do that not just once or twice but again and again over a lifetime. By necessity, this also requires being uncomfortable, and choosing to push and lead, and continuing to take actions in ways one might not have before.

By choosing to be part of the marathon of true reconciliation we are also making an important statement about where the burden of reconciliation lies.

You have read many times in this book how we all have roles to play and responsibilities to fulfil in the work of true reconciliation. This will always be the case. But too often—still—the burden for the bulk of the work is placed on Indigenous Peoples—to speak up, to push, to lead, to educate, to share, to inform, etc. Yes, Indigenous Peoples need to do these things and play their roles. But those who have suffered from colonialism are not responsible for addressing it. We need to be clear that Canadian governments and all Canadians need to do the heavy lifting in addressing this terrible legacy.

It is not about Indigenous Peoples asking for change. True reconciliation is about redressing wrongs that have created harms for Indigenous Peoples and our society as a whole. And, too often, we will use Indigenous Peoples as an excuse not to act by saying things like "Indigenous Peoples need to be in the lead," or "Indigenous Peoples need to show the way," or "Indigenous Peoples need more time," or "Indigenous Peoples want more consultation." There is a grain of truth in all of this. But only a grain. And when we use these excuses to justify our own inaction, we are not standing for change.

TRUE RECONCILIATION CHALLENGES, ELEVATES, AND ADVANCES

Tangible and coherent action is the essence of true reconciliation. It is the measure of whether we are moving forward, and how far we may get. It is through action that we address the harms, injustices, disadvantages, and lack of opportunity that are part of the legacy of colonialism.

As I said earlier, not all actions are equal. Not all actions are meaningful. Some actions can even be detrimental. And every action we refer to as reconciliation may not actually be contributing. But the answer is not found in picking and choosing just any action to take.

This is a problem we see now more and more. "Reconciliation" has become ever-present, and there is a tendency to label any and all actions regarding Indigenous matters as being "reconciliation." This is particularly and increasingly a practice of governments at all levels. They have started labelling so many things as "reconciliation"—often looking for political praise or cover in the process. When this happens, meaning is lost, along with our efforts to do what is truly impactful and important. We get confused about what we should or should not be doing. Simply stated, when everything (or nearly everything) is called "reconciliation," it is effectively the same as nothing being "reconciliation."

I witnessed this in my time as minister of justice, and it was a great source of concern. It was not just about the term *reconciliation*, but about all sorts of critical aspects of what reconciliation means. In the fall of 2018 I gave a speech about what reconciliation means between Crown and Indigenous governments. I said that at the core of "achieving reconciliation is the belief that the nation-to-nation, government-to-government, Inuit-Crown relationship must be based on the recognition of rights, respect, co-operation and partnership." I then raised the alarm that "we live in a time where language is often appropriated and mis-used, co-opted and twisted—made to stand for something it is not." Specifically:

> "Recognition" for Indigenous peoples across this country, and as a basis for true reconciliation, has meaning. It means that Indigenous peoples governed and owned the lands that now make up Canada prior to the arrival of Europeans. It means that Indigenous laws and legal orders that stewarded the lands for millenia, remain and must continue to operate in the contemporary world. It means that the title and rights of Indigenous peoples are inherent, and not dependent or contingent on court orders, agreements, or government action for their existence, substance, and effect. It means that treaties entered into historically must be fully implemented based on their spirit and intent, oral histories as well as texts, and consistent with the true meaning of a proper nation-to-nation and government-to-government relationship. It means that the distinct and diverse governments, laws, cultures, societies, and ways of life of First Nations, Métis, and Inuit are fully respected and reflected.

For Canada, recognition means resetting our foundation to properly reconcile—to finish the unfinished business of confederation. What is more, for many Indigenous peoples, recognition is the lifeline that will ensure the survival and rebuilding of their cultures, languages, and governing systems within an even stronger Canada.[3]

My point—which, frankly, was directed at the government I was a part of—was that this practice of not matching proper language with proper action is dangerous for the work of reconciliation:

> . . . too often we see the tendency—especially in politics—to use important words that have real meaning and importance, carelessly. We see them being applied to ideas and actions that in truth do not reflect their actual meaning—even, sometimes, their opposite. We see "recognition" applied to ideas that actually maintain "denial." We see "self-government" used to refer to ideas or processes that actually maintain control over others. We see "self-determination" applied to actions that actually interfere with the work of Nations rebuilding their governments and communities. We see "inherent" in the same breath as the contradictory idea that rights are contingent on the courts or agreements.
>
> When we see this being done it does not advance reconciliation. It actually undermines it. It causes confusion, chaos, and division. It treats a challenge—a challenge that is vital for the survival and well-being of children, women, families,

and communities across this country—as a "game of rhetoric." It trivializes—often out of ignorance or political expediency—a moral, social, and economic imperative for our country.

Words, in the work of reconciliation, are also cheap without real action—action that goes to the core of undoing the colonial laws, policies, and practices, and that is based on the real meaning of reconciliation. We all need to understand this.

The path of justice and equality is not advanced or achieved through half-measures, good intentions, or lofty rhetoric. And it is certainly not achieved through obfuscation or confusion about what we mean when we speak. Hard choices, innovative actions, transformations in laws and policies, new understandings and attitudes, new patterns of behavior—this is what is needed.[4]

I felt then, and feel even more so now, that we need to remain vigilant in honouring the meaning of the words we use, and translate those words into the real, transformative action that is needed.

Such vigilance is clearly still desperately needed. The tendency by governments to use "reconciliation" as a label for almost any kind of action—large or small, meaningful or not—continues. Consider some examples of things governments and political leaders have associated with reconciliation: adopting of a National Eagle Staff by the RCMP; renaming buildings, such as the former Langevin Block, where the Prime Minister's Office is located; apologizing for the residential school system; adopting a new holiday, the National Day of Truth and Reconciliation, and funding applications to raise awareness and plan celebrations; participating in the raising of a totem pole; adopting legislation to implement the UN Declaration; signing modern treaties and land claims settlements, such as with the Inuit and some First Nations in British Columbia; signing agreements regarding education with Anishinabek First Nations; signing agreements on child welfare jurisdiction, such as with the Cowessess First Nation; making new investments in First Nations housing and infrastructure; participating in book clubs; and so on. And on.

When you read this list what do you notice? Which of these actions do you think is the most important or impactful? Does calling all of these actions "reconciliation" make sense? Why or why not?

Reconciliation, ultimately, is about emphasizing the taking of certain types of actions, and not giving as much priority to others. So what are actions that support true reconciliation? How do we know our actions are coherent steps forward in the marathon?

To me, true reconciliation action *challenges, elevates,* and *advances.*

Challenges means our actions challenge oneself, and others. True reconciliation action is not comfortable or easy. For oneself, it requires some measure of discomfort, sacrifice, or change. At the same time, it challenges others to consider their own knowledge, understandings, or actions, and to consider taking their own steps in the work of true reconciliation.

The types of actions that challenge will vary for each of us, depending on who we are and the context we live in. For someone who has had little interaction or engagement with Indigenous people, their communities, and their concerns, a starting point for action that challenges could be going into new spaces where you will have opportunities to meet, listen to, and learn with Indigenous people, whether it is a rally, a meeting, a march, or a ceremony. For someone else (or organizations or communities), a challenging action might be to work to change a space or create a new space—where there hasn't been one before—that supports Indigenous people as well as opportunities for learning and understanding to be built. Indeed, we see individuals doing this more and more. For example, we see children who transform their classrooms or push their parents and families to become involved in new and impactful ways. And we see individuals in an organization who speak out when they observe forms of systemic racism or a lack of awareness, or who call for new forms of training and education, or policy and practice development.

There is another simple description and litmus test for action that challenges. Courage. Does it take courage? And, relatedly, does the action you are taking encourage others to take similar action in their own environments and contexts? If an action is not courageous and encouraging, it is likely not challenging.

Elevates means our actions elevate a shared understanding of the historic and contemporary reality of Indigenous Peoples in Canada—a growing, collective recognition of Indigenous Peoples and their worldviews, cultures, societies, governments, and laws. *Elevates* also means that we are reflecting and honouring social patterns and relations that embody our highest ideals and vision of what true reconciliation looks like, and breaking from social patterns and relations that have been entrenched as part of the legacy of colonialism. Put another way, true reconciliation actions should also promote and deepen our learning and understanding, as we discussed in parts 1 and 2. True reconciliation through learning, understanding, and acting is not linear—it is integrative. As we act, we must continue to learn and understand. As we learn and understand, we must also be taking action. By doing this, we help to ensure that our actions actually elevate patterns and relations that reconcile, as opposed to those that may, even unbeknownst to us, continue to reinforce patterns and relations that reflect the legacy of colonialism.

Actions that elevate are conscious, and not merely reactive. They are actions where—if we were asked why we were taking a particular action—it would be easy for us to say, "I am doing this because it . . . ." Those answers should be about how the action breaks from the legacy of colonization and builds the future of reconciliation. And we should mean them. The explanation of our action should be some version of: "I am doing this because it demonstrates respect for my Indigenous neighbours and understanding of the social injustices that still exist." Our answer should never be simply "because others are doing it" or "it makes me feel good" or "it benefits me" or "I feel I have to." When we are able to provide good, honest answers to questions about why we are acting as we are, we are helping to elevate because we are breaking from the motivations of the past and also building a similar awareness in others—helping them to elevate their own ability to act in impactful ways.

Again, what elevating action looks like will vary for each of us and is based on our specific contexts. The way we respond with immediate, selfless, and tangible support to a specific event, need, or challenge faced by an Indigenous family or community can be elevating. The way we recognize and respect through our actions what an individual or community says is what is needed or what is supportive can be elevating. The way we demonstrate and express consistency in our reasons for why we are doing something and ensure that our words and actions match—such as the ways a company approaches an Indigenous community about a potential resource development project—can be elevating.

Advances means our actions contribute to a proper relationship between Indigenous and non-Indigenous peoples and does this by recognizing that all actions taken must advance into other actions that build on them. In other words, our actions are coherent, not sporadic, disconnected, or ad hoc. True reconciliation requires looking into the future and seeing how we will coherently move from one action to another, and then to more actions that deepen progress.

We have to think about our "actions," and not an "action." We need to understand that true reconciliation is realized through multiple acts, over time, that build on what has already happened and lead to what is next. True reconciliation is not an event that occurs annually on a holiday, or when something occasionally happens that sparks our interest. True reconciliation sees how one step leads to the next. If we are helping educate our peers in the classroom, family, or workplace, we should already know what practical and tangible next steps this will lead to. What practices or policies will we be changing in our company? What next step will we be taking to demonstrate acceptance and care to neighbouring Indigenous families and communities that can help address or alleviate some of the needs they face? How does my action support the work an Indigenous nation is doing to ensure governments are moving down Track 1 and Track 2 properly? How do my actions support Indigenous nations in their rebuilding work?

Remember all that we have examined about how our history is filled with broken promises and a lack of follow-through—how the tendency is to default to the sprint, even when we know the marathon is the right course. When we act in ways that advance, we are always thinking steps ahead: About how we move from reading a report or studying an issue, to going to a march or rally or event, to offering some of our time or resources to support a community service initiative or project. About how we move from training ourselves within a company in cultural awareness, to having an outward orientation as a company that supports its employees and contributes tangibly, to community development. About how we move from making land acknowledgements, to having protocols with neighbouring Indigenous communities, to having joint action plans on how reconciliation will be advanced throughout the community, to actually implementing the plan as a priority and transparently measuring its progress and impact.

Through the lens of *challenge*, *elevate*, and *advance*, we can consider some of our recent actions towards reconciliation.

In recent years we have seen an increasing focus on symbolic, or what I call "performative," acts of reconciliation. Some of these are the subject of public debate and controversy—like removing statues, or changing the names of streets, sports teams, and schools, or lowering the flag. Others are not subject to as much public debate and controversy—like apologies for aspects of the past, speeches that aim to be "historic" (like the one I talked about earlier from Prime Minister Trudeau in 2018), or wearing orange T-shirts and reinforcing that "every child matters."

The debate over removing statues of Sir John A. Macdonald is perhaps the most contentious. It illustrates the full range of possible perspectives, as well as some of the limits, and even irony, of focusing so much on performative reconciliation.

Sir John A. Macdonald, Canada's first prime minister, was an architect of the residential school system. Under his tenure, practices such as relocating Indigenous Peoples from their lands and withholding of food took place. There is no question that within his legacy are horrendous actions and policies with respect to Indigenous Peoples.

When it comes to the possibility of removing statues of Macdonald, the reasons given are often focused on the message or symbolism of having a statue of someone who perpetrated such acts. You might hear, for example, how "a statue is symbolic of something, and I don't think right now that the statue is symbolic of the right things." Further, some argue that continuing to honour individuals who caused such harms can perpetuate hurt and wrongs. For this reason, some Indigenous people have been clear that, one way or another, such statues need to come down. We'll get to a place where we'll say, "We're done talking, we're done pleading, we're going to do it. . . . If you won't take it down, we'll take it down."

At the same time, there are Indigenous and non-Indigenous voices that argue that such statues should remain as an opportunity to educate: "Knocking things down, breaking things, is not my preferred option. Turning my eyes away from things is not my preferred option."

Others suggest that to focus on just one aspect of history, or what an individual did historically, is too narrow and problematic a view. Taking statues down is to risk whitewashing or potentially erasing that history.[5]

Some Indigenous leaders, such as former Senator Murray Sinclair, have stated it is a fight they would rather avoid:

The problem I have with the overall approach to tearing down statues and buildings is that is counterproductive to . . . reconciliation because it almost smacks of revenge or smacks of acts of anger, but in reality, what we are trying

to do, is we are trying to create more balance in the relationship. . . . It is not about taking off names off buildings, it is
about whether we can find a way to put Indigenous names
on buildings. . . . It is probably a fight, had I been asked,
I would have said to avoid it.[6]

Underlying these perspectives are clearly differing views
and experiences about the history of Canada, the nature of
colonization, and, in our current reality, what addressing the
legacy of colonialism involves. If anything, these debates can
be seen as a litmus test of what stage we are at in undertaking
the learning and understanding we need to do as part of true
reconciliation, and how far we must still go.

For example, the City of Victoria's removal of a statue of
Macdonald was somewhat overtaken by a controversy about
public participation in the decision to remove the statue. The
mayor of Victoria explained the rationale behind the removal
in the following terms: "The reason we're not doing a big
public consultation on the statue per se is it would become
a debate about do we keep the statue, or do we remove the
statue? That's not the debate we want to have . . . What we
want to have is a conversation about how do we as a city and as
a community have reconciliation in the city that's built on the
homelands of the Songhees and Esquimalt Nations?"[7]

But after outcry and protest, the mayor had to apologize
for making people feel they were excluded from the decision:
"As mayor of Victoria, I apologize for not recognizing that the
city family's process might make some people feel excluded

from such an important decision . . . I didn't recognize the great desire of Victoria residents to participate in reconciliation actions. The process going forward will enable this."[8]

These performative acts of reconciliation—symbolic reconciliation—can challenge, elevate, and advance, but only in very limited ways. While we need some of this form of action, it cannot be the main focus of our time, energy, and effort.

As a positive outcome, symbolic action can make people question their understanding, and can educate us about different ways of thinking. It can help us learn and understand. It can help reinforce the retelling of our history, and the shifts in worldview and awareness—the making of connections—that support better relations and healing.

Take also, for example, land acknowledgements. Not that long ago it was very rare to hear them. In recent years they have become commonplace, although not everywhere. As recently as October 2021, the government of New Brunswick ordered employees to stop making land acknowledgements because of ongoing litigation: "As a result of this litigation, legal counsel for GNB (Government of New Brunswick) and the Office of the Attorney General has advised that GNB employees may not make or issue territory or title acknowledgements." The memo went on to say that the order extends to documents and email signatures. While employees can refer to "ancestral territory," they cannot use the terms "unceded" or "unsurrendered." The memo even went so far as to say that where exceptions are given, and an acknowledgement is desirable, it must be in the following form: "We (I) respectfully acknowledge the territory in which we gather as the ancestral homelands of the XYZ. We strive for respectful relationships with all the peoples of this province as we search for collective healing and true reconciliation and honour this beautiful land together."[9]

Fortunately, and increasingly, confused perspectives like that in the New Brunswick memo are becoming rarer. This is because land acknowledgements are a form of symbolic reconciliation that do have a purpose. They provide learning about Indigenous Peoples and their connection to the land. They express an understanding of connections—to the past, the present, and the future—and an understanding of Indigenous worldviews. They reflect the importance of the work of true reconciliation. They demonstrate respect for Indigenous Peoples in a way that breaks from our legacy of colonialism. The New Brunswick example is the opposite of trying to show respect and reconcile, because it represents a failure to acknowledge basic truths of history, as we talked about in part 1. If you can't even bring yourself to acknowledge that Indigenous Peoples had an original connection with the land—as we are striving to come to terms with that reality—then you are not really trying.

That said, these acts of symbolic reconciliation do not really *challenge*. In fact, they demand very little of us (even though they may be controversial). And the ways in which they *elevate* are also quite limited; though, as I said, some of them can help reinforce the retelling of our history or support healing and understanding. They do not require or mean that anything will be done differently, that decisions will occur differently, or that anything will change in the lives or well-being of people.

Such acts also do not *advance* in significant ways—they do not clearly lead to a next step, or the next step after that, which builds the future. By and large, they are isolated, and repeated. We could spend all of our time debating what statues should remain or be removed, or renaming streets, sports teams, and places, or making land acknowledgements, and not do the actual hard work of true reconciliation.

Symbolic acts do not lift a child out of poverty or help keep them with their family. They do not address the over-representation of Indigenous people in the justice system. They do not recognize and implement Indigenous rights, uphold the human rights in the UN Declaration, or do anything else tangible. And, for these reasons, they cannot be a primary focus of our attention, energy, and effort. Yes, there is necessary value in some of these actions. We need them as part of the process of learning and understanding. But no, they should not be the leading focus of the work of reconciliation. Or taken to mean we have reconciled.

This leads to another concern with placing too much emphasis on performative reconciliation—which is that it can actually make true reconciliation action more difficult. This can occur in several different ways.

First, placing a large amount of emphasis on performative reconciliation can heighten a sense that things are changing, and expectations that things will continue to change. It looks good. It shows well. It is politically correct. Yet, because performative reconciliation does not result in tangible shifts on the ground, such an emphasis can increase legitimate frustration, anger, and conflict over the lack of real progress. It can even lead to a sense of betrayal. In some instances, it can contribute to making the real work of true reconciliation harder, because further mistrust and tension has built up around how acts of performative reconciliation did not contribute or lead to real change.

Second, overemphasizing and concentrating on performative reconciliation can send the wrong message to those who might not be as sympathetic to the work of reconciliation; it can suggest that this work is being accomplished and has an end date. And because the work is not really over and remains a focus of public pressures and demands for action, those who are not very sympathetic may be increasingly hostile to the work. In other words, it can make things harder and result in more conflict and even outright opposition to the work of true reconciliation.

We also see examples where the emphasis on performative reconciliation ends up creating controversies and distractions from the real work because the "performance" is not a good one. This is what happened on the very first National Day of Truth and Reconciliation in 2021, when the focus shifted away from the day and its meaning and to the prime minister's surfing holiday in Tofino. Much of the healing, truth-learning, and building of understanding that the national holiday could have helped to support was overtaken by that news. The spotlight was on the prime minister instead of where it should have been—on the Survivors, communities, and the work of true reconciliation.

So what kinds of actions do challenge, elevate, and advance?

Let's look at some examples of actions that individuals, communities, organizations, and governments can take that are impactful, and consider how they challenge, elevate, and advance the cause of true reconciliation. There are many remarkable illustrations of audacious action in this regard, both past and present, and I have gathered some examples below. Some are historical and well-documented. Some I know of personally. Others are those I have heard of or read about, but don't have direct knowledge of. I have included them here because not only are they illustrative of the types of actions that can challenge, elevate, and advance, but they also give us hope and show us this work can and will be done. I am sure you have read and know of many more.

Consider, for example, Maisie Hurley, who was born in Wales in 1887 and grew up in the only non-Indigenous family in a settlement in the interior of British Columbia near Merritt. While she spent much of her early years in Great Britain, the United States, and British Columbia, from the 1940s on she became a fierce advocate for and ally of Indigenous Peoples. Haida Elder Alfred Adams was the founding president of the Native Brotherhood of British Columbia, the main Indigenous rights advocacy organization in the province. After meeting Hurley in 1944, Adams asked her to educate non-Indigenous peoples about challenges and struggles being faced by Indigenous Peoples. In 1946, this led Hurley to create, publish, and edit the *Native Voice*, a national newspaper focused on Indigenous Peoples. She used the *Native Voice* to educate and advocate for Indigenous rights—including the right to vote—for the need to implement treaties, and to criticize the residential school system.

Beyond helping to bring critical attention to these issues, Hurley also was a major force in helping Indigenous Peoples navigate the legal system. As legal secretary to Tom Hurley (who would become her second husband in 1951), she helped provide free services to Indigenous Peoples, including on rights matters, even when the Indian Act prohibited such claims being supported. This was coupled with her extensive political advocacy, which continued until Hurley's death in 1964. When the first legal case about Indigenous rights took place in British Columbia—*Regina v. White and Bob*, which was referenced in the oral history—it was Hurley who supported the Indigenous hunters who were charged, arranging for Thomas Berger, a young lawyer, to represent them.

The life of Maisie Hurley is a remarkable illustration of challenging, elevating, and advancing. At a time when it was legally risky to take the stand she did, Maisie embodied true reconciliation.

Consider, also, the people we see doing novel and important things within the context of their own neighbourhoods. Like Marion Cummings, who decided at age eighty-five to leave her multi-million-dollar home in Victoria to the Victoria Native Friendship Centre as an act of reconciliation. As Marion explained, "the Indigenous connections of land across Canada have not been acknowledged in ways they should be . . . I think some of us appreciate the opportunity to return some of the land."[10]

Acts like Marion's are part of a growing recognition of innovative ways in which individuals or small groups of individuals can contribute to the economic dimensions of reconciliation. For example, beyond the formal relationships that local governments must have with Indigenous Peoples, a number of local governments are starting to look at how to facilitate ways for their citizens to contribute financially to reconciliation work. In cities such as Winnipeg and Victoria, we see proposals that include options when it comes to paying property taxes that would contribute to reconciliation initiatives with local Indigenous communities. Such initiatives have sparked debate and dialogue from many perspectives, which is important as we try to focus on actions that challenge, elevate, and advance.

We also see individuals and families who decide to look at their own daily, weekly, and monthly budgets and figure out how to support action by themselves, or others, that advances reconciliation. This might involve giving time, on a regular basis, to a community organization that helps Indigenous youth, or making a donation to support local activities for children run by a friendship centre or other community organization. By committing to support or take action consistently, over time, and building it into the rhythm of your life, you are acting with impact, and creating connections and opportunities to do even more.

New types of organizations are also emerging, designed to challenge people to think and act beyond the status quo. We see volunteer community initiatives founded by young people—initiatives that are increasingly focused on issues of Indigenous justice and reconciliation, including through supporting Indigenous political advocacy, raising funds for Indigenous charities, and driving public awareness and understanding of critical issues. The "On Canada Project" is one example. It was founded in 2020 to help disseminate information to marginalized and younger people about COVID-19, but has now expanded to a focus on work for and with Indigenous Peoples. As the project organizers see it: "Our government has a responsibility to do better, but so do we. We can't just mourn; we need to do more, individually as settlers and collectively as a settler nation. We all have a part to play in Truth & Reconciliation, and since our government isn't stepping up, then we, the people, must."[11] With a focus on Millennials and Gen Z, the On Canada Project creates tools to help them "stay informed, take up action and champion change in our country."[12]

It's worth noting that we don't all need to build digital networks to have an impact. Consider how you can help build a vibrant culture of advancing reconciliation with your neighbours and in your community. Are there ways you can open your home to dialogues about reconciliation? A book club discussion? How about creating new bridges between communities by sponsoring or hosting events where Indigenous and non-Indigenous peoples share a meal, learn from one another, and build fellowship? What about supporting opportunities for Indigenous artists, in ways that they direct and deem appropriate, to present their art in your community in ways that may not have existed before and that help build understanding between peoples?

It is often youth who are leading the world when it comes to reconciliation, and youth-driven innovation is flourishing all over Canada. In many classrooms and communities, for example, it is young people who are pushing their peers, and adults, to recognize and have conversations about the Indigenous history of Canada, and what they can do to contribute to the work of reconciliation. One example is Danii Kehler, a university student from Kawacatoose First Nation who has advocated for the use of Indigenous knowledge among young people as part of an effective response to climate change. In so doing, she is both advancing reconciliation and focusing youth on the shared environmental challenge we all face: "If we get that at a young age with Indigenous and non-Indigenous youth," she says, "then we can really create a sense of change."[13] Or we see high school students like Isaiah Shafqat, a two-spirit Mi'kmaw teen who has developed education resources about Indigenous Peoples and culture that are used on screens in elevators—reflecting the idea that every opportunity can be taken to help people learn and plant seeds of change.[14]

Innovative education efforts also challenge, elevate, and advance when they break the cycle of teaching understandings and ideas that reinforce siloes. The Regina Open Door Society is an example of an organization that works to bridge the gap between Indigenous Peoples and culture, and newcomers to Canada. They educate in order to try to prevent old and racist stereotypes and ways of thinking from being perpetuated in what new Canadians learn, while also building relations on a strong and proper footing of learning and understanding from the outset. In a nutshell, they focus on building the right relationship as early as possible in the formation of that relationship, so that we do not have to focus as much on repairing that relationship later on.[15] We need more and more of this. Consider ways in which you, too, can help support spaces and opportunities for those who are new to Canada and in your community to gain learning about the history of Canada, the territories in which they reside, the treaty and rights relationships that may exist, and the local work of reconciliation that is taking place.

It is important to remember that when we see more formal and impactful changes in communities and organizations— like new policies and agreements—there are always individual champions who are part of or integral to driving them forward. Nothing happens without individuals who are willing to push the boundaries of what has been done before and willing to think outside the same old boxes. I have seen this time and again, in so many different settings.

Consider, for example, the steps that have been taken to create new legislation and policy in Canada and British Columbia to formalize the implementation of the United Nations Declaration on the Rights of Indigenous Peoples. This would not have happened without a number of individuals choosing to accept roles and actions that differed from what had been the norm in the past. Helping drive the change in British Columbia in 2019 was the presence of a very few non-Indigenous and Indigenous leaders in the public service who were willing to challenge their colleagues in ways that had not been done before. There were also Indigenous lawyers, representing First Nations, who were willing to sit down and work co-operatively with government in ways that broke with some of the norms around how this work had been done in the past. Sometimes their work was frowned on by their colleagues, because it was challenging, and different. It required leaders on all sides to take some risks. Ten years earlier, a similar legislative initiative had been tried. It failed. There were a number of reasons for this, but a critical one was that there were not enough champions on either side—people willing to do the actual work of crafting something new—to get it across the finish line. Well, that was not the case this time, not only because the political and social context had changed, but also because more individuals felt enabled, empowered, and were present to make the change happen. People, individuals—you and us—always are driving the change. How can *you* be a champion for effecting change for reconciliation in the specific context of your community, work, and family?

This is true in the corporate world as well. We hear about the tensions and conflicts between resource development and Indigenous Peoples every day, which is understandable given how at odds the two sides can be. But there are many constructive and positive developments as well, including where we see companies—through work with Indigenous Peoples—helping to lead aspects of challenging the status quo, advancing work along both Track 1 and Track 2, and helping pressure governments, in tangible and constructive ways, to play their part.

I think it is fair to say that we have seen shifts in how industry views its role in reconciliation. For a long time, industry's position was that Indigenous relations were "the government's role, not ours." Then there were those who, over time, moved towards a different perspective: "It is still government's role, but they can't get their act together, so we will play a role." And then there were some who shifted even more: "We have a role to play also—we are using lands and resources in Indigenous territory and need to be in a sharing arrangement." Now, in at least some cases, we are seeing an even greater shift: "We need to be true partners economically, and learn to work through decision-making of Nations." Considering the current realities and what's at stake, I have no doubt that this last shift will get deeper and deeper. It is the path to certainty and clarity and prosperity. More and more, we need companies to ask themselves how their relationships and any agreements they enter into with Indigenous Peoples are enabling the solutions to the broader challenges of rebuilding Indigenous communities, governments, and nations as necessary in order to live together.

One example of this shift in thinking can be found in the concept of free, prior, and informed consent. Not so long ago, some large companies in major resource sectors had policies where they would not enter into any kind of agreement with Indigenous Peoples about use of their traditional lands and resources (because they thought it was the government's problem, not theirs). Now, many of these companies have agreed to not use traditional lands and resources unless free, prior, and informed consent has been achieved. In this regard, these companies have moved much more quickly than any government in implementing consent-based decision-making, and have put substantial pressure on governments to catch up.

Take, for example, the mining industry, where we see the adoption of sets of standards around consent by industry organizations such as the International Council of Mining and Metals.[16] We also are seeing some companies adopt consent in their policies and, more importantly, complete agreements that confirm that major mining projects will not proceed without consent.[17]

Indeed, reflecting this, British Columbia has announced the first consent-based agreement for major resource development based on the UN Declaration—with the Tahltan Nation for the review of a major mine. The agreement explicitly and legally confirms that the mine will be reviewed through a joint process that recognizes Tahltan jurisdiction, laws, and authority, and if the Tahltan do not give their consent—if they decide to say "no"—the mine will not be built.

When we see cutting-edge developments that reflect the shift to recognition and implementation of Indigenous rights, we need to take note of them and educate ourselves about these emerging trends, understand them in the context of the true history of this country and the challenges we are trying to address, and help educate others about why these developments are important. We also need to encourage further developments that recognize and implement Indigenous rights. We can do this through our political and public choices—such as what we advocate for, how we vote, how we use our voices, and what we use them for.

There are also political leaders, Indigenous and non-Indigenous, who challenge, elevate, and advance. Inevitably, these are individuals who step beyond expectations of what they will do and the positions they will advance. I have talked elsewhere about how hard it remains for Indigenous leaders to make the choice to cross over to mainstream politics—especially if they were leaders in Indigenous politics before. Not everyone in my Indigenous world wanted me to join a Crown government. As I wrote in *Indian in the Cabinet*:

> I started talking to a broader group about the possibility of running. There were many Indigenous voices who would have preferred I run for National Chief. Shawn [Atleo] was one of those. We met in Gastown in Vancouver—he was still National Chief [of the Assembly of First Nations] at the time. He pressed hard that by being the first woman National Chief I could breathe new life into the work and the organization—help with the needed institutional reform and to re-envision it. To make it less Indian Act focused.
> I thought hard afterwards about his words. I valued them. They also echoed in some ways the voice of my grandmother that I could hear in my head. "Nasty white politics!?" I could imagine her saying.
>   Some of my Indigenous friends and colleagues' observations reinforced in me a nagging fear about whether I should run or not. Would people think of me and

treat me as a "token" or a "box-ticker" candidate? As a woman, as an Indigenous person, and most certainly as an Indigenous woman? At some level, I knew this would be true, but I felt this was just the cost of politics when people like me had been excluded for so long. There would be many costs, I imagined. So it would be.[18]

But we need more and more individuals making this particular journey, including so that Indigenous worldviews, perspectives, and understandings of the world can more directly challenge and shift how decisions are made in this country.

It is not just about Indigenous leaders getting involved in mainstream politics. We also need more non-Indigenous leaders who truly understand and are willing to do the actual work that is required politically on the two tracks. Remember, the critical work is governments figuring out how to get their own "house in order"—to change laws, policies, and practices so that there can be proper relations between Indigenous and Crown governments. Like what was originally envisioned in the Two Row Wampum. And in the historic treaty relationships. And in the voices and aspirations of the Indigenous Peoples who welcomed settlers and sought a relationship between sovereigns when they arrived. We have not had many political leaders who recognized that this was the vital work that needed to be done, and then followed through and implemented it. We need leaders ready to stand up and follow through.

Challenge, elevate, and advance. That is what all of these examples—and countless others—are about. Individuals driving initiatives and action that build learning and understanding, which can and will lead to true reconciliation.

Learn, Understand, Act.

We must do all of these—with intention, consistency, and focus—if we want to be forces of true reconciliation.

In part 1, "Learn," we talked about the silos built up through our history of colonialism, and in part 2, "Understand," we talked about what we need to see in order to transcend these silos. In this part, "Act," we have identified how to translate that learning and understanding into action that challenges, elevates, and advances, and that builds new patterns of relations that reflect true reconciliation and not the reality of colonialism.

When we are active in all three of these areas, we will also begin to recognize something else: Being an agent of true reconciliation means aspiring to build unity, cohesion, and harmony between peoples. It means viewing ourselves and our purpose as being a bridge between peoples and communities that have histories of injustice, silos, and conflict. It means being "inbetween."

As in, being an "inbetweener."

There is, of course, something innately human in this. We all, throughout our lives, are striving in various ways to bring together aspects of our reality and experience that may seem or become distant or unknown. We are always aiming to build and deepen relationships. To expand our circles. We are hoping to create greater harmony, love, and joy between and among people, whether in our families or communities. We long to make sense of our present, and build our future, by understanding the connections to our past and the places from where we have come.

You have probably heard Indigenous people use the phrase "all my relations." It reflects the interconnected nature of Indigenous worldviews I described earlier—expressing the importance of sharing the connections from which we come. But it has a greater meaning, too. It is also an acknowledgement that at any moment each and every one of us is a bridge between different, disparate, and unknown realities. I exist between my known past and the unknown future of my people. I am inbetween, and I must locate myself properly in that place. And my role is to know from where I have come, to help envision and anticipate what the future may be, and to act as a bridge between them. To be an inbetweener.

In many ways, "inbetweener" is also just another word for true reconciliation.

There is something about the idea of being inbetween, and building a culture of inbetweeners, that extends beyond the work of true reconciliation. We need inbetweeners as part of revitalizing our vision of Canada as a whole—a vision of what any community of diverse and distinct peoples who are living together and interdependent can and should aspire to be.

I sometimes think of a community of interdependent, diverse, and distinct peoples through an analogy of the human body. In order for one's body to be healthy, diverse and distinct entities (such as a heart, brain, stomach, etc.) must have proper relations with one another. If one part of the body is not doing well, the whole body is sick. Similarly, if the different parts of the body are not getting along and interacting in the right way, the whole body also becomes sick. For well-being, health, and happiness, all parts of the body must be cared for in ways that consider and recognize how they are distinct.

The same is true for diverse communities. We need all peoples—along with their specific historical and contemporary realities—to be recognized, understood, and appreciated so that just conditions and proper relations can be established and maintained. When this recognition and these relations do not exist, the community as a whole—all people—suffer in various ways. Over time, if this condition persists, the challenges will build and build.

Our historical and contemporary reality is the acute, pernicious, and long-standing omission of Indigenous Peoples from the formation of a vision of Canada. This has caused tremendous harms and costs. For Indigenous Peoples. And for all Canadians. The work of true reconciliation is one part of revitalizing this vision. As part of this revitalization, we also need to ensure that other peoples and communities who have suffered injustices in the history of Canada are being recognized, and build proper relations there as well.

From this perspective, being an inbetweener also means being able to recognize and navigate between distinctive worldviews and help build understanding about how they interact, intersect, and are expressed in balance with one another in society. Yes, there is tremendous power in the historic vision of the Two Row Wampum—of peoples and societies living side by side. But today, in our complex, integrated, and diverse world, we must make sure that as we walk side by side we are doing so as part of an interdependent whole. Yes, a whole—but with distinctions and difference while being inseparable. Recognizing that means we also understand that our world-views and the ways we express them, as well the patterns we build in society, will continue to change.

More than anything, the legacy of colonialism is about two things: lack of *acceptance* and lack of *care*. For generations, the predominant reality of colonialism delivered a message to Indigenous Peoples—a message that emphasized "we don't accept you" and "we don't care about you."

Everything we read about in part 1—the policies designed to "take the Indian out of the child" and to assimilate Indigenous Peoples into other traditions—is an example of a lack of acceptance. Everything we read about in terms of taking land away, destroying economies, disrupting systems of government, and allowing severe social-economic conditions to arise is an example of lack of care.

In subtle and not-so-subtle ways, non-Indigenous Canadians have been taught to not accept and not to care, and Indigenous Canadians have been taught that they are not accepted and that they do not matter. When we talk about systemic racism—such as we saw earlier in the example of the health care system—we are talking about how lack of acceptance and lack of care have become embedded and entrenched in our social systems. When we ask ourselves why governments slip so easily into inaction and break promises, it is because of a lack of acceptance and care.

The effect of this has been to reinforce a distance between Indigenous and non-Indigenous peoples—a distance that is not just interpersonal and communal but also, as we have seen throughout this book, cultural, structural, economic, and political.

Reconciliation—true reconciliation—is about closing that distance. Through *acceptance* and *care*. And when one accepts and cares, and acts based on that, one is an inbetweener.

Inbetweeners come from all backgrounds. It does not matter what your job is or where you live. It is about who you are. When one identifies as an inbetweener one will both create spaces and opportunities to advance true reconciliation, and act in ways consistent with true reconciliation when one finds oneself in those spaces. And it is not just individuals who are inbetweeners. Organizations and companies can be inbetweeners, too. From a giant resource or tech company to a small non-profit that provides social supports, any organization can envision itself, strategize, and act as an inbetweener. They can demonstrate that breaking down the silos, closing the distance, and demonstrating acceptance and care are core to their very purpose and role. The same is true about communities. They can envision their work as creating and building inclusive inbetween spaces and modes of functioning—in how decisions are made, in how community planning takes place, and in how economic and social programs are designed.

Consider the examples from earlier in this section of actions that challenge, elevate, and advance true reconciliation. The individuals and organizations behind those examples shared something. All were consciously choosing to put themselves in the position of being "inbetween." This can be done in different ways. There are those who do it by literally being inbetween Indigenous Peoples and non-Indigenous peoples and helping build new understanding and patterns of relations. There are those who are inbetween in their communities and families, working to make them vibrant spaces where reconciliation is consistently and coherently talked about, supported, and worked on. There are those who are inbetween by occupying a space that others have been unwilling to stand in even though they should—like companies that are willing to start operationalizing consent even when governments should be leading the way. There are those who are inbetween by having the courage to break out of defined traditional roles and patterns—a few lawyers and public servants who are willing to push and pull for progress in ways that have not been pursued before. Or leaders who have taken the journey across Indigenous and non-Indigenous governing systems, or to a place of changing laws, policies, and practices that allows for the proper building of relations between Indigenous and non-Indigenous peoples.

These examples also reveal how being an inbetweener will always require challenging, elevating, and advancing. By its very nature, being an inbetweener means pushing against the entrenched and taken-for-granted patterns and norms that have been built up by our legacy of colonialism. It requires action that recognizes the critical role that Indigenous Peoples, governments, and rights must play in our shared future. And it involves actions that are helping build—tangibly—a different pattern of interacting, relating, and decision-making.

Over the years, I have come to think of my role and my work as that of being an inbetweener. I certainly did not always think of it this way. As I talked about earlier, my identity has been formed by being raised in my culture and by my family to play certain roles and take on responsibilities, particularly around leadership. My grandmother, and my dad, would never use a term such as *inbetweener* when speaking of those roles.

But I have come to see an intrinsic connection between the identity I was raised (to be a leader) and how I identify today (as an inbetweener). As I moved into different roles, especially during my time in Cabinet, I realized that this is at the core of the work we need done right now, I realized that acting, and leadership, for true reconciliation means being in the sometimes uncomfortable place of inbetween, challenging long-existing patterns, and, in doing so, helping to build new ones. I also realized when I was in Cabinet that just having an inbetweener around that table made others uncomfortable and uncertain about what they'd long believed. It challenged them to have an Indigenous woman—one who grew up in a fishing village on an island off the west coast of Canada—at that table.

When people are challenged, they must make choices. And making the right choices is hard and often uncomfortable work. Some struggle more than others in shifting their actions. But in struggling—in being challenged—they are already shifting, as it means they are questioning what they previously thought or did. On the other hand, some will fully embrace the opportunity and become inbetweeners themselves. And when there are more inbetweeners, the pace and scale of true reconciliation accelerates. And we will all be better off.

Being an inbetweener is also about our "means" matching our "ends." True reconciliation, ultimately, is about building transformed patterns of just and harmonious relations between Indigenous and non-Indigenous peoples at all levels of society. Well, we cannot build just and harmonious relations between peoples through unjust and divisive means. Just as we cannot build and nurture love between people through force, or build trust through acting in untrustworthy ways.

For most of us, the reality that our means must match our ends is common sense. As individuals, we get it. But governments have traditionally struggled with this common sense—which is why they are often viewed as hypocritical in the work of reconciliation. For example, while talk of "reconciliation" has come to the forefront over the last few decades, and governments have said they are committed to this work, they have also made choices and taken actions that appear to indicate the opposite. We see this all the time—from how much effort governments still put into fighting Indigenous Peoples in court, based on arguments that continue to deny the existence of Indigenous Peoples or their rights, to how the police are often employed and used.

How can we ever expect true reconciliation to take place if court processes are the front line in how governments and Indigenous Peoples work through the hard issues?

Litigation is predominately an adversarial, win-lose, zero-sum process. It occurs in structured, formal, and impersonal spaces that are dominated by privileged professionals who do all the talking. Lawyers are trained to identify points of division and distinction. And courts are only empowered to offer outcomes or remedies that are narrow and specific. Courts cannot make people live together. They cannot change how children are educated. They cannot determine policy on how revenues are shared, or homes are built, or suicide prevention programs are put into place.

Yes, in some instances litigation can be a vehicle for advancing dialogue and settlement. But in many respects, the "means" of using the courts can be in tension with the "ends" of true reconciliation. And while there is a necessary role for the courts, this role has at times been overemphasized and overused, particularly as a result of the behaviour of the Crown, with the result being that it has delayed the advance of true reconciliation.

The same principle holds true for individuals, organizations, and communities acting as inbetweeners. Our means must match our ends. We must act in ways that reflect the conditions we wish to help create—of acceptance and care, of greater well-being, harmony, and understanding. While true reconciliation requires acts that challenge, disrupt, and even confront, we will not advance and achieve it through means that are divisive, harmful, or violent.

Acceptance and care; and our means matching our ends.

This is what it means to be an inbetweener in the work of true reconciliation. As individuals, communities, organizations, and governments, we must increasingly embody and exemplify this standard. The more we identify and act as inbetweeners, the more our actions will be impactful in supporting real change. And the more our worldviews will change in how they are expressed.

Inbetweeners are those who know how to navigate the space of the new, the evolving, and the changing. Who embrace, at once, recognizing and respecting distinction and diversity, and interdependence, cohesion, and unity.

As we do this—as more and more of us become inbetweeners—we are also contributing to building a shared vision and reality of Canada's future. A vision of recognition and proper relations between distinct and diverse peoples who understand their interconnection and interdependence. A Canada where peoples of all backgrounds truly live in patterns of peaceful co-existence and conscious recognition of interdependence. Where we are forging an ever-changing society based on changes in our worldviews and how they are expressed as a result of learning and understanding about each other.

This is a vision that has deep roots in these lands.

It is how many of the First Nations and Inuit who lived here before the arrival of Europeans structured their relations with each other. It is a vision that is reflected in some of the early patterns of peace, friendship, and mutuality between Indigenous Peoples and Europeans. It is a vision that is reflected in the idea and understanding of treaty-making and how governments and peoples relate to one another. It is a vision that is reflected in some of the ideals at the founding of Canada—except that vision fully excluded Indigenous Peoples. It is a vision that Indigenous Peoples have advocated to see become a reality over generations. It is a vision that—because of how our learning, understanding, and acting is taking place—is being reflected in contemporary efforts to implement the rights of Indigenous Peoples in the UN Declaration and our Constitution.

It is a vision that many Canadians from all backgrounds and from all regions have increasingly been calling for and working towards. A vision of true reconciliation, in which we all have our part to play.

Acknowledgements

I thank the many people who have helped me on my journey and made invaluable contributions to the evolution and formation of the ideas in this book. There have been so many that it is impossible to acknowledge everyone by name—countless individuals who have inspired, supported, challenged, guided, and assisted me over the years. You know who you are, and I deeply thank each and every one of you.

A number of individuals directly assisted me in recent months in completing this book. I am grateful to the McClelland & Stewart team at Penguin Random House Canada for your support and passion for this project—Kristin Cochrane, Jared Bland, and, in particular, my editor, Doug Pepper, and copy editor, Linda Pruessen. Thank you as well to my agent, Stephanie Sinclair of CookeMcDermid.

To my expert, diverse, and incredibly thoughtful team of manuscript reviewers: John Borrows, Clo Ostrove, Jane Philpott, Pep Philpott, Melissa Doyle, Irene Schmid, Diana Donato, Sarah Jane Barclay, Todd Barclay, and Lea Nicholas-MacKenzie—thank you for your encouragement and for your many edits and suggestions. Having your eyes on the words of this book has made it so much better.

Also, a big thank-you to Ethan Olinga Danesh, Anna Flaišmanová, and Melissa Doyle for your most able assistance with research and (those dreaded but important) citations.

Nothing is possible without my beautiful family. My feisty and unrelenting grandmother Pugladee (Ethel Pearson); my passionate and indomitable father, Hereditary Chief Hemas Kla-Lee-Lee-Kla (William Lane Wilson); my kind and generous mother, Sandra Wilson; and my amazing sister, Kory Wilson. I am who I am because of each of you. Gilakas'la for your teachings, wisdom, and love.

And most importantly, to my husband, Dr. Tim Raybould: thank you for your fierce opinions and passion and, most of all, for your constant love and support—with this book, and throughout our lives together. Kaija, Kaylene, Kadence—you do make all sacrifices worthwhile.

I also acknowledge my community of We Wai Kai (Cape Mudge), the Musgamagw Tsawataineuk and Laich-kwil-tach Peoples, and all our friends and family. Life in our communities—on our lands and territories, among our families, our cultures, our languages, and our traditions—is a unique and precious gift, a respite from all that is everywhere else. I am so grateful.

And finally, I want to express my thanks and pride for the generations of Indigenous Peoples—past, present, and future—who have shown resilience, strength, and steadfast determination to build a more just Canada. Our work continues . . .

Notes

INTRODUCTION

1 "Terminology," Indigenous Foundations, First Nations and Indigenous Studies, University of British Columbia, 2009, https://indigenousfoundations.arts.ubc.ca/terminology/.

2 R. v. Powley, [2003] 2 S.C.R. 207 (Can.).

3 "Gathering Strength: Canada's Aboriginal Action Plan," *Aboriginal Healing Foundation* (Ottawa: Minister of Indian Affairs and Northern Development, 1997), https://www.ahf.ca/downloads/gathering-strength.pdf.

4 National Centre for Truth and Reconciliation, "What We Have Learned," 2015, http://www.trc.ca/websites/trcinstitution/File/2015/Findings/Principles_2015_05_31_web_o.pdf.

5 Haida Nation v. British Columbia (Minister of Forests), [2004] 3 S.C.R. 511 (Can.).

6 Truth and Reconciliation Commission of Canada, *Truth and Reconciliation Commission of Canada: Calls to Action* (Winnipeg, MB: Truth and Reconciliation Commission of Canada, 2015), https://www2.gov.bc.ca/assets/gov/british-columbians-our-governments/indigenous-people/aboriginal-peoples-documents/calls_to_action_english2.pdf.

7 Taiaiaike Alfred, "It's All About the Land," in *Whose Land Is It Anyway?*, eds. Peter McFarlane and Nicole Schabus (Federation of Post-Secondary Educators of British Columbia, 2017), https://fpse.ca/sites/default/files/news_files/Decolonization%20Handbook.pdf, 11.

8 Arthur Manuel and Ronald M. Derrickson, *The Reconciliation Manifesto: Recovering the Land, Rebuilding the Economy* (Toronto: James Lorimer, 2018), 56, 98–99.

9 Mary C. Hurley and Jill Wherrett, *The Report of the Royal Commission on Aboriginal Peoples* (Ottawa: Parliamentary Research Branch, 1999), https://publications.gc.ca/Collection-R/LoPBdP/EB/prb9924-e.htm#:~:text=The%20Royal%20Commission%20on%20Aboriginal%20Peoples%20(RCAP)%20issued%20its%20final.

10   Truth and Reconciliation Commisson of Canada, *Honouring the Truth, Reconciling for the Future: Summary of the Final Report of the Truth and Reconciliation Commission of Canada* (Canada: Truth and Reconciliation Commission, 2015).

11   Marion Buller, Michèle Audette, Brian Eyolfson, and Qajaq Robinson, *Reclaiming Power and Place: The Final Report of the National Inquiry into Missing and Murdered Indigenous Women and Girls* (Canada: National Inquiry into Missing and Murdered Indigenous Women and Girls, 2019), https://www.mmiwg-ffada.ca/wp-content/uploads/2019/06/Final_Report_Vol_1a-1.pdf.

12   PBS, "Seven Generations—the Role of Chief," pbs.org, 2021, https://www.pbs.org/warrior/content/timeline/opendoor/roleOfChief.html.

13   Joe Karetak, Frank Tester, and Shirley Tagalik, eds., *Inuit Qaujimajatuqangit: What Inuit Have Always Known to Be True* (Halifax: Fernwood, 2017), https://fernwoodpublishing.ca/files/Excerpt_Inuit-Qaujimajatuqangit_9781552669921.pdf.

14   Frédéric Laugrand and Jarich Oosten, "Transfer of Inuit Qaujimajatuqangit in Modern Inuit Society," *Études Inuit Studies* 33, no. 1 (2009): https://doi.org/10.7202/044963ar.

PART I: LEARN

1   Aiyana Edmund, "Maya Angelou Quotes to Live By," Literary Ladies Guide, February 22, 2018, https://www.literaryladiesguide.com/author-quotes/maya-angelou-quotes-live/.

2   "History Repeating," College of Liberal Arts and Human Sciences, 2017, https://liberalarts.vt.edu/magazine/2017/history-repeating.html.

3   Nalaga Donna Cranmer, "Dzaxwan (Oolichan Fish): Stories My Elders Told Me," in *Knowing Home: Braiding Indigenous Science with Western Science*, eds. Gloria Snively and Wanosts'a7 Lorna Williams (Victoria, BC: University of Victoria, 2016), https://pressbooks.bccampus.ca/knowinghome/.

4   Cranmer, "Dzaxwan (Oolichan Fish): Stories My Elders Told Me," 181.

5   Susan Manitowabe, *Historical and Contemporary Realities: Movement Towards Reconciliation* (Creative Commons), 9–10. https://ecampusontario.pressbooks.pub/movementtowardsreconciliation/chapter/the-creation-story/).

6   Darwin Hanna and Mamie Henry, *Our Tellings: Interior Salish Stories of the Nlha'kápmx People* (Vancouver: UBC Press, 1995), 201.

7   Jo-ann Archibald, "Coyote Learns to Make a Storybasket: The Place of First Nations Stories in Education" (PhD diss., Simon Fraser University, 1997), 10. https://firstnationspedagogy.ca/storytelling.html.

8   Canadian Press, "Alert Bay, BC, Residential School to Be Demolished," Global News, February 15, 2015, https://globalnews.ca/news/1831807/alert-bay-residential-school-to-be-demolished/.

9   Katie Raskina, "Old Residential School to Be Torn Down in Île-à-La-Crosse," CBC, September 14, 2016, https://www.cbc.ca/news/canada/saskatchewan/old-residential-school-to-be-torn-down-in-ile-a-la-crosse-1.3761840.

10 Amy Attas, "How Storytelling in Tourism Can Support Truth and Reconciliation," *West Coast Traveller*, December 7, 2021, https://www.westcoasttraveller.com/how-storytelling-in-tourism-can-support-truth-and-reconciliation/.

11 Alex McKeen, "Here's How Four Former Canadian Residential Schools Are Being Used Today to Never Forget 'the Ugly Truth'— and to Heal," *Toronto Star*, June 8, 2021, https://www.thestar.com/news/canada/2021/06/07/heres-how-four-former-canadian-residential-schools-are-being-used-today-to-never-forget-the-ugly-truth-and-to-heal.html.

12 Bob Weber, "Two Former Residential Schools Named National Historic Sites," CTV News, September 1, 2020, https://www.ctvnews.ca/canada/two-former-residential-schools-named-national-historic-sites-1.5087347.

13 "Statement of Apology to Former Students of Indian Residential Schools," Government of Canada, June 11, 2008, https://www.rcaanc-cirnac.gc.ca/eng/1100100015644/1571589171655.

14 Truth and Reconciliation Commission of Canada, *Truth and Reconciliation Commission of Canada: Calls to Action* (Winnipeg, MB: Truth and Reconciliation Commission of Canada, 2015), https://www2.gov.bc.ca/assets/gov/british-columbians-our-governments/indigenous-people/aboriginal-peoples-documents/calls_to_action_english2.pdf.

15 Canadian Press, "BC Homework Assignment Asks for 'Positive Experiences with Residential Schools,'" NanaimoNewsNOW, November 25, 2020, https://nanaimonewsnow.com/2020/11/25/b-c-homework-assignment-asks-for-positive-experiences-with-residential-schools/.

16 Allana McDougall, "Teacher, School Board Apologize to Family for Inappropriate Assignment," APTN News, June 18, 2020, https://www.aptnnews.ca/national-news/teacher-school-board-apologize-to-ontario-family-for-inappropriate-assignment/.

17 British Columbia College of Family Physicians (BCCFP), "Addressing Indigenous-Specific Racism and Discrimination in Health Care," December 2, 2020, https://bccfp.bc.ca/about-us/news/addressing-indigenous-specific-racism-and-discrimination-in-health-care/.

18 "Iroquois Creation Myth," Commack School District, n.d., https://www.cs.williams.edu/~lindsey/myths/myths_12.html.

19 Pauktuutit Inuit Women of Canada, *The Inuit Way: A Guide to Inuit Culture*, Chaire de Recherche Sentinelle Nord Sur Les Relations Avec Les Sociétés Inuit (Quebec City, QC: Université Laval, 2006), https://www.relations-inuit.chaire.ulaval.ca/sites/relations-inuit.chaire.ulaval.ca/files/InuitWay_e.pdf.

20 "Sleep Not Longer, O Choctaws and Chickasaws," History Is a Weapon, n.d., https://www.historyisaweapon.com/defcon1/tecumsehsleepnotlonger.html.

21 "Letter to Prime Minister Wilfred Laurier from the Chiefs of the Shuswap, Okanagan and Couteau Tribes," August 25, 1910, http://www.skeetchestn.ca/files/documents/Governance/memorialtosirwilfredlaurier1910.pdf.

22 "Constitution of the Iroquois Nation,"n.d., https://cscie12.dce.harvard.edu/ssi/iroquois/simple/1.shtml. The Great Law of Peace is dated 1451, though some sources say it goes back to c. 1190.

23 Franz Boas, "A Year Among the Eskimo," *Journal of the American Geographical Society of New York* 19 (1887): 383–402, https://www.jstor.org/stable/196741.

24 Quoted in Gwi'molas, "'Playing the Hand You're Dealt,'" 10–11, https://dspace.library.uvic.ca/handle/1828/11535.

25 Quoted in "The Story Box: Franz Boas, George Hunt, and the Making of Anthropology," Bard Graduate Center Gallery, February 14–July 7, 2019, https://www.bgc.bard.edu/files/Boas_PressBrochureFinal-2.pdf.

26 René Dussault and Georges Erasmus, *Report of the Royal Commission on Aboriginal Peoples*, vol. 1: *Looking Forward, Looking Back* (Ottawa: Indian and Northern Affairs Canada, 1996), as summarized

at "Highlights from the Report of the Royal Commission on Aboriginal Peoples," http://data2.archives.ca/e/e448/e011188230-01.pdf.

27 Pauktuutit, *The Inuit Way*, 4.

28 Quoted in "The Doctrine of Discovery and the Church's Complicity," Missio Alliance, October 12, 2020, https://www.missioalliance.org/the-doctrine-of-discovery-and-the-churchs-complicity/.

29 The Bull Romanus Pontifex (Nicholas V), January 8, 1455 (Granting the Portuguese a perpetual monopoly in trade with Africa), https://www.papalencyclicals.net/nicholo5/romanus-pontifex.htm.

30 "Patent Granted by King Henry VII to John Cabot and His Sons, March 1496," Heritage Newfoundland & Labrador, https://www.heritage.nf.ca/articles/exploration/1496-cabot-patent.php.

31 "Letter Addendum: Memorial to Sir Wilfrid Laurier, Premier of the Dominion of Canada, August 25, 1910," *Kamloops This Week*, February 12, 2013, https://www.kamloopsthisweek.com/opinion/letter-addendum-memorial-to-sir-wilfrid-laurier-4388477.

32 René Dussault and Georges Erasmus, *Report of the Royal Commission on Aboriginal Peoples*, vol. 1: *Looking Forward, Looking Back* (Ottawa: Indian and Northern Affairs Canada, 1996), as summarized at "Highlights from the Report of the Royal Commission on Aboriginal Peoples," http://data2.archives.ca/e/e448/e011188230-01.pdf.

33 Quoted in "Haudenosaunee to the White Brothers Two Row Wampum 1613," Onondaga Nation, n.d., https://www.onondaganation.org/history/quotes/.

34 Ellen Gabriel, "Ka'swenh:tha—The Two Row Wampum: Reconciliation Through An Ancient Agreement," in *Reconciliation and The Way Forward*, eds. Shelagh Rogers, Mike Degagné, Glen Lowry, and Sara Fryer (Ottawa: Aboriginal Healing Foundation, 2014).

35 "Royal Proclamation, 1763," Indigenous Foundations.arts.ubc.ca, First Nations and Indigenous Studies, University of British Columbia, https://indigenousfoundations.arts.ubc.ca/royal_proclamation_1763/.

36 Quoted in John Borrows, *Wampum at Niagara: The Royal Proclamation, Canadian Legal History, and Self-Government* (1997), 230, https://www.sfu.ca/~palys/Borrows-WampumAtNiagara.pdf.

37 Quoted in Borrows, *Wampum at Niagara*, 77. (Brackets in original.)

38 Quoted in "Louis Riel," Barrie Métis Council, https://barriemetiscouncil.com/metis-history/service.php?id=1.

39 Quoted in "Métis Culture Cards: The Métis Flag," Rupertsland Institute, May 29, 2019, http://www.rupertsland.org/wp-content/uploads/2019/06/Culture-Cards-29May2019.pdf?r=1.

40 Quoted in Robert Boyd, "Smallpox in the Pacific Northwest: The First Epidemics," *BC Studies* 101, no. 1 (1994): 22, https://ojs.library.ubc.ca/index.php/bcstudies/article/download/864/905/3662.

41 Quoted in Boyd, "Smallpox in the Pacific Northwest," 13.

42 Quoted in Council of the Haida Nation, *Haida Laas: Journal of the Haida Nation* (March 2009), 15, https://www.haidanation.ca/wp-content/uploads/2017/03/jl_mar.09.pdf.

43 Archibald Barclay to James Douglas, December 1849, as quoted in Derek Pethick, *James Douglas: Servant of Two Empires* (Vancouver: Mitchell Press, 1969), 77–78.

44 J. Trutch, "Memorandum on a Letter treating of condition of the Indians in Vancouver Island addressed to Secretary to the Aborigines Protection Society by Mr. Wm. Sebright Green," January 13, 1870, https://bcgenesis.uvic.ca/B70008.html.

45 Quoted in Darren R. Préfontaine with Leah Dorion, "The Metis and the Spirit of Resistance," Métis Museum, n.d., 5, https://www.metismuseum.ca/media/document.php/00740.Resistance.pdf.

46 "Louis Riel Quotes," Manitoba Métis Foundation, https://www.mmf.mb.ca/louis-riel-quotes.

47 Duncan Campbell Scott, "Indian Affairs, 1763–1841," in *Canada and Its Provinces*, vol. 4, eds. Adam Shortt and A.G. Doughty (Toronto: T. and A. Constable, 1913), 329–62.

48 Dispatch from the Earl of Gosford, Quebec City, to Lord Glenelg, Downing Street, London. Quoted in Andrew Armitage, "Canada: The General Structure of Canadian Indian Policy," in *Comparing the Policy of Aboriginal Assimilation: Australia, Canada, and New Zealand* (Vancouver: University of British Columbia Press, 1995), 75, https://files.eric.ed.gov/fulltext/ED403094.pdf.

49 British Parliamentary Papers, "Report of the House of Commons Select Committee on Aborigines, 1837," in *Correspondence Returns and Other Papers Relating to Canada and the Indian Problem Therein, 1839* (Dublin: Irish University Press, 1969), 44, quoted in Armitage, *Comparing the Policy of Aboriginal Assimilation*.

50 Duncan Campbell Scott, "Indian, 1840–1867," in Shortt and Doughty, eds., *Canada and Its Provinces*, vol. 5: 695–725.

51 "Report of the Committee of the Executive Council . . . respecting the Indian Department, Quebec City, 13 July 1837," quoted in Armitage, *Comparing the Policy of Aboriginal Assimilation.*

52 Quoted in "Inuit History and Heritage," Inuit Tapiriit Kanatami, 2016, 12, https://www.itk.ca/wp-content/uploads/2016/07/5000 YearHeritage_0.pdf.

53 Quoted in "Inuit History and Heritage," 12.

54 British North American Act, 1867, SS 1867, c 3, https://www.canlii.org/ en/sk/laws/stat/ss-1867-c-3/latest/ss-1867-c-3.html.

55 Evidence given by Deputy Superintendent-General Duncan Campbell Scott in his remarks to the 1920 Special Committee of the House of Commons, National Archives of Canada, Record Group 10, vol. 6810, file 470-2-3, vol. 7, 55 (L-3) and 63 (N-3).

56 Quoted in Robin Fisher, "Joseph Trutch and Indian Land Policy," *BC Studies* 12 (Winter 1971–72): 11, https://ojs.library.ubc.ca/index. php/bcstudies/article/download/719/761/3084.

57 Quoted in Gerry St. Germain and Lillian E. Dyck, "First Nations Elections: The Choice Is Inherently Theirs," Report of the Standing Senate Committee on Aboriginal Peoples (Ottawa: 2010), 4, https:// publications.gc.ca/collections/collection_2011/sen/yc28-0/YC28-0-403-3-eng.pdf.

58 APTN National News, "'A Lament for Confederation': A Speech by Chief Dan George in 1967," APTN News, July 1, 2017, https:// www.aptnnews.ca/national-news/a-lament-for-confederation-a-speech-by-chief-dan-george-in-1967/.

59 "The Role of the Churches," Facing History and Ourselves, 2012, https://www.facinghistory.org/stolen-lives-indigenous-peoples-canada-and-indian-residential-schools/chapter-3/role-churches.

60 "The Role of the Churches."

61 Department of the Interior, *Annual Report for the year ended 30th June, 1876,* quoted in Dussault and Erasmus, *Report of the Royal Commission on Aboriginal Peoples,* vol. 1: 255.

62 Session of the 6th Parliament of the Dominion of Canada, 1887, quoted in *Stolen Lives: The Indigenous Peoples of Canada and the Indian Residential Schools,* "Facing History and Ourselves," 2018, 37, https://www.facinghistory.org/stolen-lives-indigenous-peoples-canada-and-indian-residential-schools/chapter-3/introduction.

63 Quoted in Mark Kennedy, "'Simply a Savage': How the Residential Schools Came to Be," *Ottawa Citizen*, May 22, 2015, https://ottawacitizen.com/news/politics/simply-a-savage-how-the-residential-schools-came-to-be.

64 Canada, *Debates of the House of Commons*, May 22, 1883, 1st Session, 5th Parliament, 1376.

65 Canada, *Debates of the House of Commons*, May 9, 1883, 1st Session, 5th Parliament, 1107–8.

66 Quoted in Megan Harvey, "Story People: Stó:lō-State Relations and Indigenous Literacies in British Columbia, 1864–1874," *Journal of the Canadian Historical Association* 24, no.1 (May 12, 2014): 51–88, https://www.erudit.org/en/journals/jcha/1900-v1-n1-jcha01400/1024997ar/.

67 Quoted in Calder et al. v. Attorney General of British Columbia, [1973] S.C.R. 313 (Can.), https://www.canlii.org/en/ca/scc/doc/1973/1973canlii4/1973canlii4.html. Preceded by this statement: "The Nisga'a answer to government assertions of absolute ownership of the land within their boundaries was made as early as 1888 before the first Royal Commission to visit the Nass Valley."

68 Riel's complete speech can be found in Michael Bliss, ed., *The Queen vs. Louis Riel* (Toronto: University of Toronto Press, 1974), 311–25.

69 Crown-Indigenous Relations and Northern Affairs Canada, "The Numbered Treaties (1871–1921)," last modified May 13, 2020, https://www.rcaanc-cirnac.gc.ca/eng/1360948213124/1544620003549.

70 Quoted in Truth and Reconciliation Commission, *Final Report*, vol.1: *Canada's Residential Schools: The History, Part 1* (Montreal: McGill-Queen's University Press, 2015), 119.

71 Quoted in Truth and Reconciliation Commission, vol. 1: *Canada's Residential Schools: The History, Part 1*, 119.

72 Quoted in Truth and Reconciliation Commission, vol. 1: *Canada's Residential Schools: The History, Part 1*, 119.

73 Quoted in Truth and Reconciliation Commission, vol. 1: *Canada's Residential Schools: The History, Part 1*, 119.

74 Quoted in Truth and Reconciliation Commission, vol. 1: *Canada's Residential Schools: The History, Part 1*, 119.

75 Quoted in Harold Cardinal and Walter Hildebrand, *Treaty Elders of Saskatchewan: Our Dream Is That Our Peoples Will One Day Be Clearly Recognized As Nations* (Calgary: University of Calgary Press, 2000), 20.

76 Quoted in Cardinal and Hildebrand, *Treaty Elders of Saskatchewan*, 32.

77 Quoted in "Treaty Negotiations, July 1871 to October 1873, Between
    Canada and First Nations of Manitoba and the Northwest Territories,"
    Confederation Debates 1865–1994, 2–3 and 10, https://hcmc.uvic.ca/
    confederation/en/Morris_Chapter_05.html.

78 Quoted in Alexander Morris, *The Treaties of Canada with the Indians
    of Manitoba and the NorthWest Territories Including the Negotiations
    On Which They Were Based, and Other Information Relating Thereto*
    (Saskatoon: Fifth House, 1991), 211, 233, and 239.

79 Quoted in "Creator—Land—People: Negotiations Continue (1876),"
    Treaty 6 Education, n.d., https://treaty6education.lskysd.ca/
    negotiations.html.

80 Quoted in "Inuit History and Heritage."

81 William M. Halliday, *Potlatch and Totem, and the Recollections of an
    Indian Agent* (London: J.M. Dent & Sons, 1935), 4.

82 Quoted in Joy Inglis and Harry Assu, *Assu of Cape Mudge: Recollections
    of a Coastal Indian Chief* (Vancouver: University of British Columbia
    Press, 2006), 103–4.

83 Darcy Anne Mitchell, "The Allied Indian Tribes of British Columbia:
    A Study in Pressure Group Behaviour" (master's thesis, University of
    British Columbia, 1977), 1, https://open.library.ubc.ca/media/stream/
    pdf/831/1.0094337/1.

84 Quoted in Mitchell, "The Allied Indian Tribes of British Columbia," 130.

85 Quoted in Mitchell, "The Allied Indian Tribes of British Columbia,"
    21–22.

86 Special Joint Committee on the Senate and House of Commons
    Appointed to Inquire into the Allied Tribes of British Columbia,
    Session 1926–27 (Ottawa: King's Printer, 1927), https://parl.canadiana.
    ca/view/oop.com_SOCHOC_1601_1_1/5.

87 Indian Act, R.S.C., ch. I–5.

88 Canada, Department of Northern Affairs and National Resources,
    Annual Report, 1955, quoted in Truth and Reconciliation Commission
    of Canada, *The Final Report of the Truth and Reconciliation Commission
    of Canada*, vol. 2: *Canada's Residential Schools: The Inuit and Northern
    Experience* (Montreal: McGill-Queen's University Press, 2015), 76,
    https://indigenous.usask.ca/images/resoures-images/aVolume_2_
    Inuit_and_Northern_English_Web.pdf.

89 Quoted in Qikiqtani Inuit Association, *Qikiqtani Truth Commission: Community Histories 1950–1975* (Iqaluit: Inhabit Media, 2014), 33, https://www.qtcommission.ca/sites/default/files/community/community_histories_iqaluit.pdf.

90 Quoted in Qikiqtani Inuit Association, *Qikiqtani Truth Commission*, 26.

91 Quoted in Qikiqtani Inuit Association, *Qikiqtani Truth Commission*, 27.

92 Quoted in Truth and Reconciliation Commission *The Final Report of the Truth and Reconciliation Commission of Canada*, vol. 2: *Canada's Residential Schools*, 79.

93 Prime Minister Diefenbaker, speech to the House of Commons on January 19, 1960, as reported in Hansard, 3rd Session, 24th Parliament, 8 Elizabeth II, 1960, House of Commons of Canada Bill C-2 1952-53, c. 41; An Act to amend the Indian Act, quoted at Diefenbaker Canada Centre, https://diefenbaker.usask.ca/exhibits/online-exhibits-content/the-enfranchisement-of-aboriginal-peoples-in-canada-en.php.

94 "Memo from Ellen Fairclough, Superintendent-General of Indian Affairs and Minister of Citizenship and Immigration to PM Diefenbaker," quoted at Diefenbaker Canada Centre, https://diefenbaker.usask.ca/exhibits/online-exhibits-content/the-enfranchisement-of-aboriginal-peoples-in-canada-en.php.

95 Quoted in "First Nations Right to Vote Granted 50 Years Ago," CBC News, July 1, 2010, https://www.cbc.ca/news/canada/north/first-nations-right-to-vote-granted-50-years-ago-1.899354.

96 "Two Indians Challenge Powers of White Man," *Daily Free Press*, July 8, 1963.

97 Regina v. White and Bob, CANL11, 643 (SCC), September 12, 1963, para. 22–23.

98 Quoted in Hamar Foster, Jeremy H. A. Webber, and Heather Raven, eds., *Let Right Be Done: Aboriginal Title, the Calder Case, and the Future of Indigenous Rights* (Vancouver: University of British Columbia Press, 2007), 202, https://scholars.wlu.ca/cgi/viewcontent.cgi?article=3119&context=etd.

99 Quoted in "Honouring Our Past—Dr. Frank Calder," Nisga'a Lisims Government, n.d., https://www.nisgaanation.ca/news/honouring-our-past-dr-frank-calder.

100 Quoted in Terry Fenge and Jim Aldridge, *Keeping Promises: The Royal Proclamation of 1763, Aboriginal Rights, and Treaties in Canada* (Montreal: McGill-Queen's University Press, 2015), 109.

101 Quoted in Mark Hume, "No. 6: Frank Calder," *Globe and Mail*, April 3, 2005, https://www.theglobeandmail.com/news/national/no-6-frank-calder/article1116728/.

102 Quoted in H.A.C. Cairns, S.M. Jamieson, and K. Lysyk, "A Survey of the Contemporary Indians of Canada," vol. 1 (Canada: Indian Affairs Branch, 1966), https://caid.ca/HawRep1a1966.pdf.

103 "Prime Minister Pierre Elliot Trudeau: Remarks on Indian Aboriginal Treaty Rights: Part of a Speech Given August 8th, 1969 in Vancouver British Columbia," Internet Archive, https://archive.org/details/primeministertruoounse.

104 "Statement of the Government of Canada on Indian Policy, 1969," https://epe.lac-bac.gc.ca/100/200/301/inac-ainc/indian_policy-e/cp1969_e.pdf.

105 From the Foreword, "Statement of the Government of Canada on Indian Policy, 1969," https://epe.lac-bac.gc.ca/100/200/301/inac-ainc/indian_policy-e/cp1969_e.pdf.

106 Quoted in Dussault and Erasmus, *Report of the Royal Commission on Aboriginal Peoples*, vol. 1, 205.

107 Quoted in Martin Lawrence, *Chrétien: The Will to Win* (Toronto: Lester, 1995), 198, https://archive.org/details/chretienvolume1woooomart/page/198/mode/2up.

108 Harold Cardinal, *The Unjust Society: The Tragedy of Canada's Indians* (Edmonton: H.G. Hurtig, 1969), 139.

109 Cardinal, *The Unjust Society*, 140.

110 Quoted in Naithan Lagace, "The White Paper, 1969," Canadian Encyclopedia, last edited June 2020, https://www.thecanadianencyclopedia.ca/en/article/the-white-paper-1969.

111 Assembly of First Nations, "Charter of the Assembly of First Nations" (1985), https://www.afn.ca/wp-content/uploads/2021/09/AFN-Charter-Ammended-06JUL2021.pdf.

112 "National Representational Organization for Inuit in Canada," Inuit Tapiriit Kanatami, n.d., https://www.itk.ca/.

113 "Home," Métis National Council, n.d., https://www2.metisnation.ca.

114 Quoted in the MacKenzie Valley Pipeline Inquiry, *The Report of the MacKenzie Valley Pipeline Inquiry*, "Epilogue: Themes for the National Interest," Prince of Wales Northern Heritage Centre, 1977, https://www.pwnhc.ca/extras/berger/report/BergerV1_ch12_e.pdf.

115 Quoted in "Natives Speak Out," Canada: A People's History (CBC), n.d., https://www.cbc.ca/history/EPISCONTENTSE1EP17CH2 PA1LE.html.

116 Quoted in "Berger Commission," Canadian Encyclopedia, last edited November 12, 2020, https://www.thecanadianencyclopedia.ca/en/ article/berger-commission.

117 Union of British Columbia Indian Chiefs, Special General Assembly, May 14 and 15, 1981, Vancouver, BC, https://constitution.ubcic.bc.ca/ sites/constitution.ubcic.bc.ca/files/OCRSGA1981-05-14&15 (NoClippings).pdf.

118 R v. Secretary of State for Foreign and Commonwealth Affairs, ex parte Indian Association of Alberta, No. 82-0007, [1982] E.W.C.A. Civ Jo128-1 (U.K.), para. 13-14, http://vlex.co.uk/vid/r-v-secretary-of-793772805.

119 Quoted in Union of British Columbia Indian Chiefs, "The Indian Nations and the Federal Government's View on the Constitution," 13, https://constitution.ubcic.bc.ca/sites/constitution.ubcic.bc.ca/ files/OCRIndianNations&FederalGovView.pdf.

120 Quoted in Karilyn Toovey, "Decolonizing or Recolonizing: Indigenous Peoples and the Law in Canada" (master's thesis, University of Lethbridge, 2005), 13, https://dspace.library.uvic.ca/ bitstream/handle/1828/744/toovey_2005.pdf.

121 Constitution Act, 1982, being Schedule B to the Canada Act 1982 (U.K.), 1982, c 11.

122 Secretariat of the Conference, "Federal-Provincial Conference of First Ministers on Aboriginal Constitutional Matters," Document 800-17/004, PrimaryDocuments.ca, March 15-16, 1983, https:// primarydocuments.ca/wp-content/uploads/2018/07/1stMinConf AboVerb1983Mar15.pdf.

123 "Federal-Provincial Conference of First Ministers on Aboriginal Constitutional Matters," Document 800-17/004, PrimaryDocuments. ca, March 15-16, 1983, https://primarydocuments.ca/wp-content/ uploads/2018/07/1stMinConfAboVerb1983Mar15.pdf.

124 Quoted in Craig Baird, "Elijah Harper," Canadian History Ehx, June 18, 2022, https://canadaehx.com/2022/06/18/elijah-harper/.

125 Quoted in Allan Levine, "Native Leader Elijah Harper Helped Scuttle Meech Lake," Globe and Mail, May 20, 2013, https:// www.theglobeandmail.com/news/politics/native-leader-elijah- harper-helped-scuttle-meech-lake/article12033338/.

126 Quoted in Levine, "Native Leader Elijah Harper Helped Scuttle Meech Lake."

127 Dussault and Erasmus, *Report of the Royal Commission on Aboriginal Peoples*, vol. 1, 209.

128 "25 Years since Elijah Harper Said 'No' to Meech Lake Accord," CBC News, June 11, 2015, https://www.cbc.ca/news/canada/manitoba/25-years-since-elijah-harper-said-no-to-the-meech-lake-accord-1.3110439.

129 "Charlottetown Accord," Canadian Encyclopedia, last edited October 14, 2014, https://www.thecanadianencyclopedia.ca/en/article/charlottetown-accord-document.

130 "George Erasmus on Self-Government, 1990" (speech, Empire Club of Canada, November 29, 1990), Great Canadian Speeches, https://greatcanadianspeeches.ca/2018/03/27/george-erasmus-on-self-government-1990/.

131 Brian Mulroney to Tony Penikett (Government Leader, Yukon Territory) and Dennis Patterson (Government Leader, Northwest Territories), November 15, 1990, PCO 2150-1, Identification Number 34788, TRC Document Number TRC3379, https://www.aptntv.ca/news/wp-content/uploads/sites/4/2015/04/MulroneyletterstoNWTandYukon.pdf.

132 Dussault and Erasmus, *Report of the Royal Commission on Aboriginal Peoples*, vol. 1.

133 Delgamuukw v. British Columbia, [1997] 3 S.C.R. 1010 (Can.), para 186, https://scc-csc.lexum.com/scc-csc/scc-csc/en/item/1569/index.do?q=%5B1997%5D+3+SCR+1010.

134 Haida Nation v. British Columbia (Minister of Forests), [2004] S.C.R. 73 (Can.), https://scc-csc.lexum.com/scc-csc/scc-csc/en/item/2189/index.do.

135 Mikisew Cree First Nation v. Canada (Minister of Canadian Heritage), [2005] 3 S.C.R. 388 (Can.), para 1, https://scc-csc.lexum.com/scc-csc/scc-csc/en/item/17288/index.do.

136 Currently, there are seven First Nations implementing modern treaties under three Final Agreements signed under the BC Treaty Process: Maa-Nulth First Nations (comprising Huu-ay-aht First Nations, Ka:'yu:'k't'h'/Che:k'tles7et'h' First Nations, Toquaht Nation, Uchucklesaht Tribe, and Yuułuiłath [Ucluelet] First Nation); Tla'amin Nation; and Tsawwassen First Nation (see BC Treaty Commission,

Annual Report 2021, 12, https://www.bctreaty.ca/sites/default/files/
BCTC_Annual_Report_2021_web.pdf).

137 Quoted in "The Creation of Nunavut," Listening To Our Past, n.d.,
http://www.traditional-knowledge.ca/english/the-creation-nunavut-
s153.html.

138 Quoted in "Principals and Parties: Treaties and Agreements," BC Treaty
Commission, n.d., https://www.bctreaty.ca/principals-and-parties.

139 Douglas R. Eyford, *A New Direction: Advancing Aboriginal and
Treaty Rights* (Ottawa: Crown-Indigenous Relations and Northern
Affairs Canada, 2015), https://www.rcaanc-cirnac.gc.ca/DAM/DAM-
CIRNAC-RCAANC/DAM-TAG/STAGING/texte-text/eyford_
newDirection-report_april2015_1427810490332_eng.pdf.

140 Quoted in Katie Hyslop, "The Kelowna Accord, Racism and the
Child Welfare Crisis," *The Tyee*, May 22, 2018, https://thetyee.ca/
News/2018/05/22/Kelowna-Accord-Racism-Child-Welfare/.

141 Turtle Island Native Network, "Aboriginals and First Nations News
and Information," www.turtleisland.org, n.d., http://www.turtleisland.
org/news/kelownaaccord.html.

142 "Schedule N: Mandate for the Truth and Reconciliation Commission,"
Government of Canada, https://www.residentialschoolsettlement.ca/
SCHEDULE_N.pdf.

143 "Indian Residential Schools Statement of Apology—Prime Minister
Stephen Harper," Government of Canada, June 11, 2008, https://
www.ourcommons.ca/DocumentViewer/en/39-2/house/sitting-110/
hansard.

144 "The Day of the Apology," Government of Canada, June 11, 2008,
https://www.rcaanc-cirnac.gc.ca/eng/1100100015697/1571589725919.

145 Quoted in Joanna Smith, "School 'Atrocity' Affected Generations,
Survivor Says," *Toronto Star*, June 11, 2008, https://www.thestar.com/
news/canada/2008/06/11/schools_atrocity_affected_generations
_survivor_says.html.

146 Quoted in "Harper Apologizes for Residential School Abuse," CTV
News, June 11, 2008, https://www.ctvnews.ca/harper-apologizes-for-
residential-school-abuse-1.301603.

147 "Indian Residential Schools Statement of Apology—Mary Simon,
President, Inuit Tapiriit Kanatami," Government of Canada,
June 11, 2008, https://www.rcaanc-cirnac.gc.ca/eng/1100100015707
/1571590053915.

148 "Indian Residential Schools Statement of Apology—Beverley
    Jacobs, President, Native Women's Association," Government
    of Canada, June 11, 2008, https://www.rcaanc-cirnac.gc.ca/
    eng/1100100015717/1571590149046

149 "Closing Words," The TRC Report Online, 2015, https://nevillepark.
    github.io/trc/challenge/#closing-words.

150 Marion Buller, Michèle Audette, Brian Eyolfson, and Qajaq Robinson,
    Reclaiming Power and Place: Executive Summary of the Final Report,
    vol. 1b (Canada: National Inquiry into Missing and Murdered Indi-
    genous Women and Girls, 2019), 167, https://www.mmiwg-ffada.ca/
    wp-content/uploads/2019/06/Final_Report_Vol_1b-1.pdf.

151 "General Assembly Adopts Declaration on Rights of Indigenous
    Peoples; 'Major Step Forward' Towards Human Rights for All, Says
    President," United Nations, September 13, 2007, https://www.un.org/
    press/en/2007/ga10612.doc.htm.

152 Quoted in "Canada Votes 'No' as UN Native Rights Declaration Passes,"
    CBC News, September 13, 2007, https://www.cbc.ca/news/canada/
    canada-votes-no-as-un-native-rights-declaration-passes-1.632160.

153 Quoted in "Canada Votes 'No'."

154 "Speech Delivered at the United Nations Permanent Forum on
    Indigenous Issues, New York, May 10," Indigenous and Northern
    Affairs Canada (Hon. Carolyn Bennett), May 10, 2016, https://
    www.canada.ca/en/indigenous-northern-affairs/news/2016/05/
    speech-delivered-at-the-united-nations-permanent-forum-on-
    indigenous-issues-new-york-may-10-.html.

155 Quoted in Heather Scoffield, "Assembly of First Nations Asks
    UN to See if Ottawa's Meeting Legal Obligations," Global News,
    December 6, 2011, https://globalnews.ca/news/186079/assembly-of-
    first-nations-asks-un-to-see-if-ottawas-meeting-legal-obligations/.

156 Bill C-45 is a budget bill of the Harper government with changes
    made to environmental legislation.

157 Quoted in Sarah Van Gelder, "Why Canada's Indigenous Uprising
    Is About All of Us," *YES!*, February 8, 2013, https://www.yesmagazine.
    org/issue/issues-how-cooperatives-are-driving-the-new-economy/
    2013/02/08/why-canada2019s-indigenous-uprising-is-about-all-of-us.

158 "First Nations Meeting with PM Thrown into Disarray," CBC News,
    January 10, 2013 [video], https://www.cbc.ca/news/politics/first-
    nations-meeting-with-pm-thrown-into-disarray-1.1381808.

159 Haida Nation v. British Columbia (Minister of Forests), [2004]
     S.C.R. 73 (Can.), para 20, https://scc-csc.lexum.com/scc-csc/scc-csc/
     en/item/2189/index.do.

160 Tsilhqot'in Nation v. British Columbia [2014], 2 S.C.R. 257 (Can.),
     paras 97 and 94, https://scc-csc.lexum.com/scc-csc/scc-csc/en/
     item/14246/index.do.

161 "Remarks by the Prime Minister in the House of Commons on
     the Recognition and Implementation of Rights Framework,"
     Prime Minister of Canada, February 14, 2018, https://pm.gc.ca/en/
     news/speeches/2018/02/14/remarks-prime-minister-house-commons-
     recognition-and-implementation-rights.

162 Quoted in Jocelyn Thorpe, "Truth and Reconciliation," NiCHE,
     October 24, 2012, https://niche-canada.org/2012/10/24/truth-and-
     reconciliation/.

163 Mary Simon, "Through the Eyes of the North: Our Collective
     Responsibility" (Courchette Lecture, Queen's University, Kingston,
     ON, April 12, 2022), https://www.gg.ca/en/media/news/2022/queens-
     university-courchene-lecture-through-eyes-north-our-collective-
     responsibility.

PART 2: UNDERSTAND

1   "Chief Dan George Quotes and Sayings," inspiringquotes.us,
    https://www.inspiringquotes.us/author/3730-chief-dan-george.

2   Elder Jackie, quoted at "EMJ's Commitment to Truth and
    Reconciliation," Ethel M. Johnson School, June 21, 2021, https://
    school.cbe.ab.ca/school/EthelMJohnson/about-us/school/principal-
    message/Lists/Posts/Post.aspx?ID=81.

3   Sioux proverb.

4   Cambridge Advanced Learner's Dictionary & Thesaurus, s.v.
    "reconciliation," https://dictionary.cambridge.org/dictionary/english/
    reconciliation).

5   YourDictionary, s.v. "reconciliation," https://www.yourdictionary.com/
    reconciliation.

6   "Privilege," RationalWiki, n.d., https://rationalwiki.org/wiki/
    Privilege#Privilege_blindness.

7   Kendra Cherry, "What Is Anti-Racism?", VeryWellMind, June 16,
    2021, https://www.verywellmind.com/what-is-anti-racism-5071426.

8   Ibram X. Kendi, *How to Be an Antiracist* (New York: Random House, 2019), 9.

9   Sara Clarke-Habibi, "Transforming Worldviews: The Case of Education for Peace in Bosnia and Herzegovina," *Journal of Transformative Education* 3, no. 1 (January 2005): 33–56, https:// doi.org/10.1177/1541344604270238 (citations omitted).

10   This phrase is widely attributed to Sir John A. Macdonald. See, for example: Sean Fine, "Chief Justice Says Canada Attempted 'Cultural Genocide' on Aboriginals," *Globe and Mail*, May 28, 2015, https:// www.theglobeandmail.com/news/national/chief-justice-says-canada-attempted-cultural-genocide-on-aboriginals/article24688854/.

11   Ontario Institute for Studies in Education (OISE), "Understanding Indigenous Perspectives—Indigenous Worldviews," August 2016, https://www.oise.utoronto.ca/abed101/wp-content/uploads/ sites/9/2016/08/Module-indigenous-worldviews-plain-text-file.pdf.

12   Marie Battiste, ed., *Reclaiming Indigenous Voice and Vision* (Vancouver: UBC Press, 2009), 85.

13   Chief Crowfoot (Blackfoot), quoted in Susan Ratcliffe, ed., *Oxford Essential Quotations*, 4th ed. (New York: Oxford University Press, 2016).

14   "Piikani Blackfoot Teaching," Four Directions Teachings, 2006–2012, http://www.fourdirectionsteachings.com/transcripts/blackfoot.html.

15   Alice Williams, "The Spirit of My Quilts," *Canadian Women Studies* 10 (1989): 49–51.

16   Evelyn Steinhauer, quoted in "Our Words, Our Ways: Teaching First Nations, Métis and Inuit Learners" (Edmonton: Alberta Board of Education, Aboriginal Services Branch and Learning and Teaching Resources Branch, 2005), 16, https://education.alberta.ca/ media/3615876/our-words-our-ways.pdf.

17   Shirley Tagalik, "Inuit Qaujimajatuqangit: The Role of Indigenous Knowledge in Supporting the Wellness of Inuit Communities in Nunavut," National Collaborating Centre for Indigenous Health (Prince George, BC: National Collaborating Centre for Indigenous Health, n.d.), https://www.ccnsa-nccah.ca/docs/health/FS-InuitQaujimajatuqangitWellnessNunavut-Tagalik-EN.pdf (citations omitted).

18   "Métis Culture & Tradition," Rupertsland Institute, January 25, 2022, https://www.rupertsland.org/wp-content/uploads/2022/03/Metis-Culture-and-Traditions-Foundational-Knowledge-Themes-01.25.22.pdf.

19 Métis Family Services, in Kinai Board of Education et al., quoted in "Our Words, Our Ways," 9.

20 Andrea Bear-Nicholas, "Responsibilities Not Rights: A Native Perspective," in *Human Rights in New Brunswick: A New Vision for a New Century*, eds. John McEvoy and Constantine Passaris (Fredericton: New Brunswick Human Rights Commission, 1993), 35.

21 Ontario Institute for Studies in Education (OISE), "Understanding Indigenous Perspectives—The Power of Collective Wisdom: Power Over vs. Power With," August 2016, https://www.oise.utoronto.ca/abed101/wp-content/uploads/sites/9/2016/08/Module-indigenous-worldviews-plain-text-file.pdf.

22 Tagalik, "Inuit Qaujimajatuqangit."

23 Stephen J. Augustine, Hereditary Chief and Keptin of the Mi'kmaq Grand Council, quoted in "Oral Traditions," Indigenous Foundations, First Nations and Indigenous Studies, University of British Columbia, https://indigenousfoundations.arts.ubc.ca/oral_traditions/.

24 "Storytelling," Métis Gathering, Métis Nation-Saskatchewan and Canadian Geographic, 2022, https://metisgathering.ca/history-culture/storytelling/.

25 Maria Campbell, Métis author, playwright, broadcaster, filmmaker and Elder, quoted in "Storytelling."

26 Greg Young-Ing, quoted in "Our Words, Our Ways," 25.

27 Leroy Little Bear, "Jagged Worldviews Colliding," in Marie Battiste, ed., *Reclaiming Indigenous Voice and Vision*, 79, 90–91.

28 Harold Cardinal and Walter Hildebrandt, *Treaty Elders of Saskatchewan: Our Dream Is That Our Peoples Will One Day Be Clearly Recognized as Nations* (Calgary: University of Calgary Press, 2000), 16.

29 Anne Poonwassie and Ann Charter, "An Aboriginal Worldview of Helping: Empowering Approaches," *Canadian Journal of Counselling/Revue Canadienne de Counseling* 35, no. 1 (2001): 63–73, https://files.eric.ed.gov/fulltext/EJ622699.pdf (citations omitted).

30 Jody Wilson-Raybould, *Indian in the Cabinet: Speaking Truth To Power* (Toronto: HarperCollins, 2021), 130–31.

31 "Consensus Government," Government of Nunavut, n.d., https://www.gov.nu.ca/consensus-government.

32 Kevin O'Brien, "Some Thoughts on Consensus Government in Nunavut," *Canadian Parliamentary Review* 26, no. 4 (2003), http://www.revparl.ca/english/issue.asp?param=60&art=26.

33 O'Brien, "Some Thoughts on Consensus Government in Nunavut."

34 Duane Champagne, "Markets, Change, Economic Development: Politics and Business" (lecture given at Banff Centre, AB, 2008).

35 John Ralston Saul, *A Fair Country: Telling Truths about Canada* (Toronto: Penguin, 2009), 3.

36 Saul, *A Fair Country*, 55.

37 Saul, *A Fair Country*, 236.

38 Bev Sellars, *Price Paid: The Fight for First Nations Survival* (Vancouver: Talonbooks, 2016), 16.

39 Daniel JK Beavon, Cora Jane Voyageur, and David Newhouse, eds., *Hidden in Plain Sight: Contributions of Aboriginal Peoples to Canadian Identity and Culture* (Toronto: University of Toronto Press, 2005), 8.

40 Mahad Arale, "Quebec Probes Incident of Indigenous Woman Who Filmed Abuse from Nurses in Hospital," Reuters, October 1, 2020, https://www.reuters.com/article/global-race-canada-nurse-idINKBN26M4DP.

41 Quoted in "In Plain Sight: Addressing Indigenous-Specific Racism and Discrimination in BC Health Care" (Addressing Racism Review Summary Report), Government of British Columbia, November 2020, https://engage.gov.bc.ca/app/uploads/sites/613/2020/11/In-Plain-Sight-Summary-Report.pdf.

42 Quoted in "In Plain Sight."

43 Quoted in "In Plain Sight," 12.

44 Quoted in "In Plain Sight," 12.

45 United Nations General Assembly, Resolution 61/295, "United Nations Declaration on the Rights of Indigenous Peoples," October 2, 2007, https://www.un.org/development/desa/indigenouspeoples/declaration-on-the-rights-of-indigenous-peoples.html.

46 "Frequently Asked Questions: Declaration on the Rights of Indigenous Peoples," 2007, https://www.un.org/esa/socdev/unpfii/documents/faq_drips_en.pdf.

47 "The UN Declaration," Coalition for the Human Rights of Indigenous Peoples, n.d., https://www.declarationcoalition.com/the-un-declaration.

48 Royal Commission on Aboriginal Peoples, "Public Policy and Aboriginal Peoples, 1965-1992 Vol. 2: Summaries of Reports by Federal Bodies and Aboriginal Organizations," Minister of Supply and Services Canada, xi, http://central.bac-lac.gc.ca/.redirect?app=rcap&id=512&lang=eng.

49 "*Truth and Reconciliation Commission of Canada: Calls to Action*"
    (Winnipeg, MB: Truth and Reconciliation Commission of Canada,
    2015), https://www2.gov.bc.ca/assets/gov/british-columbians-our-
    governments/indigenous-people/aboriginal-peoples-documents/
    calls_to_action_english2.pdf.

50 Marion Buller, Michèle Audette, Brian Eyolfson, and Qajaq Robinson,
    *Reclaiming Power and Place: The Final Report of the National Inquiry
    into Missing and Murdered Indigenous Women and Girls*, vol. 1a (Canada,
    2019), https://www.mmiwg-ffada.ca/wp-content/uploads/2019/06/
    Final_Report_Vol_1a-1.pdf.

51 "Murray Sinclair Says It'll Take a While to Figure out What to Do
    with Sept. 30," APTN News, September 30, 2021, https://www.aptn-
    news.ca/featured/its-like-renewing-our-vow-murray-sinclair-says-it-
    will-take-a-while-to-figure-out-sept-30-but-we-shouldnt-give-up/.

52 Lenard Monkman, "5 Years after Report, Truth and Reconciliation
    Commissioners Say Progress Is 'Moving Too Slow,'" CBC News,
    December 15, 2020, https://www.cbc.ca/news/indigenous/trc-5-years-
    final-report-1.5841428.

53 Dennis Ward, "National Inquiry Lacked Federal Support from the
    Beginning: Commissioner," APTN News, February 16, 2022, https://
    www.aptnnews.ca/facetoface/mmiwg-national-inquiry-lacked-federal-
    support-from-the-beginning-says-former-chief-commissioner/.

54 Jody Wilson-Raybould, *From Where I Stand: Rebuilding Indigenous
    Nations for a Stronger Canada* (Vancouver: UBC Press/Purich Books,
    2019), 197.

55 "Remarks by the Prime Minister in the House of Commons on the
    Recognition and Implementation of Rights Framework," February 14,
    2018, https://pm.gc.ca/en/news/speeches/2018/02/14/remarks-prime-
    minister-house-commons-recognition-and-implementation-rights.

56 Richard Nixon, "Message from the President of the United States
    Transmitting Recommendations for Indian Policy (8 July 1970),"
    H.R. Doc. No. 91-363, 91st Congress, 2nd Session.

57 John Borrows, "Policy Paper: Implementing Indigenous Self-
    Determination through Legislation in Canada," April 20, 2017, https://
    www.afn.ca/wp-content/uploads/2018/09/2017-04-20-Implementing-
    Indigenous-self-determination-through-policy-legislation.pdf.

58 Tsilhqot'in Nation v. British Columbia, [2014] 2 S.C.R. 257 (Can.),
    para. 73.

PART 3: ACT

1   It seems likely that this quotation has been incorrectly attributed to Mahatma Gandhi, although it is in fact a clear interpretation of his thoughts; see Brian Morton, "Falser Words Were Never Spoken," *New York Times*, August 29, 2011, https://www.nytimes.com/2011/08/30/opinion/falser-words-were-never-spoken.html.

2   Government of Canada, "Remaining Long-Term Drinking Water Advisories," February 26, 2021, https://www.sac-isc.gc.ca/eng/1614387410146/1614387435325.

3   Government of Canada, "Recognition, Reconciliation and Indigenous People's Disproportionate Interactions with the Criminal Justice System," September 17, 2018, https://www.justice.gc.ca/eng/news-nouv/speech.html.

4   Government of Canada, "Recognition, Reconciliation and Indigenous People's Disproportionate Interactions with the Criminal Justice System."

5   Michelle Lalond, "Not Sir John A. Macdonald's Canada Anymore: Statue Reignites Debate on History Lessons," *Montreal Gazette*, September 2, 2020, https://montrealgazette.com/news/local-news/not-sir-john-a-macdonalds-canada-anymore-statue-reignites-debate-on-history-lessons.

6   Canadian Press, "Honour Indigenous Heroes, Sinclair Says," *Red Deer Advocate*, August 29, 2017, https://www.reddeeradvocate.com/news/honour-indigenous-heroes-sinclair-says/.

7   "Debate Flares as Victoria Votes to Remove Macdonald Statue from City Hall," CTV News, August 9, 2018, https://vancouverisland.ctvnews.ca/debate-flares-as-victoria-votes-to-remove-macdonald-statue-from-city-hall-1.4047105.

8   Lisa Helps, "Reconciliation Is a Learning Process for Us All," Lisa Helps—Victoria Mayor, August 29, 2018, https://lisahelpsvictoria.ca/2018/08/29/reconciliation-is-a-learning-process-for-us-all/.

9   Mrinali Anchan, "New Brunswickers Turn To Social Media to Defy Provincial Directive around Indigenous Land Title," CBC News, October 17, 2021, https://www.cbc.ca/news/canada/new-brunswick/new-brunswickers-refute-provincial-directive-1.6214009.

10 Jeff Bell, "Oak Bay Senior Puts Reconciliation in Action, Leaves Her Home to Native Friendship Centre," *Times Colonist*, September 26, 2021, https://www.timescolonist.com/life/oak-bay-senior-puts-reconciliation-in-action-leaves-her-home-to-native-friendship-centre-4692354.

11   "Settlers Take Action," On Canada Project, n.d., https://
     oncanadaproject.ca/settlerstakeaction.

12   "Our Growth," On Canada Project, n.d., https://oncanadaproject.ca/
     whoweare.

13   Nick Pearce, "'You Are Our Future,' Indigenous Youth Told at
     FSIN Conference," *Saskatoon StarPhoenix*, April 20, 2022, https://
     thestarphoenix.com/news/local-news/you-are-our-future-indigenous-
     youth-told-at-fsin-conference.

14   Janice Golding, "'They're On Land That Is Indigenous and They
     Probably Don't Even Know': Company Brings Teen on Board to
     Mount Education Campaign," CTV News (Toronto), November 3,
     2021, https://toronto.ctvnews.ca/they-re-on-land-that-is-indigenous-
     and-they-probably-don-t-even-know-company-brings-teen-on-
     board-to-mount-education-campaign-1.5651051.

15   Moreen Mugerwa, "Regina Open Door Society Building Connections
     between Newcomers and Indigenous People," CBC News, April 28,
     2022, https://www.cbc.ca/news/canada/saskatchewan/newcomers-
     connecting-to-indigenous-culture-1.6422944.

16   "Indigenous Peoples and Mining: Position Statement," International
     Council on Mining and Metals, May 13, 2016, http://www.icmm.com/
     en-gb/about-us/member-requirements/position-statements/indigenous-
     peoples.

17   "Our Approach to Relationships with Indigenous Peoples," Teck, 2020,
     https://www.teck.com/media/teck_approach_to_Relationships_with_
     Indigenous_Peoples_2020.pdf.

18   Wilson-Raybould, *Indian in the Cabinet*, 130–31.